Comparative Literary Dimensions

Comparative Literary Dimensions

Essays in Honor of
Melvin J. Friedman

Edited by
Jay L. Halio and Ben Siegel

DELAWARE

Newark: University of Delaware Press
London: Associated University Presses

Associated University Presses
440 Forsgate Drive
Cranbury, NJ 08512

Associated University Presses
16 Barter Street
London WC1A 2AH, England

Associated University Presses
P.O. Box 338, Port Credit
Mississauga, Ontario
Canada L5G 4L8

The paper used in this publication meets the requirements of the American National Standards for Permanence of Paper for Printed Library Materials Z39.48-1984.

Library of Congress Cataloging-in-Publication Data

Comparative literary dimensions : essays in honor of Melvin J. Friedman / edited by Jay L. Halio and Ben Siegel.
    p.   cm.
  Includes bibliographical references and index.
  ISBN 0-87413-715-2 (alk. paper)
  1. European literature—History and criticism.   I. Friedman, Melvin J.
  II. Halio, Jay L.   III. Siegel, Ben, 1925–
PN36.F75C66   2000
809—dc21   99-088010

PRINTED IN THE UNITED STATES OF AMERICA

Contents

Comparative Literary Dimensions

Part I
Introduction

Introduction

JAY L. HALIO AND BEN SIEGEL

THIS IS THE SECOND OF TWO VOLUMES COMMEMORATING THE LIFE AND work of noted scholar and critic Melvin J. Friedman. We began our introduction to the first volume, *American Literary Dimensions*, as follows: "Melvin Friedman passed away on March 25, 1996, from Lou Gehrig's disease. There was a certain irony in Mel having been stricken by a disease bearing the name of a great athlete, as he was an avid sports fan and critic. He was also one of the most respected, best-liked, and truly beloved individuals in American academic life. Academe lost a major moving spirit with his death. In addition to his numerous published books, essays, and reviews, Mel was always ready, if not eager, to help friends, colleagues, and students. A recommendation from Mel Friedman always proved meaningful. Of course, his loss was compounded for those of us who knew Mel intimately and cared deeply about him."

The essays in *American Literary Dimensions* focused mainly upon Mel's wide-ranging interests not only in American writers like Ernest Hemingway and Scott Fitzgerald but also in Jewish American writers like Saul Bellow, Philip Roth, and Arthur Miller. Also included were tributes to Mel as a person—a teacher and friend—as well as several essays on Mel's lifelong interest in sports and the literature of sports. But Mel's literary expertise extended beyond our national borders to French, Irish, and British writers as well. He also knew personally the leading scholars, critics, and teachers in these areas. Not surprisingly, therefore, when we issued a call for contributions to a Mel Friedman *festschrift*, the response was such that we quickly became aware that we would need a second volume to accommodate all the outstanding people who wanted to show their admiration and respect for him.

It seemed logical to devote the first volume to American literature, and the second to comparative literature, and that is how this second collection, *Comparative Literary Dimensions*, came into being. We would like to thank Professors Donald Mell and Leo Lemay and their editorial board colleagues at the University of Delaware Press, and Mr. Julien Yoseloff, director of Associated University Presses, for their understanding and cooperation. They have made possible the publication of this two-volume tribute to Mel Friedman.

The first two essays suggest Mel Friedman's varied literary interests. Haskell Block begins, as his title suggests, by tracing a theory of comedy from Dante in the Middle Ages to Joyce in the twentieth century. Block delineates the theory as it developed from some notes by Aristotle and was expanded and modified by subsequent writers, particularly German theorists such as Immanuel Kant, Friedrich Schiller, Friedrich Schlegel, and Georg W. F. Hegel. Block explains how neo-Hegelian thought directly influenced nineteenth-century British thinkers like Bernard Bosanquet and Samuel Butcher; he points out that while Joyce drew many of his own ideas from their works, he also admired and was influenced by the work of George Meredith, namely the latter's essay on comedy and uses of the comic spirit.

Clayton Koelb finishes the first essay group with "The Medium of History: Robert Graves and the Ancient Past," using Graves's early short story "An Imperial Tale" (later renamed "The Apartment") as a text to understand better what is happening in *I, Claudius*. According to Koelb, Graves considers the role of the author "a modern dwelling place for [the] ancient ghosts" of characters that populate his novel. If all fictional creations, moreover, have their "ontological homes" inside the minds of their creators, this metaphor of the creative imagination also suggests something about the ontology of history and then about the relation between the historian and his or her readers.

Joyce and the development of the novel were two of Mel Friedman's major interests, and Zack Bowen, in compelling fashion, here considers Bakhtin's views on the epic and the novel. Bowen notes the special relevance of Bakhtin's arguments to *Ulysses* and, citing Bakhtin's discussion of the open-endedness and contemporaneity of the novel as opposed to the epic, he explains that he finds it hard to believe that Joyce never read Bakhtin or Bakhtin, Joyce.

Michael Patrick Gillespie offers a somewhat different perspective on Joyce's creative genius. Gillespie deals cogently with *Finnegans Wake* and the aesthetics of aging. He examines the images of age and the aging process in the final ten pages of Joyce's last book. Gillespie then considers that account of physical disintegration as it matches the figurative break-up of relationships in the course of the narrative. In his analysis, Gillespie emphasizes the nonlinear dynamics of the novel as contrasted with Cartesian cause-and-effect interpretations, which, though still capable of producing logical explications, lead to less full readings.

Perhaps the most varied approach to Joyce and *Finnegans Wake* is that of musician/composer Margaret Rogers. She describes her means of creating a performance version of "The Washerwoman" segment of the ALP section of *Finnegans Wake*. Her objective, she states, "was to separate and delineate the voices of the two women." She wanted to "accentuate the powerful rhythms inherent in words and sentence structure, highlight linguistic attributes and (when appropriate) set portions to music." She offers the reader musical notations to illustrate her key points.

The genius of James Joyce, then, is amply treated in this volume. But Mel Friedman was also one of the first American scholars to recognize the importance of Samuel Beckett. Therefore, that the next group of essays deals with Beckett and his work is fitting. The first essay in this cluster, by James Acheson, focuses on Beckett's *Happy Days*. Acheson cites two quotations—one from Robert Burton and the other from Arthur Schopenhauer—that Beckett, in his final transcript of the play, did not identify as sources for his allusions. Schopenhauer's lines are from *The World as Will and Idea*, in which the philosopher heaps scorn upon the confirmed optimist; the other quote is from *The Anatomy of Melancholy* wherein Burton indicates that happiness is a function not of a person's circumstances but of his or her state of mind. Both references are relevant to Beckett's protagonist, Winnie, who embodies the deluded optimist refusing to face the unpleasantness of her situation.

Raymond Federman, in "Beckett [f]or Nothing," begins with the question: "What form can fiction take when it encounters everywhere nothing but verbal dust?" Federman himself writes fiction in a vein that Beckett would have understood and appreciated—as did Mel Friedman. Here Federman explores two of Beckett's most significant later texts, *The Unnamable* and *Texts for Nothing*; he uses the former to help explicate the latter and answer the questions it poses. These include such queries as "What will become of the speaking/ writing I, if he blots out, negates, cancels the words that have been him—his life?" Livio Dobrez, in "Beckett Briefly on the Nature of Everything," also considers *Texts for Nothing*, viewing it not only as a parody of the realist tradition (particularly in the novel form), but also as an anguished parody, not a facile one. In his analysis, Dobrez pinpoints the pattern of Beckett's "Texts," a pattern that remains constant from the third to the thirteenth; it is a pattern of "a dynamic absence, a gaping hole in the middle of the narrative, thirteen times patching itself up, thirteen times reopening." The Text, according to Dobrez, is precisely this failure *to be*.

James Liddy sets himself to tracking the echoes in Beckett of his playwriting predecessors and then Beckett's influence on the Irish dramatists who followed him. In "A Sup of the Hawk's, or the Saints': Beckett and Irish Theater," Liddy summarizes succinctly his approach. "The before-relationship within the Irish Dramatic movement of Synge and Yeats to Beckett can be paralleled by the later adoption of Beckett by the group associated with Friel. As Beckett added an extra isolated voice to Synge's original characters . . . so Friel and the younger playwrights take from Beckett tactical silence, pauses in monologue and duet, and abrupt and rhetorical philosophical discourses. Thus the last great Anglo-Irish writer is delivered into the hands of that other island of folklore and nationalist politics, and closer to that fated island's soil ambivalence."

Richard Pearce leads off another miscellany of essays. He uses a different—indeed, a postmodernist—critical approach in his "Virginia Woolf's Construction of Masculinity: A Narrative Model—A Reading of *Mrs Dalloway*." He points out that Woolf employs a range of narrative strategies to position her readers "in a fictional world predominantly framed by a woman's experience focalized from a woman's perspective. Nor do we simply experience Woolf's world from a woman's perspective passively as voyeurs." For Woolf turns "us into active readers, or leads us to collaborate in constructing a present and past," one derived from her women characters' experiences and perspectives. In the process, she develops "not only a female sentence to counteract the sentence used by 'all great novelists like Thackeray and Dickens, and Balzac' but also ways of undermining traditional male story conventions."

In "Zangwill's *The Melting Pot* and Nichols's *Abie's Irish Rose*," Owen Aldridge explicates Zangwill's well-known metaphor, one that the English author also used for the title of a play dealing with Jewish immigration and assimilation and reflecting his own disenchantment with Zionism. Tracing the stage history of Zangwill's play, Aldridge ends by comparing it with Anne Nichols's *Abie's Irish Rose*, another—if quite different—drama designed to promote cultural assimilation.

David Hayman has chosen to treat the work of one of the most difficult—as well as distasteful—French writers of this century, Louis-Ferdinand Céline. But Céline's work is really only the vehicle for Hayman's theory regarding paranoid writing. Admitting that this theory or construct is both unscientific and metaphorical, Hayman still believes it helps explain how paranoia fuels a good deal of our best fiction, as well as other aesthetic forms. Céline's novels *Bagatelles pour un Massacre* and *Féerie pour une autre fois* are prime examples. Debra Castillo then shifts the focus to South America, as she discusses the work of the contemporary Argentine novelist Luisa Valenzuela. (Though not a card-carrying feminist, Mel Friedman always showed great sympathy for and understanding of women writers.) Castillo concentrates on the ironically titled "A Place of Quietude," the last story in Valenzuela's collection *Strange Things Happen Here* (1979; reprinted in *Open Door,* 1988). It is a chilling autobiographical fantasy about the roles of writing and the writer in a police state. Castillo explains that "A Place of Quietude" derives from the author's experience of returning to her native city, Buenos Aires, after a long absence and just before the crackdown that led to the "dirty war" (1976–83). The story not only deals with different meanings and with ways for writing "to overcome," but also with two different types of writing: one is a secret writing for no audience but the author herself; the other is imagined as "a public rehistorization that will redirect the nation's understanding of itself."

Finally, Mark Williams, in "Ethnicity and Authenticity: Wilson Harris and Other 'Black' Writing," extends his discussion beyond the work of the Caribbean author in his title to the literary efforts of such other writers as Salman Rushdie, Derek Walcott, Epeli Hau'ofa, Charles Johnson, and Keri Hulme. Williams wishes to formulate, if possible, a useful definition of "authenticity" as related to the concepts of "identity" and "negritude." After exploring the subjects as thoroughly as possible within the compass of a short essay, Williams ends as he began—with Wilson Harris, who rejects all simplistic or reductionist definitions. In his model, "the world is grasped as the relentless movement of informations from a huge variety of cultures and sources across national and ethnic barriers, yet allowing for a flourishing of cultures as they intersect." This "opening out to reality" is, moreover, an "optimistic act of faith in the human capacity to be enriched by experience, painful as well as consoling, to make new, provisional wholes out of the fractures of history, to draw on, imitate, and celebrate the past without seeking to close the world around some nostalgic conception of its meaning for the present." This is what Wilson Harris's fiction does, argues Williams, and this is what the best literature does, as any comparatist knows. Certainly Mel Friedman knew this. He taught it and, equally significant, he lived it.

Reenforcing this point is the detailed and revealing bibliography of Mel Friedman's publications that concludes this *festschrift.* It was compiled by Jackson Bryer, with the cooperation of Judith Friedman

Theory of Comedy from Dante to Joyce

Haskell M. Block

THE YOUNG JAMES JOYCE—AGED 21—WAS KEENLY INTERESTED IN AESTHETics. In a letter from Paris to his mother on 20 March 1903, he describes his literary activities and plans as follows: "My book of songs will be published in the spring of 1907. My first comedy about five years later. My 'Esthetic' about five years later again. (This *must* interest you!)."[1] Joyce never completed the comedy or the projected treatise. His notes on aesthetics, composed mainly in 1903 and 1904, were communicated to Herbert Gorman for inclusion in his biography of Joyce of 1941, and are reprinted in *The Critical Writings of James Joyce*. To this collection of close to 300 pages should be added Joyce's *Scritti Italiani*, published in 1979, which overlaps considerably with the Mason–Ellmann volume. Along with early essays and passages from notebooks, the *Critical Writings* includes 23 book reviews, all published in the Dublin newspaper the *Daily Express*. Joyce's critical writings provide important insight into his literary development. Some of the early essays, notably "Ibsen's New Drama," published in *The Fortnightly Review* in 1900, are illuminating interpretations of their subject. The Ibsen essay is a truly remarkable achievement for a writer only 18 years old. The reflections on aesthetics were to be embodied in *Stephen Hero* and, with both transference and modification, in *A Portrait of the Artist as a Young Man*. The final chapter of this novel is concerned in large part with the aesthetics formulated by Stephen Dedalus as a central affirmation of his artistic calling.

Joyce's Paris notebooks include reflections on both tragedy and comedy. The remarks on comedy are quite brief and are limited to generalities. Most students of Joyce's aesthetics have viewed his discussion of comedy in a cursory way. As in other areas of theory, Joyce's approach to comedy depends in great part on his careful study of Aristotle. The polarization of comedy and tragedy is a direct reflection of the *Poetics*, reinforced by developments in critical theory between Aristotle and Joyce. Joyce's brief but arresting observations on comedy are part of the long history of the subject. Some attention to this history should help in understanding both the traditional elements in Joyce's theory and its originality.

The strict separation of literary genres, along with the opposition of tragedy and comedy, begins with Aristotle. We are told in the *Poetics* that comedy aims at representing men as worse, tragedy as better, than in actual life. While comedy imitates characters of a lower type than tragedy, it issues in a happy ending, in which "no one slays or is slain." Sufficient remarks on the nature of comedy in the *Poetics* account for the subsequent elaboration of a theory of comedy along Aristotelian lines. Essential aspects of Aristotle recur in Roman and medieval criticism, as in Horace's insistence that a theme belonging to comedy not be set forth in the verses of tragedy, although he also admits that comedy may sometimes raise its tone. The classical theory of comedy persists in the Middle Ages, notably in the essays of Evanthius and Donatus.[2] Evanthius's *De Fabula*, a fourth-century commentary on Terence, sets forth the sharp opposition of tragedy and comedy according to subject matter and effect:

> In comedy the fortunes of men are middle-class, the dangers are slight, and the ends of the actions are happy; but in tragedy everything is the opposite—the characters are great men, the fears are intense, and the ends disastrous. In comedy the beginning is troubled, the end tranquil; in tragedy events follow the reverse order. And in tragedy the kind of life is shown that is to be shunned; while in comedy the kind is shown that is to be sought after.[3]

A similar formulation can be found in Donatus's *De Comedia*. Evanthius's allusion to the kind of life to be sought after as the concern of comedy points unmistakably to the notion of comedy in Dante.

Mary T. Reynolds's study, *Joyce and Dante: The Shaping Imagination* (1981), has demonstrated the fundamental importance of Joyce's study of Dante for every aspect of Joyce's literary thought and art. Not only citations and allusions, but also theme, structure, style, and implication all reflect Joyce's deep immersion in Dante. Joyce's assertion in the Paris notebooks that "the feeling which is proper to comic art is the feeling of joy" is a direct consequence of his appreciation of Dante's *Commedia*. Dante's definition of comedy is both stylistic and structural. In *De Vulgari Eloquentia* he distinguishes tragedy and comedy according to higher and lower stylistic levels.[4] He enlarges on the contrast of tragedy and comedy in the letter to Can Grande, which also provides the explanation for the title of his poem: comedy, he declares, "introduces a situation of adversity, but ends its matter in prosperity, as is evident in Terence's comedies."

After again differentiating the styles of tragedy and comedy, he adds: "So from this it should be clear why the present work is called the *Comedy*. For, if we consider the matter, it is at the beginning, that is, in Hell, foul and conducive to horror, but at the end, in Paradise, prosperous, conducive to pleasure, and welcome."[5]

In the later nineteenth century the letter to Can Grande was accepted by *Dantisti* as authentic and was quoted at length in commentaries. Thus, in his introductory notes to his 1873 edition, Eugenio Camerini cites from the letter and sets forth the traditional contrast between tragedy and comedy. Mary Reynolds has called attention to the presence of a copy of the Camerini edition in Joyce's Trieste library. She has shown that the edition was in common use in Dublin at the end of the nineteenth century as a school text for the study of Dante. The notion of comedy as marked by a happy ending is commonplace in the late Middle Ages.[6] The culmination of comedy in joy is attended by the glory of eternal beatitude. The pattern of comedy is a celebration of human salvation. Other medieval texts support this view. In an early fifteenth-century English dialogue by Henry Parker, *Dives and Pauper,* mirthful plays are praised as a figuration of the joy of man's ultimate redemption:

> the rest the mirth the ese and the welfare
> that god hath ordeyned in the halidayes
> is token of endlesse reste ioye and myrthe
> and welfare in heunes blisse that we hope to
> haue withouten ende.[7]

We should note that Joyce's distinction of improper and proper art depends on the antithesis of desire and rest. All art, he insists, is static. Joy is a condition of absolute rest "which does not urge us to seek anything beyond itself." It is this joy that is proper to comedy.

Dante's title created problems of genre classification of his poem for subsequent generations of critics. Bernard Weinberg has shown at length how vexing the questions of Dante's genre and title were for sixteenth-century Italy. Thus, Carlo Lenzoni viewed the title as appropriate because Dante himself is an actor in the poem; hence the poem is "representative."[8] Others saw the poem as closer to epic, although some contended that it failed to conform to the requirements of an epic poem. Whether considered comedy or epic, Dante's poem was defined in relation to external and universal notions of genre.

The conception of comedy as issuing in joy continues to be restated in comic theory after the Renaissance. In the preface to *The Conscious Lovers* (1723), Richard Steele declares:

> any thing that has its Foundation in Happiness
> and Success, must be allow'd to be the Object
> of Comedy, and sure it must be an Improvement
> of it, to introduce a Joy too exquisite for
> Laughter, that can have no Spring but in Delight. . . .[9]

In his book *The Amiable Humorist,* Stuart Tave singles out Corbyn Morris's *An Essay towards Fixing the True Standards of Wit* . . . (1744) as "historically the most interesting piece of comic criticism in the eighteenth century."[10] Morris's contrast of Ben Jonson and Shakespeare is essentially a contrast of preachment and joy: "Johnson in his COMIC Scenes has expos'd and ridicul'd *Folly* and *Vice; Shakespear* has usher'd in *Joy, Frolic* and *Happiness.* . . . With Johnson you are confin'd and instructed, with *Shakespear* unbent and dissolv'd in Joy."[11] Morris's essay was not well known in his time, but it constitutes a striking link between medieval and early modern theory.

The theory of comedy in the late eighteenth century was shaped by two principal developments: the assertion of the autonomy of art, reflecting Kant's formulation in *The Critique of Judgment* of "purposefulness without purpose," and the realignment of the hierarchy of genres, which from the sixteenth to the eighteenth centuries placed epic poetry at the apex, followed first by tragedy and then by comedy.[12] Both in the liberation of art from didacticism or any conscious moral purpose, and in the claim that comedy is superior to tragedy, the German idealist tradition—and particularly the criticism of Schiller—is of special importance. Much of the discussion of these topics in the Schlegels, Schelling, Hegel, and Schopenhauer, among others, is an elaboration of positions set forth by Schiller, mainly in "On Naive and Sentimental Poetry" and in "On the Aesthetic Education of Man," both published in 1795. In his account of rest or stillness in poetry, Schiller seems to reflect Winckelmann's ideal of "silent grandeur," and more especially Kant's conception of beauty in *The Critique of Judgment.*

In contrasting the sublime and the beautiful, Kant asserts that the sublime brings with it a movement of the mind, "while in the case of the Beautiful taste presupposes and maintains the mind in *restful* contemplation."[13] For Schiller, naive art is marked by the "restfulness of completeness." Freedom from passion is for Schiller the basis of the superiority of comedy over tragedy. Tragedy creates continual excitement, but comedy subdues passion and thereby allows the poet greater freedom. The opposition of tragedy and comedy is that of passion and calm:

The aim that comedy has in view is the same as that of the highest destiny of man, and this consists in liberating himself from the influence of violent passions, and taking a calm and lucid survey of all that surrounds him, and also of his own being, and of seeing everywhere occurrence rather than fate or hazard, and ultimately rather smiling at the absurdities than shedding tears and feeling anger at sight of the wickedness of man.[14]

Schiller goes on to state in notes to his essay on naive and sentimental poetry that while tragedy makes us godlike men, comedy makes us gods: "Our condition in comedy is calm, clear, free, cheerful, we feel neither active nor suffering, we gaze, and everything is outside of us. This is the condition of gods, who do not trouble over anything human, who hover over all, whom no destiny touches, no law compels."[15] Comedy here becomes art at its highest reach. In the letters *On the Aesthetic Education of Man,* notably in letter 22, Schiller again emphasizes the freedom of art from both desire and tendentiousness:

There is a fine art of passion, but an impassioned fine art is a contradiction in terms; for the inevitable effect of the Beautiful is freedom from passions. No less self-contradictory is the notion of a fine instructive (didactic) or improving (moral) art, for nothing is more at variance with the concept of Beauty than that it should have a tendentious effect upon the character.[16]

Clearly, we are very close here to the central position of Joyce on comedy and the aims of art as set forth in the Paris notebooks of 1903. Joyce makes no explicit reference to Schiller in these formulations, but Schiller's major critical essays were readily available in English translation in the later nineteenth century, and the young Joyce may well have been familiar with them.[17]

Other German idealist thinkers set forth similar convictions. In an essay of 1794, "On the Aesthetic Worth of Greek Comedy," Friedrich Schlegel asserts that "beautiful joy is the highest object of fine art." The freedom and joy of Old Comedy expresses "the infinite fullness of life," recognized as holy and divine. This joy is "in itself beautiful."[18] The young Friedrich Schlegel seems to place comedy at the apex of literary genres, but he does not develop his theory by contrast to tragedy, as is more usually the case in German literary theory of the time. Hegel, in his *Aesthetik* (first published in 1835), sees comedy, unlike tragedy, marked by calm and cheerfulness, but in the course of its development comedy has moved from strength and freedom to the prosaic and ordinary, pointing in this decline to the dissolution of art. Hegel contends that art at its highest reach cannot last; perforce it passes "from the poetry of the imagination to the prose of thought."[19]

The capacity of comedy to dissolve itself as representation while maintaining a consciousness of its identity reflects the subjectivity of comedy; this capacity is in contrast to the objective art of tragedy, which is dissolved by the Absolute.[20] Apart from his history of early dramatic genres, Hegel does not seem to value one genre above another. In his *Aesthetik* he sets forth a trichotomy of tragedy, comedy, and drama ("Schauspiel"), the last falling between the first two types and constituting tragicomedy. Hegel not only points to a new dramatic genre; he also anticipates the move from genre to mode, from comedy to the comic, or from tragedy to a "tragischen Anschauungsweise," thereby displacing genre by vision, apart from the requirements of any fixed form.[21] In many important ways Hegel anticipates crucial developments in modern literary theory.

Neo-Hegelian thought was an important part of aesthetics in England in the late nineteenth century. It can be seen most notably in Bernard Bosanquet's *A History of Æsthetic* (1892) and in Samuel H. Butcher's translation and commentary, *Aristotle's Theory of Poetry and Fine Art* (1895). Jacques Aubert has argued convincingly that Joyce drew substantially on both works, especially the history of Bosanquet, in constructing his own aesthetics.[22] Francis C. McGrath, in a study devoted mainly to Walter Pater, has similarly argued for the central importance of German idealist thought in the aesthetics set forth by Joyce. Indeed, McGrath contends that Joyce went to great trouble "to camouflage his Romantic sources" by means of constant references to Aristotle and Aquinas.[23] This may or may not be the case, but the simultaneous presence of multiple currents of aesthetic thought in the formulations of the young Joyce cannot be doubted. He was unusually well read, and he was directly or indirectly familiar with virtually all major formulations in literary theory from classical antiquity to modern times. Indeed, it is by no means certain that Joyce's view of tendentious art as improper was derived from his reading of Bosanquet. This conviction was commonplace in the late nineteenth century; furthermore, no awareness can be found in Bosanquet's account of Schiller of the distinct character of Schiller's theory of comedy.[24] Schiller's theory points far more directly to the formulations of Joyce than do the passages from Hegel cited in Bosanquet.

It is interesting to note in passing Bosanquet's discussion of the problem of genre in Dante. He considers the *Divine Comedy* unique in form and not subject to traditional notions of genre:

He himself called his great work a Comedy first because it begins grimly and ends pleasantly; and secondly, because it is written in the vernacular, in which even women converse, and therefore must be regarded as, in a humble style, contrasted with that of tragedy.

But we need not say that it is not a comedy; for it is not even a drama, having neither dramatic form nor dramatic unity.[25]

Epic is also ruled out, "for the incidents are not in any normal sense parts within a single action." Lyric plainly will not do. Bosanquet concludes that the *Divine Comedy* is a unique form in open defiance of traditional classification. Very much the same position was held, as Bosanquet recognizes, by Schelling in his essay on Dante of 1803. There Schelling claimed that Dante's poem constitutes a wholly new genre, "eine Gattung für sich," for which traditional forms are inadequate.[26] Schelling's view of Dante, like that of Bosanquet, is part of an assault on the traditional view of genres that was to gain ground in the years ahead.

As we have seen, the movement from genres to modes as primary terms of critical discourse reflects the dissolution of the traditional concept of genre. A major contribution to the transformation of comedy to the comic as a critical norm was George Meredith's essay, *An Essay on Comedy and the Uses of the Comic Spirit,* published in magazine form in 1877 and republished as a book in 1897. Here Meredith extols "the calm, curious eye of the Comic Spirit," and does so without any reliance on the contrast with tragedy or any restriction of the comic to dramatic representation. The comic is a principle of both life and art, Meredith reasoned, social in its origins and expression, an idealization rather than a replica of experience, and appealing primarily to the intellect. It is for Meredith the most civilized of arts and indeed the measure of a civilization. While some of his examples are drawn from the whole range of stage comedy, especially Molière, he also includes Chaucer, Rabelais, Cervantes, Pope, Fielding, and Sterne as masters of the comic spirit. The same large perspective is set forth in Meredith's "Prelude" to his novel *The Egoist* (1879) and in other novels such as *The Tragic Comedians* (1892), which the young James Joyce especially admired.[27] Here Meredith points to tragicomedy as the appropriate art of modern times, in accord with a new complexity of character to be rendered in fiction. Among the books reviewed by Joyce for the Dublin *Daily Express* was Walter Jerrold's critical study, *George Meredith* (London, 1902); this study was concerned mainly with Meredith's novels but dealt also at length with the essay on comedy and the comic spirit. The displacement of genre by mode that we see in Meredith is also apparent in the early writings of Joyce.

According to the recollections of his brother, Stanislaus, the young Joyce was fond of comedy and played the lead role in a one-act comedy by a friend.[28] He may have attempted to write a comedy as well. In a letter to W. B. Yeats of August 1902, George Russell (AE) states that Joyce is "engaged in writing a comedy,"[29] and we have noted that Joyce alludes to a projected comedy in a letter to his mother from Paris the following year. Stanislaus Joyce mentions "dialogue in the style of Ben Jonson," which the young Joyce composed in Paris,[30] but the text has not survived. In his first major critical essay, "Drama and Life" (1900), Joyce sees drama as the primary element of life apart from any dependence on literary forms. His subject here is "the great human comedy,"[31] but as an expression of the comic spirit rather than of the genre. Referring to Ibsen's heroines in the essay "Ibsen's New Drama," Joyce remarks: "Gina Ekdahl is, before all else, a comic figure, and Hedda Gabler a tragic one—if such old-world terms may be employed without incongruity."[32] Joyce casts doubt on the validity of the traditional concepts even in the act of using them. Apart from the brief remarks in the Paris notebooks, the young Joyce wrote very little about comedy. No discussion of the subject is in the extant chapters of *Stephen Hero,* even when Stephen sets forth a theory of genres that he rapidly transforms into the modes of lyrical, epical, or dramatic.[33] The same trichotomy is present in *A Portrait of the Artist as a Young Man,* where only an oblique reference is made to comic art.[34]

In the Paris fragment, Joyce both asserts and subverts the opposition of comedy and tragedy. Their differentiation is based on contrasting means and ends. In their modes of operation, comedy and tragedy are countergenres, yet in claiming the superiority of comedy to tragedy, Joyce argues for the autonomy of comedy even as he subverts the traditional generic hierarchy.[35] Considering that most theorists place tragedy on a higher plane than comedy, Joyce's claim is a bold one, prefigured in so unqualified a way perhaps only by Schiller. Indeed, Joyce reduces his claim somewhat when he states that "even tragic art may be said to participate in the nature of comic art so far as the possession of a work of tragic art (a tragedy) excites in us the feeling of joy." Mason and Ellmann comment on this passage: "That joy may result from tragedy as well as from comedy does not follow well from what he has said."[36] In the preceding paragraph Joyce declares that tragic art excites in us feelings of pity and terror. Joy would seem to be a higher feeling, in keeping with Dante's view of comedy and the pattern of his poem. In addition, Joyce asserts that all proper art, tragic or comic, aims at a state of rest, at what Stephen describes in *Portrait* as "the luminous silent stasis of esthetic pleasure."[37] Initially, at least, Joyce's theory of comedy is a central part of his elaboration of a static theory of art.

In defining comedy at its highest reach as the feeling of joy, Joyce parts company with any theory of comedy based simply on laughter. A striking anticipation of this position can be found in the correspondence of Flaubert, in a letter of May 8, 1852: "Le comique arrivé à l'extrême, le comique qui ne fait pas rire, le lyrisme dans la blague, est pour moi tout ce qui me fait le plus envie comme écrivain."[38] Joyce knew Flaubert's correspondence and on occasion cited from it; he may well have been familiar with Flaubert's arresting formulation. In any event he shares with Flaubert the enlargement of the scope of the comic to embrace elements seemingly foreign to it.

For strategic purposes the young Joyce set forth a theory of genres that a recent analyst of genre theory, Jean-Marie Schaeffer, would describe as "essentialiste," according to an Aristotelian model.[39] Joyce seems to have thought of genres as constants, just as he viewed classicism as "a constant state of the artistic mind."[40] Comedy and tragedy are for him fixed and permanent forms. Joyce does not discuss the ways and means of their possible transformation, nor does he say anything about devices of technique or style by which a genre may attain its end. The processes of generic art simply are not discussed. Joyce's theory of comedy is much too brief to constitute more than notes toward a theory, but his refusal to develop these remarks is itself a comment on the enterprise. His easy movement on occasion from genre to mode points to a serious questioning of the viability of genre criticism.

Any discussion of theory of genre in the twentieth century must confront the lion in the path. Benedetto Croce's *Estetica* was published in 1902, and in the course of its many editions and reformulations has come to constitute the central assault on the theory of genres in our time. We should note that Joyce read Croce's *Estetica* during his Trieste years, mainly for its discussion of Vico, at a time when questions of literary theory were no longer among Joyce's primary concerns.[41] For Croce, comedy and the comic, like all generic concepts, have no meaning. They are arbitrary, extrinsic, contingent, and lacking any validity.[42] Croce insists genres are abstractions without any historical reality.[43] Their use as critical norms he finds totally pernicious. Without accepting Croce's extreme position, we should recognize that Joyce himself suffered from the abuse of genre at the hands of those critics who declared of *Ulysses* in 1922: "I do not know what sort of work this book may be but it is assuredly not a novel." Croce's insistence that great art is always a violation of a genre recalls previous defenses of Dante. At the same time, as some earlier critics also recognized, much can be gained by viewing Dante's poem within the framework of epic poetry.

The breakdown of the once firm distinction of tragedy and comedy has extended to modes as well as forms. Writing in 1925, Thomas Mann declared that the modern spirit of art "no longer recognizes the categories of the tragic and the comic, and also the theatrical forms and genres of tragedy and comedy, and sees life as tragicomedy."[44] Here genre has been redefined as vision, itself subject to further transformation. The theory of comedy from Dante to Joyce exhibits both continuity and radical change. For Joyce, the theoretical preoccupation we have considered found new expression in *Ulysses* and in *Finnegans Wake*, both rich in their evocation of humor amid the trials of existence. *Ulysses* may well be viewed as a comic epic, Leopold Bloom a comic hero, and the novel itself an assertion of the dignity and affirmation of the comic spirit.[45] In this concrete manifestation, theory and expression converge.

Notes

1. James Joyce, *Letters,* ed. Richard Ellmann (New York: Viking Press, 1966), 2:38.

2. Alex Preminger, O. B. Hardison, Jr., and Kevin Kerrane, eds., *Classical and Medieval Literary Criticism* (New York: Frederick Ungar, 1974), 299–309.

3. *Ibid.,* 305.

4. *Literary Criticism of Dante Alighieri,* ed. Robert S. Haller (London: University of Nebraska Press, 1973), 39.

5. *Ibid.,* 100–101.

6. Paget Toynbee, "Dante's Obligations to the Magnae Derivationes of Uguccione da Pisa," *Romania* 26 (1897): 543.

7. Cited in V. A. Kolve, *The Play Called Corpus Christi* (Stanford: Stanford University Press, 1966), 133.

8. Bernard Weinberg, *A History of Literary Criticism in the Italian Renaissance* (Chicago: University of Chicago Press, 1961), 2:824. For detailed discussion of the quarrel over Dante, see 2:819–911.

9. Richard Steele, *Plays,* ed. Shirley Strum Kenney (Oxford: Oxford University Press, 1971), 299.

10. Stuart M. Tave, *The Amiable Humorist* (Chicago: University of Chicago Press, 1960), 118.

11. *Ibid.,* 138.

12. Alastair Fowler, *Kinds of Literature* (Cambridge: Harvard University Press, 1982), 216.

13. Immanuel Kant, *Critique of Judgment,* trans. J. H. Bernard (London: Macmillan, 1931), 105–6. Cf. Kant, *Kritik der Urteilskraft* (Frankfurt am Main: Suhrkamp Verlag, 1974), 168.

14. Friedrich Schiller, "On Simple and Sentimental Poetry," in *Essays, Aesthetical*

and Philosophical (London: George Bell, 1900), 294. Cf. "Über naive und sentimentalische Dichtung," in *Werke,* Nationalausgabe (Weimar: H. Böhlaus Nachfolger, 1962), 20:472–73.

15. Schiller, "Aus dem Nachlass. Tragödie und Komödie," *Sämtliche Werke,* Säkular-Ausgabe (Stuttgart: J. G. Cotta, 1905), 12:329–30, my translation.

16. Schiller, *On the Aesthetic Education of Man,* trans. Reginald Snell (New Haven: Yale University Press, 1954), 106–7. Cf. *Sämtliche Werke,* Säkular-Ausgabe, 12:86.

17. Schiller's essays were first published in English translation in London in 1844. His *Essays, Aesthetical and Philosophical* was published in London in 1875 in "Bohn's Standard Library." This edition was reprinted in 1884, 1900, and 1903. See Robert Pick, *Schiller in England 1787–1960. A Bibliography. Publications of the English Goethe Society,* n.s., 30 (1961).

18. Friedrich Schlegel, *Kritische Ausgabe,* ed. Ernst Behler (Paderborn: Ferdinand Schöningh, 1979), 1.1:19–33.

19. Georg Wilhelm Friedrich Hegel, *Aesthetics,* trans. T. M. Knox (Oxford: Oxford University Press, 1975), 1:89.

20. See Richard Collins, "The Comic Dissolution of Art: The Last Act of Hegel's Aesthetics," *Theatre Journal* 33 (1981): 60–68; Walter Hinck, "Einführung in die Theorie des komischen und der Komödie," in Hinck, ed., *Die deutsche Komödie* (Düsseldorf: August Bagel, 1977), 1–31; Anne Paolucci, "Hegel's Theory of Comedy," *New York Literary Forum* 1 (Spring 1978): 89–108.

21. Hegel, *Aesthetik* (Berlin: Duncker und Hamblot, 1843), 3: 533. A similar view of the mixture of the tragic and the comic as "a fundamental principle of modern drama" is set forth by Friedrich Wilhelm Schelling in his lectures of 1802 on the philosophy of art. See Schelling, *Sämmtliche Werke* (Stuttgart: J. G. Cotta, 1859), 5:718.

22. Jacques Aubert, *Introduction à l'esthétique de James Joyce* (Paris: Librarie Marcel Didier, 1973); *The Aesthetics of James Joyce* (Baltimore: Johns Hopkins University Press, 1992).

23. F. C. McGrath, *The Sensible Spirit: Walter Pater and the Modernist Paradigm* (Tampa: University of South Florida Press, 1986), 281.

24. Benedetto Croce criticizes Bosanquet severely for his omissions. See Croce, *Estetica come scienza dell'espressione e linguistica generale* (Milano: R. Sandron, 1902), 518–19. Croce's account of Schiller emphasizes theories that strikingly anticipate those of Joyce, *Estetica,* 299–301.

25. Bernard Bosanquet, *A History of Æsthetic* (London; S. Sonnenschein, 1892), 152.

26. Schelling, 5:152.

27. Eugene Sheehy, *May It Please the Court* (Dublin: C. J. Fallon, 1951), 28.

28. Stanslaus Joyce, *My Brother's Keeper: James Joyce's Early Years,* ed. Richard Ellmann (New York: Viking Press, 1958), 124.

29. Cited in Robert Scholes and Richard M. Kain, eds., *The Workshop of Daedalus* (Evanston: Northwestern University Press, 1965), 166–67.

30. Stanslaus Joyce, 224–25.

31. James Joyce, *The Critical Writings,* eds. Ellsworth Mason and Richard Ellmann (New York: Viking Press, 1959), 45.

32. *Ibid.,* 64.

33. James Joyce, *Stephen Hero,* eds. Theodore Spencer, John J. Slocum, and Herbert Cahoon (New York: New Directions, 1955), 77.

34. James Joyce, *A Portrait of the Artist as a Young Man,* ed. Chester G. Anderson (New York: Viking Press, 1968), 214.

35. See Michael Silk, "The Autonomy of Comedy," *Comparative Criticism* 10 (1988):3–37.

36. James Joyce, *The Critical Writings,* 144 n.4.

37. James Joyce, *Portrait,* 213.

38. Gustave Flaubert, *Correspondance,* ed. Jean Bruneau (Paris: Gallimard, 1980), 2:85.

39. Jean-Marie Schaeffer, *Qu'est-ce qu'un genre littéraire?* (Paris: Editions du Seuil, 1989), 13.

40. James Joyce, *Stephen Hero,* 78.

41. Richard Ellmann, *James Joyce,* new and rev. ed. (New York: Oxford University Press, 1983), 340 n.

42. Croce, *Estetica,* 89–93.

43. Gian N. G. Orsini, *Benedetto Croce: Philosopher of Art and Literary Critic* (Carbondale: Southern Illinois University Press, 1961), 96–111.

44. Thomas Mann, *Altes und Neues* (Frankfurt am Main: S. Fischer Verlag, 1961), 472–73, cited in Silk, 12–13.

45. For discussions of comedy in *Ulysses,* see Harold Kaplan, *The Passive Voice: An Approach to Modern Fiction* (Athens: Ohio University Press, 1966), 80–91; Zack Bowen, *Ulysses as a Comic Novel* (Syracuse: Syracuse University Press, 1989); Robert H. Bell, *Jocoserious Joyce: The Fate of Folly in Ulysses* (Ithaca: Cornell University Press, 1991).

The Medium of History:
Robert Graves and the Ancient Past

CLAYTON KOELB

IN 1960, TWO AND A HALF DECADES AFTER THE PUBLICATION OF HIS CLAU-
dius novels, Rober Graves published a short story set in the time of
Claudius called "An Imperial Tale." The story was later revised as
"The Tenement: A Vision of Imperial Rome" and later still as "The
Apartment House." It is a first-person narrative recounted by Egnatius, a young client of Lucius Vitellius and manager of a Roman
apartment house owned by his father-in-law.

Egnatius describes one day in his life, from his awaking to an evening dinner party, touching only on what he considers the salient
points, including particularly his loveless marriage to the philander-
ing Arruntia. The story appears to be a straightforward attempt to
reconstruct a typical day in the life of a typical Roman right up until
its end, when it takes a distinctly odd turn. The apartment house
Egnatius manages and in which he lives collapses in the midst of his
dinner party, apparently killing everyone then present: "Did any of
us survive? I doubt it. My next distinct memory is of being a child
once more. Martial music sounds. Mother lifts me up to watch,
through a well-glazed English nursery window, the decorated car-
riages and red-coated soldiers of Queen Victoria's Diamond Jubilee
procession."[1] The narrating consciousness elides both the temporal
gap between the reign of Claudius and that of Victoria, and the conventional boundary separating the author of a fiction from the characters in it. The elision is surprising and uncomfortable. The reader
has assumed that the first-person pronoun belongs exclusively to a
fictional person of first-century Rome named Egnatius; indeed, that
assumption is necessary for the story to be readable in the conventional way. The ending, though, pulls the rug out from under the
reader, reminding everyone that Robert Graves, a modern Englishman, has written all these words. Are we to suppose that Graves and
Egnatius are really one and the same, the former a reincarnation of
the latter?

Of course, the story prompts us to believe exactly that. The "Robert Graves" whose name appears on the by-line is the product of metempsychosis, retaining through the journey across death the memories of Egnatius, a contemporary of Claudius the emperor. The protagonist of the story, then, is not the Roman only but the composite psyche Egnatius-Graves. The modern author, or at least some part of him, has the same ontological status as the ancient character—whatever we suppose that status to be. Does Egnatius's psychic communion with Graves make him more real and tangible, or does it instead make "Graves" into a character in a fiction? This Egnatius-Graves composite seems to dwell in a peculiar liminal space between fiction and fact, and between then and now.

It is worth noting that the ancient Roman and the late-Victorian Englishman bearing his memories perform one, and only one, act in common: they both look through a window. The story opens with Egnatius's servant, Sophron, opening "the shutters of an unglazed window" through which the protagonist views his balcony and the balcony of a house across the street. It ends with the English child looking through a "well-glazed English nursery window" at a parade. This detail suggests that the most tangible point of contact between these two persons might be their position at or near the boundary between two locations, between inside and outside, for instance, or between past and present. Since the final paragraph opens the question as to what is inside and outside the bounds of the story, as well as to what belongs to the present and what to the past, the image seems particularly appropriate. It is all the more so when we consider that the narrating voice of Egnatius hovers somewhere on the border between life and death, since on the one hand he reports the catastrophe that brings about his own demise and on the other asserts his continued existence "now" despite his death "then."[2] Even Egnatius's physical position is uncertain at the end of his Roman life. With the collapse of the apartment house, one cannot say for sure whether his body ends up "in" it (covered by its remnants) or not.

Egnatius may or may not be buried, and indeed he may or may not be in the grave, but he does appear to be "in" Graves, and in several ways. As a figment of discourse he is certainly "in Graves," in the sense that the text that comprises his literary being is part of the oeuvre one can designate metonymically with its author's name. One could properly answer the question "Where can I find the character Egnatius?" by saying, "in Graves." But if we accept the implication of the story's conclusion, Egnatius is "in" Graves by reason of his psychic transmigration. His soul is now laterally contained within the Englishman born in 1895 near the end of Victoria's reign. We may read this as a metaphor of artistic imagination whereby we understand all fictional creations to have their ontological homes in the minds of their creators, but the story does not urge us to do so. On the contrary, by proposing the priority of Egnatius's existence to that of the Englishman, it suggests that Graves is not the origin of this personality but its (perhaps temporary) terminus.

Egnatius has exchanged one kind of apartment house for another in the moment of the story's climax. The later tenement happens to be a container of the dead named by an English word denoting containers of the dead, "Graves." "The Apartment House" thus makes good a reading of the author's name through the figure of autonomasia, a reading of which we can be confident the English poet was acutely aware. How could he fail to understand his name this way when his character Claudius repeatedly proposes precisely analogous interpretations of Latin names? Indeed Claudius is a vigorous adherent of the doctrine of the fitness of names:

"Why do you call me by my last name?"
"Because it's the more appropriate one."
"How do you make that out, clever?"
"Because among the Etruscans 'Camilla' is what they call a young hunting priestess dedicated to Diana. With a name like Camilla one is bound to be a champion runner."
"That's nice. I never heard that. I shall make all my friends call me Camilla now."
"And call me Claudius, will you? That's my appropriate name. It means a cripple. My family usually call me Tiberius, and that's inappropriate because the Tiber runs very fast."[3]

On another occasion he reminds the reader that "the name 'Livia' is connected with the Latin word which means Malignity,"[4] the appropriateness of which connection Claudius's history goes on to document. He remarks again in later pages of *Claudius the God* "how appropriate some people's names are," noting the resemblance between Asinius Gallus and the animals (*asinus* ["donkey"] and *gallus* ["rooster"]) suggested by his name. Gallus, he says, "was the most utter little donkey-cock for his boastfulness and stupidity that one could find in a month's tour of Italy."[5] The author of *I, Claudius* would inevitably understand "Graves" to refer to both his own person and to a set of habitations for the dead. These two apparently incompatible concepts suddenly come together at the conclusion of "The Apartment House," when the protagonist exchanges his dwelling in the collapsed tenement—apparently his body's physical grave—for a place in the memory (or imagination) of a Victorian

Englishman named Graves. The apartment house becomes, as a consequence of its fall, an unplanned necropolis, the psychic contents of which take up residence inside the British author. One can understand, then, why Graves decided to change the focus of his title from the "Imperial" idea (the equation of imperial Rome and imperial Britain) to the figure of the tenement or apartment house; the central idea is really the role of the author as a modern dwelling place for these ancient ghosts. Robert Graves is the apartment house cited in the title.

All this should prompt us to reconsider the implication of Graves's choice of a title for his earlier, immensely popular novel, *I, Claudius*. Certainly it is proper to think of the title as an abbreviated *incipit:* the first words of the text are "I, Tiberius Claudius Drusus Nero Germanicus This-that-and-the-other. . . ." Numerous ancient texts bear titles of this kind, and Graves surely liked this touch of scholarly authenticity. This assumption entails ascribing the first-person pronoun to the narrating voice of the fictionalized Claudius. But, proper as that assumption might be, the improper notion that Graves's own voice speaks in the title as well cannot be suppressed. If Egnatius has managed to set up psychic housekeeping in the tenement of Graves's mind, so too might other Romans of the time, including the emperor himself. The "I" of the title becomes shared property in such circumstances, since the self named Graves carries within it also some portion of a self named Claudius.

The existence of an Egnatius and a Claudius inside the modern British poet is more than a figure for the creative imagination: it is a suggestion about the ontology of history. Actually, Graves clearly would reject out of hand the notion that the historical characters in his fictions are simply the products of his own fancy. He asserts flatly in the "Author's Note" at the head of *Claudius the God* that "no character is invented in either volume." He attacks the opinion expressed by some reviewers of *I, Claudius* that he had gleaned facts from Tacitus and Suetonius "and expanded the result with my own 'vigorous fancy,' " listing an impressive array of classical writers he consulted.[6] At the back of the volume he appends not only a set of three texts describing Claudius's death, by way of completing the story Claudius himself could not, but also his own translation of Seneca's satire "The Pumkinification of Claudius," which served as a source for certain important details. He stresses his reliance on primary sources, not on his imagination: "The most difficult part to write, because of the meagreness of contemporary references to it, has been Claudius's defeat of Caractatus." But even in that case he did not turn to "vigorous fancy" but to alternative scholarly authority: "I have had to help out the few Classical notices of [British Druidism] with borrowings from archaeological works, from ancient Celtic literature and from accounts of modern megalithic culture in the New Hebrides, where the dolmen and menhir are still ceremonially used."[7] Claudius the historian also prizes scholarly rigor over the creative imagination. He expresses a preference for the historiography of Asinius Pollio over that of Livy, though the latter is a far more popular writer. Livy defends his method as one which produces an account that "may not be true in factual details, [but] is true in spirit." Pollio, on the other hand, claims that history is "a true record of what happened, how people lived and died, what they did and said," with no rhetorical embellishment or invented speeches. Pollio takes Livy to task for modernizing men of the past: "You credit the Romans of seven centuries ago with impossibly modern motives and habits and speeches. Yes, it's readable all right, but it's not history." Pollio's factual approach gets him the reputation of belonging to the company of "mere truthtellers—'undertakers who lay out the corpses of history' (to quote poor Catullus's epigram on the noble Pollio)—people who record no more than actually occurred."[8]

Claudius's preference for Pollio does not, however, lead him to reject out of hand Livy's belletristic style. His most telling comment on the two approaches poses the possibility that "perhaps they are not irreconcilable." The Claudius who writes the autobiography shows himself at the outset to be aware of the dangers of laying out the facts of history like a corpse: he had already done so himself in an "official" chronicle of his life dictated to his secretary Polybius. It was, he confesses, a very dull book:

> I let it be a dull book, recording merely such uncontroversial facts as, for example, that So-and-so married So-and-so, the slaughter of Such-and-such who had this or that number of public horrors to his credit, but not mentioning the political reasons for the marriage nor the behind-scene bargaining between the families. Or I would write that So-and-so died suddenly, after eating a dish of African figs, but say nothing of poison, or to whose advantage the death proved to be, unless the fact were supported by a verdict of the Criminal Courts. I told no lies, but neither did I tell the truth in the sense that I mean to tell it here.[9]

It had to be dull, Claudius acknowledges, because for reasons of state he could not report the unflattering truth about Augustus or his wife Livia and felt it would be unjust to spare them and give the unvarnished truth about others.

The problem is the relation between the historian and his readers. Livy writes highly readable history, but he sacrifices factuality.
Pollio writes only what he is confident is correct, but he must ignore
the interests of his readers. Claudius the emperor must be dull not
to disrupt the functioning of the state for which he is responsible.
But Claudius the autobiographer has found in his old age a way to
get around the problem of the historian's concern for the welfare of
his readers: he addresses his work to a set of "confidants" who can
be relied upon for discretion:

> But who, it may be asked, are my confidants? My answer is: it is addressed
> to posterity. I do not mean my great-grandchildren, or my great-great-
> grandchildren: I mean an extremely remote posterity. Yet my hope is
> that you, my eventual readers of a hundred generations ahead, or more,
> will feel yourselves directly spoken to, as if by a contemporary: as often
> Herodotus and Thucydides, long dead, seem to speak to me.[10]

Claudius needs an audience whom the truth cannot help or hurt,
an audience that is, therefore, "extremely remote" from his own
place and time. To such distant readers he can address a history that
is not only factual but also complete in the sense that it offers a look
at the "behind-scene" goings-on that often determine the course of
events.

At the same time, however, the emperor-historian requires intimacy with his audience; he hopes his readers will have the sense of
being "directly spoken to, as if by a contemporary." Claudius feels
such an intimate connection with Herodotus and Thucydides, dead
though they may be. Clearly help will be needed for this effort to
succeed, as Claudius recognizes in his resolve not to bury his manuscript in a sealed container but instead simply to leave it lying
around in the hope that chance will deliver it to a remote posterity.
But more than good fortune will be needed if the autobiography
of an early Roman emperor is to seem "contemporary" nineteen
hundred years later. Claudius must become somehow a voice belonging as much to the twentieth as to the first century, must acquire
somehow the ability to speak the vernacular of his distant audience.

He accomplishes this by taking up residence in the apartment
house offered by Graves. Claudius propels himself away from his
own time and place by addressing the future and by using a language other than Latin for his chronicle. But the language-other-
than-Latin he thinks he is using—Greek, the language of Herodotus
and Thucydides—undergoes a transformation into a language non-
existent in his own time—the English of Graves. Claudius speaks to

us like a contemporary because he *is* our contemporary in the sense that he has merged with the mind of a twentieth-century British writer. This union allows Claudius to "speak directly" to a posterity still extremely remote from him, to preserve the distance necessary for frankness while establishing the intimacy required by the role of confidant. Claudius, for all the modernity of his language and his feeling of kinship with the posterity living nineteen hundred years after his death, retains a certain residuum of alienness that Graves takes care not to minimize. It is not simply that Claudius is dead—though that does indeed represent a gap between him and us that we are in no hurry to bridge—but that he is a god. Certainly Claudius shows plenty of modern skepticism about his divinity, but he does not reject the idea completely. As he says of Augustus, "if a man is generally worshipped as a god then he is a god";[11] and it is more than self-deprecatory irony that prompts him to style himself "God of the Britons" in the novel's closing sentence.[12] The interplay between intimacy and distance that Graves figures as psychic subtenancy explicitly in "The Apartment" and implicitly in *I, Claudius* appears elsewhere in Graves's writing as the poetic trance. Indeed, it seems likely that Graves meant the conclusion of "The Apartment" to suggest that the poet has a kind of mystical access to the past that corresponds to his access to the totality of his experience in the poetic trance:

> In the poetic trance, [the poet] has access not only to the primitive emotions and thoughts that lie stored in is childhood memory, but to all his subsequent experiences—emotional and intellectual; including a wide knowledge of English won by constant critical study. Words are filed away . . . and as soon as the trance seizes him he can single out most of the ones he needs. Moreover, when the first heavily blotted draft has been copied out fairly before he goes to bed, and laid aside for reconsideration, he will read it the next morning as if it were written by another hand. Yet soon he is back in the trance, finds that his mind has been active while he was asleep on the problem of internal relations, and that he can substitute the exact right word for the stand-in with which he had to be content the night before.[13]

The trance is the means by which that which is alien in the psyche is made familiar. It calls the truce between "two separate and usually warring entities" of conscious and unconscious mind, allowing a productive traffic to develop. The results of these forays into alien territory will still have a distinct air of otherness about them: they look as if they "were written by another hand." One might, on occasion, give this "other hand" a local habitation and a name, and if the trance prompted the poet to consider the "internal relations" among all the facts he had gathered relating to the early Roman empire, that name might properly be Egnatius or even Claudius. It is, however, still and always *Graves* who focuses the trance.

The balance between intimacy and distance that Claudius wants in his relationship to his readers and which he attains by using an English poet as his medium reproduces the balance necessary to every act of reading. The relation between past and present is always necessarily legendary for the truth-telling historian who on the one hand cannot tolerate an audience with a real *interest* (in the root sense of the word) in the events related, but on the other must not fail to *excite* interest (in the more familiar sense). The material such a historian relates must be legendary in so far as it lingers on the distant horizon of his audience's reality, but legendary also in that it must compel a reading (*legenda* = "that which must be read") to establish that audience. The situation of reading, which presupposes both the absence of the author and the compelling presence of the author's signs and traces, is what Claudius seeks in its purest form. The great gap of time purifies it of all inappropriate forms of interest, of course. Claudius cites this purifying power of time when he explains his motive for burying his book in obscurity for nineteen hundred years: "And then, when all other authors of to-day whose works survive will seem to shuffle and stammer, since they have written only for to-day, and guardedly, my story will speak out clearly and boldly."[14] The shuffle and stammer that contaminate the physical body of the living Claudius migrate in the course of the centuries to the textual bodies of others; Claudius, writing only for posterity, will speak unstammeringly in his textual voice.

It is worth noting that the impetus for composing such a legible history for posterity comes from an act of reading. Claudius relates how he made a visit years earlier to the Cumaean Sibyl, asking the pythoness to prophesy about "Rome's fate and mine." She answers with a set of "Greek" verses:

> Who groans beneath the Punic Curse
> And strangles in the strings of purse,
> Before she mends must sicken worse.
>
> Her living mouth shall breed blue flies,
> And maggots creep about her eyes.
> No man shall mark the day she dies.
>
> Ten years, fifty days and three,
> Clau—Clau—Clau—shall given be
> A gift that all desire but he.

To a fawning fellowship
He shall stammer, cluck, and trip,
Dribbling always with his lip.

But when he's dumb and no more here,
Nineteen hundred years or near,
Clau—Clau—Claudius shall speak clear.[15]

The text is by no means self-explanatory, and Claudius must make use of all his experience as "a practiced diviner, a professional historian and a priest who has had opportunities of studying the Sibylline books" to interpret it.[16] The most difficult verses of all are the last three, which propound the riddle of clear speaking arising out of absence and silence. If we reformulate the verses in a standard riddle-form ("Who speaks clear when he is dumb and no more here?"), it becomes evident that indeed Claudius has hit upon the proper solution: an author.

But Claudius, experienced as both author and reader, knows this solution to the Sybil's riddle needs substantial refinement. Not just any act of writing will do. Claudius already is an author many times over, even the author of another autobiography, but he has no confidence that those other works will speak clearly to posterity. He will need to do two things to transform himself from the present stammerer into the future clear-speaker: first, he must make a special effort to address the posterity that will be his audience, and, second, he must let the same divine agency who made the prophecy provide for the text's reception: "Apollo has made the prophecy, so I shall let Apollo take care of the manuscript."[17] Apollo does so, but not in just the way Claudius expects. Instead of preserving the manuscript physically and transmitting it to the future, Apollo bridges the temporal gap in the same way he is accustomed to bridging the gap between his divine knowledge of the future and mortals' bounded present: he selects a human medium. As Claudius must read the divine wisdom of Apollo not from a document delivered from Olympus but through the mortal speech of an inspired woman, so must posterity read the history of Claudius not from an ancient manuscript miraculously preserved but through the contemporary English of an inspired poet. The Sybil's prophetic poem thus is a proleptic figure of Graves's historical poem. Both deliver out of a trance the truth of another time.

This striking use of the Sibyl as a figure for poetic mediation is evidence enough, I think, that Graves already at this relatively early stage in his career consciously was working out the notion of poetry that would become a decade later the core of *The White Goddess*. The poetic trance that produces modern poetry is, according to this idea, a development of a widespread ancient religious practice:

> The poetic trance derives from ecstatic worship of the age-old matriarchal Greek Muse. . . . A male dance-leader, originally her sacrificial victim, invoked the Muse by improvising hexameter verses to a lyre accompaniment that set an ecstatic round dance in motion. Presently the Muse . . . entered into, or "rode," some woman dancer, who now acted, spoke and sang on her mistress's behalf.[18]

Later, Muse-worship was assimilated to the cult of Apollo, and that god took on the role of leader of the Muses and principal inspirer of prophetic speech. "Yet Apollo," Graves contends, "though the patron of formal verse . . . , was incapable of supplying the authentic trance, and discouraged ecstatic utterances except from his own highly tendentious oracles."[19] But all genuine poetry remains for Graves intimately connected to the ancient cult of the White Goddess: "Poets who serve the Muse wait for the inspired lightning flash."[20]

The historical novel, no less than any other form of poetic activity, participates in the mystery of the poet's possession by a powerful Other. Graves makes this explicit in the opening of *Hercules, My Shipmate*, where he places a forthright "Invocation" of the spirit of one of Jason's shipmates, a certain Ancaeus, buried at Deia on the island of Majorca. A fictional supplicant, apparently a Greek of the second century B.C., begs the spirit to "speak to us visitants, speak clearly from your rocky tomb" and "unfold the whole story of that famous voyage," presumably through the mediation of that second-century Greek.[21] Ancaeus apparently grants the request, for the narrator, though no witness himself to the great doings aboard the Argo, speaks with the authority of such a witness. But the narrator, too, enters the tomb, and his possessed spirit possesses that of another resident of Majorca in yet a latter day: Graves himself. The chain of mediations is reminiscent of Plato's description of poetic inspiration in the *Ion*, where Socrates analogizes the power of the Muse to that of the lodestone magnetizing iron rings, each in turn magnetizing another. The ultimate beneficiary of this process is the audience, who may feel through all these mediations—though in a highly attenuated form—the power of the divine inspiration. The reader of *Hercules* or the *Claudius* books attains, with Graves's help, a certain intimacy with the past.

That Graves felt a genuine mystical intimacy with antiquity is, I think, clear enough. But it should also be clear that such an intimacy did not just come upon him out of nowhere. It did not happen that way with the Sibyl either, she had to prepare herself carefully, and she needed access to the holy place where Apollo, for his own reasons, preferred to engage with the mortal realm. Graves's preparations for his mystical union with Claudius were characterized by an attempt at scholarly thoroughness. He immersed himself in the documents available to him, just as Flaubert had done with the Punic materials he gathered for *Salammbô*. He did not, however, suppose that these studies in themselves could bring the past into sharp focus. Actually, for all of Graves's learning and despite his assurance that "historical authority of some sort or other"[22] supports nearly every incident in his novel, Graves maintains considerable skepticism about the reliability of such historical witnesses. The epigraph to *I, Claudius,* a passage taken from Tacitus, expresses the most radical doubt:

> A story that was the subject of every variety of misinterpretation, not only by those who then lived but likewise in succeeding times: so true is it that all transactions of preeminent importance are wrapt in doubt and obscurity; while some hold for certain facts the most precarious hearsays, others turn facts into falsehood; and both are exaggerated by posterity.[23]

Perhaps most interesting about this passage is its skepticism about contemporary interpretations of events. Tacitus finds no special privilege in eyewitnesses, at least when it comes to interpreting what they have experienced. Even those who see something happen do not necessarily know what they are seeing.

The implication is that the obscurity of the historical record is not only the product of failing memories and the physical losses occasioned by time but also, and perhaps more importantly, the result of the interests of those who interpret. Claudius suggests that he necessarily misinterprets his own life in his "official" autobiography because he must write with an awareness of his interests as emperor. He is only free to speak the truth when he imagines himself dead and therefore disinterested. "The dead may speak the truth only," says the supplicant in his prayer to Ancaeus, "even when it discredits themselves."[24] But the truthful dead, when they are given speech by means of poetic inspiration, tell their truth in a context already saturated by "every variety of misinterpretation" perpetuated and promulgated by uninspired historiography. The "facts" of history are more often a tissue of legends only tenuously connected to the reality of the past.

But if the past is legendary in this sense of history's unreliability, it is also legendary in that it is readable. The "doubt and obscurity" that envelop important events leave an opening for new acts of interpretation. The epigraph to *Hercules* makes this point even more clearly: "But as a rule the ancient myths [that is, *muthoi*, 'stories'] are not found to yield a simple and consistent story [*historia*], so that nobody need wonder if details of my recension cannot be reconciled with those given by every poet and historian."[25] Didorus Siculus may have been offering an excuse for the divergences between his version of the tale of the Argonauts and those of other authorities, but Graves is doing something else. He is stressing that the material treated in his novel is both unreliable and in need of interpretation: it is, in short, legendary. A creative act of reading must intervene to turn the ancient *muthoi* into *historia*. Graves presents his historical novels as such acts of reading, where the creativity is provided by the mystic process of poetic inspiration.

This inspiration is characterized by the interpenetration of living and dead, past and future. The author can be a grave (as the "original" narrative of Jason's story issues from the grave of Ancaeus) or Graves the medium, the living necropolis of ancient personalities. The author is necessarily touched by death to become one who "may speak the truth only," and indeed must descend into the land of the dead, like Mann's narrator in *Joseph* or his Professor Cornelius, to make contact with his subject. One of Graves's most profound perceptions is that death makes history, and this in every sense. Death not only transforms the present into the past, but also and more importantly death provides the magic that allows a set of random events to become *historia*, a true and consistent story. Death is the essential creative moment: "Now, to make yourself responsible for your entire life, and all your stupidities, successes, ill luck, joys and sufferings, puts you in a very strong position, because you can blame nobody else. But then the question arises: when were these decisions taken? . . . Then precisely when did I make myself? . . . At the moment of my death."[26] One might suspect that Graves is pulling the leg of his interviewer, especially since he prefaces these remarks with the rhetorical question, "But would you like to know how crazy I am?"[27] But Graves, in good Platonic style, finds the appearance of craziness in the most serious matters, such as this one. It is not just the old Graves (he gave this interview in 1970) who links death with the moment of self-creation. In 1929 the relatively young poet wrote an autobiography that makes a story out of the life he wished to renounce definitively. *Good-Bye to All That* posits a figurative death in the manner of Goethe's "Stirb und werde," a break in one's life so abrupt that what came before is "what I was, not what I am."[28] The moment of actual death is also a figurative death in this sense. It is the ultimate "good-bye" to all that: "That's the only time when life is complete. . . . Very well! That gives you a neat package all tied up."[29] Claudius only can tie up his package when, at the end of *Claudius the God,* the portents of his death appear in profusion about him.

Graves viewed the moment of death as one among several nodes at which linear time could be overcome. One of the "crazy" ideas he expressed to Edwin Newman was that "time is only a convenience, having no absolute sense."[30] This convenience can be dispensed with in the special and relatively rare moment when "one does any real thinking"—and the prospect of imminent death does, it has been said, focus the mind wonderfully. The poetic trance dissolves time in its way too, working through what Graves calls "the fifth dimension, independent of time."[31] Scientific insight can work similarly. Graves's favorite example, which he cited on more than one occasion, was Rowan Hamilton's discovery of Quaternions: "He was strolling across Phoenix Park, Dublin [in 1842], when suddenly this important formula came into his head. He happened to have a penknife with him, and cut the formula in stone on the bridge across the Liffey, now called Quaternion Bridge. Quaternions are among the chief mathematical props in nuclear physics."[32] Such sudden flashes of brilliance "plainly derive from fifth-dimensional thinking: they are not built up from any similar theories but make a leap into the future."[33] The moment of death opens the possibility of a leap into the past that enables one to "take sole responsibility for having been born."[34] The poetic trance that generates historical fiction allows another leap into the past that enables one to take sole responsibility for the existence of an ancient epoch.

Graves's forthright mysticism harbors no embarrassment for the belief in a supernatural power required to overcome the "convenience" of linear time. Such a belief was not at all uncommon among Graves's contemporaries, though it was perhaps less common in intellectual circles. But Graves, ever the eccentric, found the source of supernatural power not in the traditional Christian context one might have expected from a man of his background but in the unabashedly pagan White Goddess. The power of poetry cannot be separated from the primal force of the great female divinity, which is love: "The basis of poetry is love, but love between men . . . is seldom more than a metaphor. . . . Love between men and women is a fundamental motion, strong enough to transcend social contracts; and the love bestowed on a poet, however briefly, by a Muse-

possessed woman, heightens his creative power to an unparalleled
degree." This Muse-possessed woman is a kind of incarnation of the
Goddess herself, who is not only the bestower of love but also its
object. The Muse is "the perpetual Other Woman" who "scorns any
claim on her person or curb on her desires." She often appears to
be "a vixen, a bitch, a bird of prey" and will "multiply her evasions
and broken promises, while still demanding the poet's absolute
trust; take gifts as her right, rule him with a whim of iron, and subject him to almost insufferable ordeals."[35] The Muse is obviously a
harsh mistress, sometimes even a downright evil one: "her eventual
function and fate is to betray him." She would seem to have only
limited attractiveness to a sober Englishman born in the reign of
Victoria and possessed of an interest in ancient history. This very
Muse, however, presides prominently over both volumes of the *Claudius* novels and is in an important sense the story's central topic. The
story of the Roman emperors is of course a story of struggles for
power, but in Graves's version the most important and fundamental
power struggle goes on behind the scenes and involves figures to
whom traditional history has ascribed only marginal importance.
These marginalized figures are women, who occupy the secret center of the ancient world.

The Muse who rules over the *Claudius* novels appears most dramatically in the guise of the implacable, horrifying, yet somehow attractive Livia. She is so often the subject of Claudius's discourse that
he feels guilty about it: "I must apologize for continuing to write
about Livia, but it is unavoidable."[36] Everything of major importance
that occurs in the early empire proves her doing, so naturally Claudius must keep returning to her. She is most directly the Muse who
drives Augustus to the pinnacle of power and the one who keeps
him there, demanding and receiving absolute trust, ruling him
(without his ever realizing it) with a whim of iron. Her efforts represent an attempt by female power, once dominant in Europe but long
since overthrown by patriarchy, to reassert itself. It is the vengeance
of the White Goddess, who will not tolerate male rule without ex-
tracting a terrible price. Livia declares herself to be "perhaps the
greatest ruler that the world has ever known,"[37] and enough
grounds for the claim exist to keep Claudius (and the reader) from
dismissing it.

Livia does not seem to be the object of Claudius's love; quite the
contrary, he seems to despise her. And yet, once Livia is dead and
Claudius is emperor, he makes sure to comply with her wish to make
her a goddess: "I had not changed my opinion of the ruthlessness
and unscrupulousness of the methods that she used for gaining con-

trol over the Empire and keeping it in her hands for some sixty-five years; but . . . my admiration for her organizing abilities increases every day."[38] When he considers the matter in detail, as in the speech he makes to the senate proposing her deification, Claudius finds her faults to be consistent with her divinity:

> Heartlessness is a grave human fault and is unforgivable when combined with profligacy, greed, sloth and disorderliness; but when combined with boundless energy and a rigid sense of order and public decency, heartlessness takes on a different character altogether. It becomes a divine attribute. Many gods do indeed possess nearly so full a measure as my grandmother did. Then again, she had a will that was positively Olympian in its inflexibility, and though she never spared any member of her own household who failed to show the devotion to duty that she expected of him, or who created a public scandal by his loose living, neither, we must remember, did she spare herself. How she worked![39]

He goes on to remind the senate of how much Augustus relied on Livia's advice and benefited from her "divine wisdom."

This may seem like grudging admiration, and it may be so, but Claudius demonstrates the depth of his attachment to his grandmother by emulating Augustus's reliance on his spouse. In the paragraph that directly follows the one reporting the deification of Livia, Claudius informs us: "I trusted Messalina so completely that I allowed her to use a duplicate seal for all letters and decisions made on my behalf."[40] We ought to remember that the full title of the second volume of the *Claudius* novels is *Claudius the God and His Wife Messalina*. In many important respects Livia and Messalina are the same woman, both avatars of the powerful, terrible White Goddess. A third incarnation appears near the end, when Claudius marries his kinswoman Agrippina, the mother of Nero and reputed poisoner of Claudius. She reminds one of Livia not only in her penchant for poison but also her formidable administrative skills: "I must say at once that Agrippinilla has shown herself a remarkably able ruler of the tyrannical sort. . . . She no longer needs to pretend affection for me. I soon made her realize that I married her purely on political grounds. . . . I was quite frank about it. I explained: 'The fact is, that I got tired of being Emperor. I wanted someone to do most of the work for me. I married you not for your heart but for your head. It takes a woman to run an empire like this.' " This realization that women are more suited than men to the exercise of power is Claudius's ultimate compliment to the memory of the deified Livia. It is an acknowledgement that the woman whom he helped make a goddess was right from the beginning an earthly aspect of the Goddess to whom all poets and historians owe allegiance.

The *Claudius* novels embody Graves's belief that the pursuit of history and devotion to the Muse who rules with a whim of iron are essentially the same. Ancient history is the particular realm of the Goddess, both because in ancient times her cult was most visible and because her nature is to be remote, difficult, and "wrapped in doubt and obscurity." She is the paradigm of the legendary, and therefore the object of both Graves's and Claudius's desire. For Claudius, the physical object of his erotic longing resides in Messalina, as for Graves it was (or had been) Laura Riding. But in both cases physical attraction emerges as secondary to an intellectual longing for something ultimately even more enigmatic, more demanding, more heartless than any living woman. The relation between history and the "perpetual Other woman" is one of mutual figuration in which each is vehicle for the other's tenor. The relation of the present and past, like that between man and woman, is one of intimacy between two entities that always remain fundamentally alien to each other. Claudius may share Messalina's bed, but he never understands her. And Claudius (or Egnatius) may share Graves's consciousness, making the modern Englishman the medium of history, a living necropolis housing the spirits of ancient Rome, but those spirits will always belong to another world that remains accessible only in acts of inspired imagination.

Notes

1. Robert Graves, *Collected Short Stories* (Garden City: Doubleday, 1964), 153.

2. It is worth noting that Graves was so seriously wounded by bursting shells in World War I that he lay in a coma for twenty-four hours and was given up for dead. An official letter of condolence was sent to his mother. Graves therefore knew firsthand the experience of living on in the "now" despite being apparently dead "then." See Katherine Snipes, *Robert Graves* (New York: Ungar, 1979), 3.

3. Robert Graves, *I, Claudius: From the Autobiography of Tiberius Claudius, Born B.C. X, Murdered and Deified A.D. LIV* (New York: Random House, n.d.), 93.

4. *I, Claudius*, 28.

5. Robert Graves, *Claudius the God and His Wife Messalina* (New York: Random House, n.d.), 431.

6. Ibid., 5–6.

7. Ibid., 6.

8. *I, Claudius*, 108–9, 115.

9. Ibid., 4–5.

10. Ibid., 5.

11. *Claudius the God*, 393.

12. Ibid., 559.

13. "The Poet in a Valley of Dry Bones," in Robert Graves, *Mammon and the Black Goddess* (London: Cassell, 1965), 88–89.

14. *I, Claudius,* 8.

15. Ibid., 7.

16. Ibid., 8.

17. Ibid., 8–9.

18. "Intimations of the Black Goddess," in *Mammon and the Black Goddess,* 145.

19. Ibid., 146.

20. Ibid., 147.

21. Robert Graves, *Hercules, My Shipmate* (New York: Creative Age Press, 1945), 2.

22. *Claudius the God,* 6.

23. *I, Claudius,* unnumbered front matter.

24. Ibid.

25. *Hercules, My Shipmate,* vii. Graves gives both the original Greek and the English translation cited here.

26. "Speaking Freely: Interview by Edwin Newman on the American Air," in Robert Graves, *Difficult Questions, Easy Answers* (London: Cassell, 1972), 206–7.

27. Ibid., 206.

28. Quoted in Snipes, *Robert Graves,* 8. Graves's *vita nuova* posited by the book tacitly recapitulates in the spiritual realm the physical resurrection he experienced after his "fatal" wounding during the war.

29. "Speaking Freely," 207.

30. Ibid., 206.

31. "What Has Gone Wrong?," in *Difficult Questions, Easy Answers,* 118.

32. "Speaking Freely," 206.

33. "What Has Gone Wrong?," 118.

34. Ibid., 118.

35. The quoted material above and immediately following is from "Intimations of the Black Goddess," 146–56.

36. *I, Claudius,* 29.

37. Ibid., 312.

38. *Claudius the God,* 144.

39. Ibid., 146.

40. Ibid., 149.

Part III
Fresh Glances at James Joyce

Bakhtin, Joyce, and the Epic Tradition

Zack Bowen

THAT JOYCE NEVER READ BAKHTIN NOR BAKHTIN JOYCE IS HARD TO believe. Evidence, of course, exists that Bakhtin was prevented from writing on Joyce, but Joyce's work virtually cries out for recognition in the pages of "Epic and Novel,"[1] Bakhtin's analysis of the historical and substantive differences between the two genres. The relevance of his arguments to *Ulysses* and its special place in modern literature seems inescapable. Central to his discussion is the open-endedness and contemporaneity of the novel as opposed to the epic, which is frozen in an inflexible past as a segment of the ur-tradition defining a civilization or nation's history of "beginnings" and peak time in nationhood as represented to its descendants. The epic was not even about a time contemporaneous with its writing, but about a past period and the heroes who came before the descendants for whom it was composed. For Bakhtin the epic relies on personal and sacrosanct tradition. It relies on a commonly held evaluation and point of view that excludes any possibility of another approach, therefore displaying a profound piety toward the subject described and toward the language used to describe it, the language of tradition.

Bakhtin traces the roots of the novel at least to the Socratic dialogues and Menippean satire, which even in classic Greek times posed alternatives to national origins in epic poetry. The issues he discusses focus on the closed system of the epic, its quasi-religious insistence on conventions of form, language, and its unchangeable didactic history spelling out the prime exemplars of nationhood as moral–religious paradigms for descendants. The novel, as the only genre still evolving and hence open to an ever-changing world of contemporary circumstances, without closure, is always looking to the future, and is self-reflexive in its constant critique of the human condition and its relation to the narrative itself. It has it own sanctions of conduct, notably its lower, irreverent comic aspect, and is companion to Bakhtin's concept of the carnivalesque and Foucault's subjugated knowledges.

51

According to Bakhtin, Socrates's dialogues show this tendency to debunk pretenders to absolute knowledge serio-comically by assuming the guise of a know-nothing, ignorant of the topic of conversation, bringing the antagonist—with his pretense of infallibility—to defeat, a variation on Peter Falk's television detective Columbo. Parody and satires had the same function, of course, providing the background of the novel, beginning with originals in Cervantes and Rabelais. My argument is, of course, that what Bakhtin so cogently describes as the novel reached its modern zenith in *Ulysses,* because it so precisely defined the genre as Bakhtin did: its comic representation of self-referentiality and realistic contemporary life, its concentration on the future by refusing closure in the present, and its consciously offering only ambiguity as its conclusion. *Ulysses* not only accomplishes everything that Bakhtin claimed for the genre as a whole, but also, more astoundingly, did it all self-consciously, almost as if Joyce had himself taken Bakhtin to heart and written a parody of Bakhtin's diology between epic and novel forms. Either by happenstance or because they were both right, the writer and critic mirror each other's ideas. Joyce made certain that his readers knew that the title of his novel was more than just a name when he discussed his Homeric parody with Stuart Gilbert. In doing so he broke ground for the contemporary epic novels of Barth, Pynchon, and García Márquez, parodic works that comically treat the contemporary human condition in a way satirizing the solemn pronouncements not only of their epic predecessors but also of their classical forbears in the novel itself—and in the process satirizing themselves. This claim for comic modernism will, I hope, occupy a booklength manuscript, out of what begins as the foul rag and bone shop of Joyce/Bakhtin's egalitarian vision.

Keith Booker, in his groundbreaking *Joyce, Bakhtin, and the Literary Tradition,* covers many of the same fields retilled here for slightly different purposes.[2] Booker stands midway between my reading of *Ulysses* not only as a comedy, but also as the modern comic work that dictated the later comic-epic novels of the mid- and late twentieth century, and Julia Kristeva's position that comedy is not the primordial expression of life, but in its conflation with Menippean satire exists only as a serious (i.e., righteous) expression of opposition to confound the authoritarian pronouncements of whatever hegemony bears examining.[3]

For this paper reexamining Bakhtin's arguments in "Epic and Novel" more or less seriatim, discussing each relevant idea in relationship to Joyce's composition of *Ulysses,* is enough. Early in the essay Bakhtin made the first iteration of the centrality of the novel's essentially comic approach to life:

> Parodic stylizations of canonized genres and styles occupy a central place in the novel. In the era of the novel's creative ascendancy—and even more so in the periods of preparation preceding this era—literature was flooded with parodies and travesties of all the high genres . . . parodies that are the precursors, "companions" to the novel, in their own ways studies for it. . . . This ability of the novel to criticize itself is a remarkable feature of the ever-developing genre. (6)

Joyce, of course, by titular admission parodied the epic, but hardly stopped there. After Sirens, Joyce devoted the rest of the book to comic parodies not only of former classics and authors such as the Rabelaisian giganticisms in Cyclops, the Sternean postponements of vital information throughout Ithaca, the Cervantes's Quixote–Panza aspects of the dual protagonists, and the plethora of literary parodies in Oxen, but also of turn-of-the-century news headlines in all their permutations in Hades, periodical advertising in Nausicaa, clichéd literary speech in Eumaeus, science and religious language in Ithaca, newspaper language and evangelical oratory in Cyclops, and parodies of stage language and effects from pantomime through *Faust* in Circe, as well as countless others. *Ulysses* contains so many parodies, including those created by the characters themselves (i.e., Mulligan's parody of priest/Stephen, Stephen's parody of Simon on family relations) that, besides the all-encompassing parody of the *Odyssey,* more lines of internal parody than of nonparodic text can be found in *Ulysses.* Even Bloom's and Molly's seemingly original images come from popular clichés such as song memories, often presented as original thoughts. A scholar at the recent Rome symposium declared that Joyce lacked linguistic training. What had Joyce been doing all his life *but* absorbing and uncannily reproducing in parody form an inordinate cross-section of linguistic styles and ideas in his last two books? Since a much fuller discussion of specific parodies in a Bakhtinian context appears in *Ulysses as a Comic Novel,* I will let the matter rest, except to say that, even with all the literary parodies, the voices of common people in all their parodic wisdom and stupidity are just as vital a source of satiric fun, and even closer to the contemporaneity of the work.

Bakhtin makes the point that the novel becomes free and flexible when its language renews itself by incorporating extraliterary heteroglossia (common language) and by engaging the "novelistic" layers of literary language in a diologized interaction. It is an interaction

permeated with laughter, irony, humor, [and] elements of self-parody.
. . . [F]inally . . . the novel inserts into these other genres an indeterminacy, a certain semantic openendedness, a living contact with unfin-
ished, still-evolving contemporary reality (the openended present). (7)

Joyce's combination of comedy, popular culture, and literature of
every canonical rank mixed together with common activities and
speech in *Ulysses* helps explain why, despite its difficulty, the book
makes such an appeal to Joycean nonprofessionals. It goes beyond
Stephen's promise in *Portrait* by recreating life out of life and literary
history. According to Bakhtin, the novel (read *Ulysses*) is the product
not of epic monoglossia—or set of ossified verbiage—but of polyg-
lossia where interaction of language and dialects provide multiple
points of view and meanings (13). Just as the term *epic* in the vernacular has come to mean "all inclusive," "big," or "comprehensive"
in today's colloquial and advertising argot, so has *Ulysses* taken on
those vulgar proportions, polyglossic attributes that bestow on this
hybridized mock epic the qualities of modern-age genius. It authentically represents everyday life, it is skeptical of everything including
itself, it embodies tradition and a great deal more, and it recognizes
and represents comedy as the vital, salvational force of life. Booker's
example of Bloom's checking out the number of orifices in the mu-
seum statue, as a paradigm for Joyce's comic literalization of classic
art(s), draws a brilliant analogy to Joyce's essentially comic process.

I have no intention of expressing any fundamental disagreement
with Booker's approach to Bakhtin and Joyce except for Booker's
assertion that "Joyce is not so much leaning on Homer's authority
as trying to undermine it and thereby to contribute to breaking the
hold that the past exerts on the present of Ireland" (13). Joyce is
comically capitalizing on Homer's epic authority not to accord it the
honor of some full-blown dialogic opposition, but to play with it as a
means of comically redirecting its authority to encompass Ireland's
microcosm as the basis of the rest of Western civilization, thus bringing all of us into sync with the realities of modern-day life. Bloom is
not merely an Irish Everyman but also a comically messianic Sancho
Panza whose outlook combines mundane irreverence for the traditional classical romances of his boss with having to cope with the
conditions of everyday life. By extending that literary metaphor
from sixteenth-century Spain to modern Dublin, Joyce forges a conscience for his race and at the same time prepares an elixir for everybody from here to Vladivostok.

In composing a mock epic, Joyce turned the original genre 180
degrees. As Bakhtin tells us,

Epic discourse [as] . . . a discourse handed down by tradition . . . is given solely as tradition . . . sacred and sacrosanct, evaluated in the same way by all and demanding a pious attitude toward itself, which excludes the possibility of another approach . . . and which therefore displays a profound piety toward the subject described and . . . toward the language of tradition. (17)

When Joyce would not succumb to demands to rewrite tradition to the tune of national propaganda but promised to forge the conscience of his race, he may not have thought that race would encompass Western civilization. Irish epic poetry during the Irish Renaissance was a major source of the nationalistic movement, and writers were expected to devote their talents to nationalist literature akin in purpose to what Bakhtin describes as the prime purpose of the epic: to create a national history and identity for racial descendants. Since the original story already is common knowledge, epics do not need to establish final closure but may be fragmentary aspects of the entire history, such as the *Iliad*'s conclusion with Hector's death. The plethora of Deirdre stories, poems, and dramas are just such partial segments of Irish epic history as it comes down from the *Tain*, etc. Joyce chose to take the epic beyond its national boundaries and raise his sights beyond Dublin or Ireland to bring the tradition of the West under comic scrutiny, and by microcosmic parodic extension make Dublin the Ithaca of Europe and ur-home of a civilization, bringing the sacrosanct piety of the epic under the cleansing comic laser focus of his satire. By relegating the Ur-religion/tradition of the Western world in the mundane terms of Dublin's citizens' idiosyncratic, subjugated, subaltern knowledges, he encompassed several hemispheric leaps—geographical and linear, into the twentieth century and beyond. As Bakhtin put it,

The novel comes into contact with the spontaneity of the inconclusive present: this is what keeps the genre from congealing. . . . He may turn up on the field of representation in any authorial pose, he may depict real moments in his own life or make allusions to them, he may interfere in the conversations of his heroes, he may openly polemicize with his literary enemies and so forth . . . for the "depicting" authorial language now lies on the same plane as the "depicted" language of the hero. (27)

This, of course, precisely describes Joyce's use of Stephen Dedalus in both *Portrait* and *Ulysses*.

What Joyce did is what many of us who teach classical literature to undergraduates do in our classrooms—that is, we try to give epics such as the *Odyssey* the immediacy of a novel by representing it as a

universal homecoming and reassertion of patriarchal rights of possession. In effect, Joyce not only universalized the traditional in
terms of time and place, but his comedy also provided the hard-
headed verisimilitude of modern reality. His work created serio-
comic veracity embracing everybody from artists to ad salesmen to
Andrew J. Pisser Burke. Each reader can create his or her own Penel-
ope/Ulysses satirically shorn of propaganda, cant, and pomposity—
fantasizing, defecating, urinating, masturbating—engaging in all
human activities and feeling the whole range of emotions. It's a new
Bloomusalem.

Embodying all that "contemporaneity," the "flowing and transitory, 'low present,'—this 'life without beginning or end' was the basic
subject matter in that broadest and richest of realms, the common
people's creative culture of laughter" (20). The contemporaneity
and its attendant laughter become for Bakhtin the evolving embodiment of the future out of the present, the persistence of common
experience always relevant to reality, future as well as present. If anything like the continuum of life exists, a sort of immorality of the
evolving mundane, it lies in the ever-changing comic debunking of
shibboleths, past and present. According to the personal admissions
of such comic writers as Angela Carter, John Barth, and Gabriel
García Márquez, as well as a host of others, Joyce's parodic examples
and ideas live on in their works, and their characters, like Joyce's
Bloom, are not frozen in time as epic heroes whose fate is already
assigned, but heroes who retain a happy surplus of their own, their
rudimentary but inexhaustible "human face" capable of more than
developing a set plot but instead a whole realm of transient possibility, "heroes of free improvisation and not heroes of tradition, heroes
of a life process that is imperishable and forever renewing itself, forever contemporary—these are not heroes of an absolute past" (36).
Joyce passed this vital legacy on to the future of literature.

Joyce's work set new standards of freedom and "plasticity itself . . .
[for] a genre that is ever questioning, ever examining itself and sub-
jecting its established forms to review" (39) and along the way finding and forging new ways to extract new wine out of old bottles, as
Barth claims in the "Literature of Replenishment." In *Ulysses,* trivia
made epic accord the mundane epic importance. The self-referentiality of examining motives of characters, their ways of expressing
themselves, and the comic parody of internal and external self-ex-
amination, of language itself, and of inviting readers to seek nonexistent conclusions, even as no ultimate answers exist for the
characters, all establish their own contingent if irrefutable comic
truth. The relationship of modern society to the ancient made mani-

fest in Joyce's *Ulysses/Odyssey* parody is about a dialogue between modern transient reality and antique notions of a social ur-contract with history. For Bakhtin such a dichotomy has always existed in the unruly common comic mind, whose consciousness of reality has been subjugated by hegemonic claims for some sort of perfection in the ur-past and its solemn prophecies of the future, and whose present has been bounded only by circumstance and lack of innovation. Joyce's combination provided the innovation to move into a future of comic possibilities. The idea did not dawn all at once as an epiphany, but rather, gradually throughout his early career.

In *Dubliners* Joyce did not begin his description of common city life with a crowd of essentially comic citizens, but by the time the penultimate trio of stories was written, his satire and irony had begun to take on aspects of comedy. For instance, the reader must closely read the newspaper account of "A Painful Case" to understand how ridiculous an official coverup could be, with its touches of official newspeak in providing an exculpation of the railroad for any blame in Mrs. Sinico's death. According to the account, the testimony established that the train, starting from a dead stop, had, in the second or two before the engineer stopped it, gathered enough speed to knock Mrs. Sinico flying. A series of increasingly funny descriptions of the hearing follow until the account with journalistic delicacy touches on the wages of her intemperate sins, the whole programmed to turn the death into a justifiable homicide: "No blame attached to anyone." By attaching blame to Mrs. Sinico, the article managed to unattach blame to anybody else, especially the railway's employee. Duffy recapitulates the blame motif in initially taking the story at face value and blaming Sinico. Then, in an outburst of self-importance, he attributes her heartbroken bibulous behavior to her loss of his own scintillating company, even though she had only been drinking for two years and the breakup occurred two years before that. The underlying ludicrousness of nipped-in-the-bud carnality is underscored by the final metaphor of a phallic train winding through the darkness "obstinately and laboriously."

The newspaper account in "A Painful Case" begins Joyce's shift from satire to parody as the predominant tone in the last half of *Dubliners*. "A Mother," "Ivy Day," and "Grace" become increasing comic in their parodic behavior, so that what might have been taken as a sentimental high point in Gabriel's vision of universality in the all-encompassing snow of death is comically undermined by two phallic boots, one on its side to represent the departed, and the other with a limp erection.

The irony of *Portrait* falls far short of thigh-slapping comedy in

Joyce's bildungsroman depiction of artistic youth and zeal. Stephen does not have the seasoning to see (read) himself as others do, and his solipsistic reality dominates the narrative, just as the middle-aged Joyce's softened and outward-oriented Bloom dominates *Ulysses*. Life in that book, despite inward suffering, shifts to a nonjudgmental perception closer to Bloom's; it affords the spotlight to surroundings existing in and of themselves, not as trials and tribulations of middle age, but as manifestations of life independent of, although impinging on, the protagonist. All this action occurs in a novel of becoming—of the future. In the novel, one protagonist may learn something about reality, and, given Stephen's own theory of authorial detachment, unrealized in practice up to this point, that protagonist may write a novel about the mundane man he himself may or may not become.

The book leaves us with only questions about the future: Will Bloom get his breakfast? Will Molly continue her liaison with Boylan? Has Stephen learned enough to write *Ulysses*? Will anyone vaguely like Bloom—putative author of *My Experiences in a Cabman's Shelter*—write *Ulysses*? Will Deasy's letter about hoof-and-mouth disease cure Ireland's economic problems? Who was M'Intosh? Will Bloom dream *Finnegans Wake* nestled between the plump, mellow, yellow smellonous melons of Molly's behind? Ultimately we are made to realize that the answers we had so long sought in vain in Ithaca mean far less than the comedic unimportance of the questions. We have been fed a dose of parodic reality to temper our own view on the future, even as we glimpse its affinity to the past in the form of the epic homecoming the novel satirizes.

Thus, *Ulysses*, like the novel form Bakhtin describes, offers an alternative to closure and the closedness of the epic tradition—as the genre turns toward indeterminacy, interpretation, new points of view, and evaluations (17). As Bakhtin tells us,

> Laughter is a vital factor in laying down the prerequisite for fearlessness without which it would be impossible to approach the world realistically. As it draws an object to itself and makes it familiar, laughter delivers the object into the fearless hands of investigative experiment—both scientific and artistic—and into the hands of free experimental fantasy. Familiarization of the world through laughter and popular speech is an extremely important and indispensable step in making possible free, scientifically knowable and artistically realistic creativity in European civilization. (23)

In terms of *Ulysses*, Joyce's choice of comedy opened the way to the great experimental innovations of the second half of the book, and ultimately to perhaps the greatest novelistic experiment of modern times, *Finnegans Wake*. It could not have been so effective without having reduced the world it investigates to the familiarity comedy provides. Goethe only touched on comedy in his experimental fantasy in the Walpurgus Nacht scene in *Faust I* and the fantasia pageantry of *Faust II*. But Goethe had a serious message: to get back to the important but mundane vocation of sewer building, which finally satisfies Faust's longings.

The *Faust* model in Joyce's comedic hands in Circe led, from my point of view, to a far more insightful sojourn through the libidinous avenues of human fantasy in Bella Cohen's. To paraphrase Stephen, by thinking of things comically, you can understand them, strip them of their traditional superstitions, and examine them in the freedom of the creative imagination. Masochism, sado- and otherwise, can be more realistically represented and understood through the comic lens than through all the piety in the world. Fetishism, guilt, vaulting ambition, scapegoating, and all the other ills/joys that flesh is heir to are acceptable to the superegos of Joyce readers because Joyce presented them as part of the realistic human comedy, making us realize that they are as funny as they are sad. So Joyce cast his Circe play on the old familiar comic pantomime stage, regarded by Irish and English citizenry as being as wholesome as Disneyworld. Admittedly, the realities of the carnivalesque origins of both are not every clergyman's cup of tea, any more than is the threat to religio-political hegemony of comedy in general.

Joyce set the stage for Circe's liberties with pious tradition in the diology of Cyclops, where the low cantankerousness of the barfly vies with the stentorian aggrandizements of newspaper and periodical writers, like those of the reporter in "A Painful Case." One narrator is funny in his scrupulous meanness, the other in his pomposity. The diology of Nauscicaa shifts genders between another kind of advertising writing, which has made such inroads on its audience that it gives voice and meaning to Gerty McDowell's thoughts. The other voice, Bloom's own, is the product of a middle-aged man, preoccupied with his own marital solipsistic problems, not unlike the ones that must have plagued Odysseus on the Phoenician beach. The voyeurism of the Greek hero is made comically explicit here by Bloom's masturbatory response and the Lacanian gaze, with its own combination of sexual pyrotechnics, as Bloom picks up where Odysseus and Stephen at the end of chapter four of *Portrait* left off (pun intended).

Oxen introduces us to heteroglossia with a vengeance, as parodied language over the centuries obscures meaning, and parody of classical precursors becomes an end in itself. Reality here is buried in the past, even harder to resurrect given the present dialects and speech variations, until we are offered the consoling balm of John Alexander Dowie's elixir in evangelical terms we *can* understand, even as we know its comedic import is advertising sham. Better this than bee-sting dragon-smites, or obfuscated sardines, or the reappearance of that holiest of ghosts, M'Intosh.

After Circe is the heteroglossia of Eumaeus, the voice of the old tarpaulin, Sinbad/Odysseus, comically obfuscating with his nautically tinged verbiage amidst a mountain of contemporary clichés. This journalistic idiom arises from a common, if comically ostentatious narrator who is *not* James Joyce.

The Ithaca diology between two points of view variously described by critics as scientific, catechismal, and so forth, is Joyce's final attempt to frustrate closure or afford anything but the merest ground for speculation on what the book is about—its "meaning." The issue of what can be trusted as empirical, or scientific, or mathematical, or historical truth has only in the last decade come under critical scrutiny, with "errors" pointed out, beginning with the list of Molly's putative lovers. By this time some people still did expect that at least some questions as well as answers would yield truths in a context, even if totally irrelevant—as most of the relationship between Ithaca's questions and answers are—to the perennial issue of life itself. To what expectant readers deem meaningful questions, answers were afforded in contexts other than what they expected to hear, and, to what appeared to be irrelevant questions. These answers, pregnant with potentially deep meaning, were given in this exceptionally funny frustration of readers' demands for traditional closure. In the end most of us "get it": that this is not an epic; that there is no traditional closure; that this a modern novel in the process of becoming a post-modern novel, and now a post–post-modern novel; and so on into the Bakhtinian future. The only thing (apparently) certain is that, like the *Wake*, the last word is a woman's. But of course in the *Wake*, whose comic manifestations dwarf those of *Ulysses*, the last word is the first, and who knows what gender inspired that? One more thing—the last word is "Yes." I leave it at that.

Notes

1. M. M. Bakhtin, *The Dialogic Imagination*, ed. Michael Holquist (Austin: University of Texas Press, 1981).

2. M. Keith Booker, *Joyce, Bakhtin, and the Literary Tradition: Toward a Comparative Cultural Poetics* (Ann Arbor: the University of Michigan Press, 1997).

3. For a fuller discussion of Julia Kristeva on Bakhtin see my "Word, Dialogue, and Novel," in *Desire in Language: A Semiotic Approach to Literature and Art*, ed. Leon S. Roudiez (New York: Columbia University Press, 1980).

"I pity your oldself I was used to": *Finnegans Wake* and the Aesthetics of Aging

Michael Patrick Gillespie

Images of age and aging fill the final ten pages of *finnegans Wake*, the portion of Joyce's narrative devoted to the valedictory soliloquy of the female principal, Anna Livia Plurabelle (ALP):

> O bitter ending! I'll slip away before they're up. They'll never see. Nor know. Nor miss me. And it's old and old it's sad and old it's sad and weary I go back to you, my cold father, my cold mad father, my cold mad feary father. . . . (627.34–628.02)[1]

Further, the position of this passage in the book and its insistent reference to time passing and to individuals growing old lead conventional readers to see it as a description of entropic decline. They view it as an account of physical disintegration that matches the figurative break-up of the narrative that has transpired over the course of *Finnegans Wake*. Indeed, in the first book-length commentary on *Finnegans Wake* to appear after its publication, Joseph Campbell and Henry Morton Robinson endorse this linear tone and apply it to an assessment of ALP's monologue; they call it "the elegy of the River Liffey as she passes, old, tired, soiled with the filth of the city, through Dublin and back to the sea."[2]

The inclination to identify these lines as the book's denouement doubtless grows out of a strong tradition in Western literature that sees unambiguous dissolution—physical and mental—as the inexorable consequence of the passage of time and the inevitable conclusion in tragedy. Indeed, easy analogies occur between the funereal tone of the closing pages of *Finnegans Wake* and, for example, that which dominates the final scene of *King Lear*. One must, of course, engage in a slight inversion of events—Lear joins his daughter in death, while ALP returns to a life with her father. Nonetheless, for conventional readers, Albany's bitter question, "Is this the promised end?," might apply equally well to either passage. Further, such a view makes perfect sense in a linear world where Cartesian cause-and-effect logic and Newtonian science bring a measure of predictability to our lives.

However, while Shakespeare wrote at the beginning of the Enlightenment with Baconian science displacing Scholastic thinking, Joyce writes in an entirely different era. In 1905 Albert Einstein discovered that time, which had always seemed an unvarying condition, a constant in an otherwise contingent world, had the unsettling habit of varying with its context. Subsequently, theories of relativity, of quantum mechanics, and of uncertainty have radically altered assumptions about how one can perceive the physical world. In consequence, contemporary readers face a situation where elements previously presumed to be stable benchmarks do not in fact offer consistent assessments of reality.

Although only one in a series of dramatic reassessments of the physical world that took place in the early decades of the twentieth century, Albert Einstein's work on relativity forcefully demonstrates this reconfiguration of perceptions. Einstein demonstrated his premise of time's elasticity with a thought experiment involving the kinetic actions of trains and lightning bolts. Allow me to offer tamer illustrations of his theories based upon stasis but no less reflective of chronological relativity. All our senses tell us that a boring sixty-minute lecture given in an overheated room filled with a restive audience does not encompass the same amount of time as an hour spent enjoying a wonderful meal at a four-star restaurant. Analogously, fourteen days waiting for a biopsy result do not pass nearly as quickly as two weeks vacationing in Florida in mid-winter. To say that the gauges or mechanisms we use to measure time confirm these experiences to be of equal duration imposes artificial mechanistic boundaries upon the comprehension of duration that our senses do not readily accept.[3]

For literary critics, however, the specifics of Einstein's scientific theory or of those of other twentieth-century physicists do not emerge as important features of such discoveries. Rather, the broader impact of their work exerts significant influence on how we think about physical reality. In particular, their discoveries compel us to change the manner in which we speak not simply about time but also about concepts located in time, like aging. For the sake of accuracy, we must now acknowledge the contextual elasticity that shapes perceptions at any given instant.[4] For example, as one moves contemporaneously from context to context, changing roles evoke patterns of behavior originating in different periods in one's life. (When I travel with my wife and daughter to visit my parents' home or to visit my brothers and sisters, I alternate between being spouse, parent, child, sibling.) The process, however, is not linear or unidirectional. Sitting at the Thanksgiving dinner table we might, in successive moments, assume all these roles and in doing so occupy different periods in our lives. In essence we would inhabit contiguous spaces of time differently. In the process we reject as too narrow the limitations of defining aging by a unidirectional insistence of biology.

Perceptions of and responses to one's environment stand as significant to humanists because we fabricate so much of the language of our discipline—certainly its principal metaphors—from images of the physical world. If science now offers a more detailed and sophisticated conception of physical reality, should we not acknowledge this change in our imaginative fields as well? To some degree, of course, we have already implemented those changes in perception by unconsciously accommodating them to our ways of seeing the world, as in the examples just cited of perceptions of passing time or of ostensibly chronological roles. Nonetheless, formal recognition of this shift would enhance the way we speak of writers like Joyce who have already adopted into their narratives this new way of perceiving.

Just as Shakespeare wrote out of a period when a new science was reforming the imaginative consciousness, so also did Joyce. A Scholastic could read and enjoy *Hamlet,* but a Humanist would have a greater sense of the intellectual scope of the play. Similarly, while linear, cause-and-effect thinking can still produce logical interpretations of Joyce's writing, approaches sensitive to nonlinear dynamics lead to much fuller readings.[5]

In terms of age and aging, for example, a reader able to circumvent the Cartesian impulse for closure will see that the more flexible metaphors that appear in the narrative of *Finnegans Wake* go well beyond simply intensifying the impact of exclusionary images. They enforce a pluralistic view of the impact of gerontology and chronology within the narrative that creates a concept of age moving multidirectionally, reversing itself as easily as it progresses. Joyce's mode of discourse would seat us at that Thanksgiving dinner table with our multiple roles comfortably occupying a single chair.

As noted previously, however, for years a tendency toward exclusionary, cause-and-effect thinking has dominated criticism of *Finnegans Wake.* Joyce himself anticipated this inclination and tried to forestall it, a decade before *Finnegans Wake* was published, with a collection of critical essays he commissioned.[6] Although in many ways these pieces reflect the intellectual dynamics dominating Joyce's writing, their avant garde tone daunted even intellectuals like Edmund Wilson, whose contemporaneous essay, "The Dream of H. C. Earwicker," adopted the approach to reading *Finnegans Wake* that has become the norm.[7]

Even critics writing in a post-Structural period have continued efforts to circumscribe Joyce's narrative. In particular, many attempt to make ALP's soliloquy more accessible through the familiar critical position of bracketing, in this case seeing *Finnegans Wake* as a dream sequence. Kimberly Devlin urges us, for example, to consider "the fact that the closing monologue contains reversals and contraries which make little sense on the level of realistic or waking narrative." She holds "that it generates multilayered images typical of condensed, overdetermined visions of dream."[8] Devlin goes on to use this concept of the dream language of ALP's soliloquy to legitimize its translation into the ostensibly more comprehensible vernacular of critical discourse, reconfiguring the multiplicity and pluralism of ALP's words into the singularity and exclusivity of the critic's. Analogously, Margot Norris defines ALP and her male counterpart, HCE, as mirror figures, each reflecting the central attributes of the other.[9] Sheldon Brivic does the same with Lacanian psychoanalysis, offering transitional terminology for glossing ALP's discourse, seeing it from a slightly different perspective as psychodrama.[10]

These critics have done important initial interpretive work in delineating selected complex aspects of the passage, and one should not discount these endeavors simply because of their linear aspect. Indeed, as noted above, one can derive a fairly straightforward narrative picture from the rambling remarks that ALP offers. She awakens to a rainy day: "Soft morning" (619.19). She begins a conversation with her husband, Humphrey Chimpden Earwicker (HCE), first about his clothing (619.24) and then about their sons (620.20). She turns her conversation to a recollection of their sex life—"But that night after, all you were wanton! Bidding me do this and that and the other" (620.23–24)—and suggests that they use the time while the children are still asleep to renew sexual activity. "We'll not disturb their sleeping duties. Let besoms be bosuns. It's Phoenix, dear. And the flame is, hear! Let's our journee saintomichael make it" (620.36–621.02). Over the next few pages, with no apparent response from her husband, ALP's discourse oscillates from thoughts of breakfast (621.12) to an attempt at foreplay—"So. Draw back your glace. Hot and hairy, hugon, is your hand! Here's where the falskin begins. Smoos as an infams" (621.24–26). With still no response her mind turns to a visit to Howth Castle (623.04), which reminds her of the letter she wrote long ago (623.29). She makes a final, fruitless effort to arouse HCE by reminding him of her past loves (624.25). The narrative then begins ALP's leave-taking (626.01), which continues through the final pages of the mono-logue.

Nonetheless, while this paraphrase gives a rough idea of a portion of the action, the basic methodology of such an approach—unrelentingly Cartesian and thematic—oversimplifies Joyce's work. It privileges one point of view over another, and thereby runs di-rectly contrary to the grand lexical and perceptual disposition of *Fin-negans Wake*. A more effective approach seeks out ways of sustaining this multilayered, multidirectional discourse while keeping the need to maintain its integrity foremost in our consciousness.

Such an approach necessarily operates at several levels simultane-ously. Extratextually, it must survey the evolutionary process that shaped the writing of this passage. Intratextually, it must recognize the way metaphors in the narrative operate to foster ambiguity rather than certainty. To meet these demands, nonlinear concepts of time and age can serve as anchors for diverse views while them-selves embodying a pluralistic concept—"Time after time. The sehm asnuh" (620.15–16). That is, repeatedly the narrative puts ideas into an original condition—the same as new—meaning both familiar and novel.

At several levels, ALP's final soliloquy reflects important elements of the argument I seek to make regarding the need to reconfigure our conceptions of features like time and aging along nonlinear lines. The extratextual relation of both conditions to Joyce and to the imaginative evolution of the episode offers useful examples of just how these elements shape the comprehension of the final ver-sion of the episode. Specifically, a quick recollection of the composi-tion history of this passage reinforces the need for an elastic understanding of time, for it reminds us that the extratextual aging of the author—as the creation of the passage spans the transition in Joyce's life from early middle age to his approaching old age—turns the narrative towards this multidirectional, multilayered view.

The passage was begun, according to David Hayman, when Joyce was forty-one as one of the earliest sketches of the project that would evolve into *Finnegans Wake*.[11] The version took shape during 1923 as an episode intended for inclusion in ALP's letter (now appearing in fragmented form at various points throughout the book). For what-ever reason, Joyce set the episode aside until 1938 when he was fifty-six. Only then, after *Finnegans Wake* had moved toward completion, did Joyce return to the passage, incorporating it into the narrative as ALP's last words, revising it extensively as it became, according to Hayman, "the last passage to be written for the *Wake.*"[12] In consequence, its imagery necessarily traces Joyce's responsiveness to alternative concepts on age that a more localized composition would not capture. (Hayman notes, for instance, that the first holograph version of the episode is signed and dated "Paris 1922–1938."[13])

During the sixteen-year period bounded by those dates, Joyce's world changed radically. His daughter Lucia experienced a complete breakdown and was institutionalized. On 4 July 1931 Joyce married Nora Barnacle, the woman who had been his common-law wife since 1904, and Joyce's father died in December of that year. On 6 December 1933 Judge John M. Woolsey of the U.S. District Court at New York ruled that *Ulysses* was not pornographic, and by early 1934 Random House had made the first American edition of the book available to North American readers. During the decade of the 1930s, Joyce's son Giorgio married, had a son, and separated from his wife. And over the full sixteen-year period Joyce became increasingly afflicted with eye ailments and other health problems.

Over this same period, the creative milieu in which *Finnegans Wake* evolved also changed. Most of a *Work in Progress* (the provisional title that Joyce had given to his book) was serialized in little magazines like *transition.* Increasing opposition arose to the form that Joyce's writing was taking from former staunch supporters like his brother Stanislaus and the poet Ezra Pound. Joyce even reached a point where he toyed with the idea of having Irish writer James Stephens complete the project for him. Developing out of the context of this personal and artistic turmoil, the imaginative elements of the final ten pages of *Finnegans Wake* inevitably retain reminders of the significant shifts in perspective that took place over the temporal length of the work's composition.

Was the author who in 1938 took up the passage for revision the same one who wrote its original version in 1922? Was the passage itself, even before a word was changed, the same as the version composed shortly after the publication of *Ulysses?* Can one derive a satisfying reading of the passage from a linear recapitulation of its action? In each of these instances, I think the answer is no.

Being present in the initial stages and going through a form of retro-fitting as the book came to a close give these final ten pages of *Finnegans Wake* positions in and out of time. In words reprising the narrative's central concerns, ALP's monologue overturns conventional, linear narrative strategies and rejects impulses to impose closure or to acknowledge culmination. Her discourse offers a new system of metaphors, but it does so not by introducing completely unfamiliar forms of representation but by demonstrating how pluralistic expressions can go further than conventional images in sustaining complex, multiple perceptions. Any reading striving toward a full aesthetic response to Joyce's prose must engage that pattern of representation.

As I have suggested from the beginning of this essay, one can undertake this new interpretive process thematically. In the case of the passage under consideration here, this would involve acknowledging how ALP's final monologue highlights the manner in which time and age bring a mutability rather than stability to Joyce's characters throughout *Finnegans Wake*. Certainly a new sense of chronology underscores ALP's pluralistic nature, and rebuts efforts to explain that multiplicity by assigning to her a stratified series of roles based on chronological seniority. The nonlinear view of time and aging takes a more flexible position: We are not as old as we feel. Age is contextualized, so we are as old as we feel like being. Significantly, seeing age and time as relative, reversible conditions overturn linear habits of reading that rely on the narrowing inclinations of archetypal associations to circumscribe the genuine character.

In her detailed glosses of the character references that punctuate the discourse of *Finnegans Wake*, Adaline Glasheen's justifiably renowned census has done much to solidify this notion of an archetypal view of characterization.[14] Glasheen's study, however, does not stop with a detailed catalogue of allusions. Her approach imposes an archetypal structure as the controlling matrix of readings of *Finnegans Wake*. Organizing her scheme around various personifications of HCE, Glasheen finds corresponding roles for his sons (Shem and Shaun), his daughter (Issy), and his wife (ALP).[15]

Because of the laudable quality of Glasheen's scholarship, however, readers have accepted the interpretive implications of her delineations without the scrutiny necessary to assess their validity. In fact, the images that run throughout this final monologue provide ample evidence that one cannot accurately see ALP as simply the mother figure, the female principal, or the middle-aged wife. By extension this calls into question the practice of associating any character with a series of archetypes that he or she purportedly assumes at various points in the narrative. All these types rely on fixed conditions of time and aging to contextualize them. That unifying aspect no longer obtains in Joyce's narrative, and interpreting ALP, or any other character, in this fashion in effect ignores a major portion of her nature.

Ideas of individuality or even types are difficult to sustain when characters keep overstepping the defining limits of their natures.

The "liddle phifie Annie" mentioned in the opening pages of *Finnegans Wake* (4.28) bears no more resemblance to the speaker on the final page than she does to "this man of hod" (4.26) identified as her husband. Recognizing the relativity of time and aging in the narrative leads one both to a deeper awareness of this relativity in characterization and to concepts on how best to read it.

Acknowledging the mutability of age and time in *Finnegans Wake* marks the first step toward displacing antiquated Victorian approaches to interpretation camouflaged by opaque jargon. Genuine readings (if that itself is not a contradiction) find in the nonlinear metaphors of *Finnegans Wake* the lexicon of post-Einsteinian discourse. Anna Livia Plurabelle modulates her voice to suit polyphonic entities, moving back and forth through the roles of wife, lover, acolyte, and seer without at any point relinquishing any. As characterization piles on characterization, ALP supplants the reader's linear conceptions of time and aging with a view that sustaining a variety of human conditions, crossing perceived boundaries set down by time, become as easy as recognizing and attending to the polyphony in a room filled with diverse speakers. Ranging easily from an old woman to a young girl, ALP presents cyclical alternatives to the serial roles generally assigned by the aging process.

As previously noted, on one level at least, the soliloquy contains a discernible linear discourse, one that acknowledges ALP's predicament as the older mother figure who must confront the fact that a younger woman has usurped her position in the household. At the same time, however, while sustaining that narrative image, it also suggests that unidirectional entropy no longer serves as a guiding principle for transformation: "Yes, you're changing, sonhusband, and you're turning, I can feel you, for a daughterwife from the hills again" (627.01–03). That is, ALP sees those around her in multiple roles unrestrained by unidirectional entropic time. If we wish to go beyond simplistic responses to her narrative, we must follow her lead. Readings that step outside the Enlightenment mode of analysis prove the best model for achieving such results.

Two decades ago, in a close reading of another passage of *Finnegans Wake* (185.14–186.10), Father Robert Boyle introduced a concept for understanding the discourse that very neatly addresses the condition outlined here. Instead of offering an exclusionary reading that privileged a single point of view, Boyle set up an analogy with a central tenet of Catholic dogma—the power of the Holy Eucharist—to illustrate what occurs in Joyce's narrative. As Boyle notes, in an inversion of the Christian mystery of transubstantiation—whereby during the mass, the host and wine are consecrated to become, respectively, the body and blood of Christ while retaining the accidents of bread and wine—a transaccidentation occurs here. Feces and urine become ink. The writer, Shem, uses that ink to write "over every square inch of the only foolscap available, his own body" (185.35–36), so that "his own individual person life unlivable [becomes] transaccidentated through the slow fires of consciousness into a dividual chaos, perilous, potent, common to allflesh, human only mortal" (186.04–06).[16] The scene is not a simple celebration of Rabelaisian excess. It stands rather as a representation of the transformative power of art. Joyce reverses the disintegrative impetus characterizing feces and urine, the final form of narrative entropy. He combines them into a creative fluid capable of generating imaginative development.

Four hundred and thirty pages later, with a transaccidental gesture that collapses the authority of a linear process of aging, ALP's protean discourse does very nearly the same thing as she deftly reconfigures impressions that would relegate her to the single role of aging female. As her soliloquy progresses, her age regresses: "Carry me along, taddy, like you done through the toy fair" (628.08–09). It then seems to jump forward toward a conclusion: "End here" (628.13) only to move the narrative cyclically back to the beginning: "A way a lone a last a love a long the . . . riverrun, past Eve and Adam's, from swerve of shore to bend of bay, brings us by a commodius vicus of recirculation back to Howth Castle and Environs" (628.16–17). In this break with chronological determinism, ALP's monologue invites one to read her and the broader narrative both proleptically and retrospectively.

As is the case throughout the discourse of *Finnegans Wake,* the cyclical rhythm of ALP's soliloquy acknowledges decay without precluding reinvigoration. In this gesture it rejects linearity and invites us to do the same. ALP speaks as an old woman moving toward youth, and makes both positions viable: "And it's old and old it's sad and old it's sad and weary I go back to you my cold father, my cold mad father, my cold mad feary father. . . . Carry me along, taddy, like you done through the toy fair!" (627.36–628.10). Whether that becomes for readers a physical or a metaphysical journey matters little in the context of the narration, for her words renounce any perspective founded on closure.

The consequences of the multiplicity that she advocates go beyond simply interpretive double-vision, giving lip-service to the both/and view of the discourse. Without finality, without closure, terms like *pathos, tragedy, characterization, ideology, disposition,* and any others that impose fixed traits on the narrative or the individuals within it have no significance. The transformative nature of figures, actions, and settings precludes the sort of linear judgments that have become an integral part of conventional criticism. As ALP oversteps Newtonian laws of science, she also reconstitutes the metaphysics of reading. This creates for us a fundamental epistemological problem. We must discover new ways of assessing the new things we are seeing.

From the very opening of her soliloquy, ALP's voice introduces concepts that both endorse and run counter to the presumption of entropic decline. Repeatedly, her discourse suggests how oscillating perspectives undermine the hegemony of views of time and of aging that follow patterns of unidirectional movement. In the space of eight lines, for instance, between direct references to falling leaves and changing seasons, Anna Livia rouses HCE with a resurrection-like summons:

> Only a leaf, just a leaf and falling. (619.22–23)
> Rise up, man of the hooths, you have slept so long! (619.25)
> I am leafy, your goolden, so you called me, may me life, yea
>   your goolden, silve me sove, exsogerriader! (619.29–30)

Shifting images create multiple impressions meant to coexist and complement rather than to displace one another. The falling leaf of the first example introduces a downward movement toward decay and death. It is immediately counterbalanced in two lines by the upward thrust of awakening with its blend of physical, sexual, and spiritual connotations. In four more lines the leaf/Liffey is now golden, but its color now denotes peak, not decline.

In keeping with their pluralistic identity, the phrases just quoted may merit little more than passing notice, but they assume far greater significance when one pursues the implications of a world without time's conventional influence on individuals. Even with the offhanded glosses previously offered, one can see that each of the phrases quoted precludes a familiar categorical response through its aggressive indeterminacy. Each encourages inclusive readings in terms of discerning fundamental elements, but those readings hamper our ability to judge in the traditional fashion: Is it a good or a bad thing to be an old leaf? Even if one can decide this, what can one say when confronted with the idea that old or new are transitory qualities that can be reversed any number of times? Can one find anything more than linguistic significance in these lines, or is literary criticism relegated to abstractions?

These questions form the literary legacy of a post-Einsteinian world, the consequences of perceptions that see greater logic in a point of view dictated by quantum mechanics than in one set by Newtonian physics. They reflect our own theories of chaos and complexity. Like analogous views in physics, small variations in the expected pattern can lead to enormous changes.[17]

Indeed, a subtle shift in typography underscores the narrative's relation to the reader, signaling new rhythms of presentation and trusting in a satisfactory completion of the imaginative process. One finds the programmatic form of sentences prematurely interrupted by periods, for example, "Since the lausafire has lost and the book of the depth is. Closed" (621.02–03) and "I won't take our laddy's lampern. For them four old windbags of Gustsofairy to be blowing at" (621.05–06). Likewise, many of ALP's thoughts are only half-expressed, broken off in mid-sentence as if she knew that her listener could finish it for her. "Maybe that's why you hold your hodd as if" (621.27–28). These breaks in expected cadence should do more than makes us aware of how we habitually read. They should bring us to question the efficacy of those patterns of reading.

Hugh Kenner's critical commonplace that Joyce's works—especially *Ulysses* and *Finnegans Wake*—devote much of their narrative energy to teaching us how to read them operates with new force here. We are not simply learning how to rehabilitate fractured syntax or imprecise metaphors to discern a privileged meaning. We are also learning how to enjoy our inability to impose the closure that those methods require.

As noted already in the "son/husband" passage, throughout the soliloquy ALP describes the roles of a number of characters in a fashion both sharply defined and fundamentally unstable. Readers seeking an effective response to her discourse must necessarily adopt language that accommodates this condition of mutability. Each of Joyce's images contains not simply its opposite but multiple variations. They are not, strictly speaking, alternatives, since they exist consubstantially within the narrative. Even if one gives emphasis to a particular image, the others remain in one's consciousness and continue to influence one's overall perception of the passage. Not only does this pluralism preclude completely privileging one view above the rest, but the transition from one image to another also elides boundaries and affirms ambiguous coexistence: "If you spun your yarns to him on the swishbarque waves I was spelling my yearns to her over cottage cake" (620.34–36).

The oscillation of this phrase invites us to see a series of superimpositions upon its basic structure. From the syntactic to the metaphoric, the sentence disrupts predictable patterns without simply negating them. The subordinate conditional "If" clause that opens the sentence does not find a clear anchor in the subsequent clause that follows, yet the analogous structure allows for the possibility of an implicit "then" and consequent resolution. Contextually, the sentence seems to be contrasting HCE's education of one of their sons with ALP's instruction of their daughter, Issy. At the same time the distance between tale-telling at sea and heart-to-heart talks at home raises a sense of polarization, even competition, while yarns and yearns go on to imply a form of manipulation. Suggesting the possibility of hostility inculcated into traditional family roles brings a kinetic quality to the phrases, which causes our conceptions of their meaning to shift during the very process of perception.

We can, of course, confront this radically new epistemology without necessarily feeling alienated from common interpretive habits. Once we accept the move toward amalgamation rather than exclusion, we have the option of perceiving it at a number of different levels. ALP's soliloquy encourages us to adopt such flexibility by repeatedly playing off potentiality and predictability. It also implicitly enforces the concept that by selecting one response to the exclusion of all others, we inevitably slip into a reductive view.

Her discourse, for example, invites us to consider the contingency of one's nature and its reconfiguration over time. Simultaneously, the narrative reminds us that reconfiguration does not eliminate the past but rather amalgamates it. When images shift, the potential for meaning continues to expand in an inverse relation to the possibility for closure. As she lies in bed, ALP ruminates about coming events, telling her husband that "next peaters poll you will be elicted or I'm not your elicitous bribe" (622.02–03). Does this reflect her hope for a public vindication of the family's reputation? Is it the promise of erotic pleasure? Is it a combination of electoral ambitions and dubious practices? One might easily respond, "All of the above," and in that fashion sustain a range of distinct but not exclusive readings.

Further, the discourse leads us to see that as the impermanence of communal roles emerges, views of individuals also change. "How you said how you'd give me the keys of me heart. And we'd be married till delth to upstart" (626.30–31). The image of the transference of keys is repeated later in the monologue, but the sense of the phrase as it is conveyed here seems to invert the conventions of the marriage ceremony. HCE promises ALP the keys to her own heart and seems to swear fealty only until some upstart appears. The marriage then begins with assurances of its impermanence, and the cynical calculations of HCE break down the suppositions about newlyweds' feelings.

This gesture is typical of the rhetoric of the final pages of *Finne-*

gans Wake. Familiar words and common meanings are not dismissed. They are represented as elaborations by the speaker. The act of self-construction reforms impressions generated by cliches. This becomes amply clear when one examines the final page and a half of *Finnegans Wake.*

Beginning with the lines "But you're changing, acoolsha, you're changing from me, I can feel" (626.35–36), the discourse seems to settle into a linear pattern, an emotional unraveling that ends with ALP's dissolution: "A way a lone a last a loved a long the" (628.16–17). A closer look at this section, however, reflects a much higher level of complexity. As ALP ostensibly describes her response to her husband's rejection of her for a younger woman, instead of a progressive direct movement toward despair, resignation, or anger— indeed instead of any single-minded emotional response—one sees a deft oscillation among various moods, characters, and situations. ALP slips from one role to another and from one attitude to the next in a fashion that shows the complete independence of one from another.

While the fluctuating movement of the final pages stands as emblematic of the imaginative structure of the entire work, merely identifying this vacillation does not produce a clearcut interpretive methodology. Indeed, I do not presume in these few pages to lay out an alternative program for reading *Finnegans Wake.* That in itself would run the risk of taking on prescriptive tones counter to the pluralistic methodology I have advocated throughout the essay. Rather, I endeavor to offer a prolegomenon to such work. In pointing out the limitations of conventional approaches to reading *Finnegans Wake,* I hope to encourage others to explore further the imaginative possibilities that arise from adopting an alternative point of view.

Notes

1. James Joyce, *Finnegans Wake* (New York: Viking, 1939). All subsequent references will appear in the body of the essay, designated by page and line numbers alone.

2. Joseph Campbell and Henry Morton Robinson, *A Skeleton Key to Finnegans Wake* (New York: Viking, 1944), 355.

3. For a detailed explanation of Einstein's special theory of relativity, see John Gribbin's *In Search of Schrödinger's Cat: Quantum Physics and Reality* (London: Corgi Books, 1984), 43–44.

4. For a detailed discussion of the alternative ways our culture perceives aging, see the essays in Kathleen Woodward and Murray M. Schwartz's *Memory and Desire: Aging—Literature—Psychoanalysis* (Bloomington: Indiana University Press, 1986).

5. For one example of this, see Thomas Jackson Rice's *Joyce, Chaos, and Complexity* (Urbana: University of Illinois Press, 1997).

6. Samuel Beckett et al., *Our Exagmination Round His Factification for Incamination of Work in Progress* (Paris: Shakespeare and Company, 1929).

7. Wilson's essay appeared in his collection *The Wound and the Bow* (New York: Oxford University Press, 1947).

8. Kimberly Devlin. "ALP's Final Monologue in *Finnegans Wake:* The Dialectical Logic of Joyce's Dream Text," in *Coping with Joyce: Essays from the Copenhagen Symposium,* eds. Morris Beja and Shari Benstock (Columbus: Ohio State University Press, 1989), 233–34.

9. See, for example, Margot Norris's "Anna Livia Plurabelle: The Dream Woman," in *Women in Joyce,* eds. Suzette Henke and Elaine Unkeless (Urbana: University of Illinois Press, 1982), 197–213.

10. Sheldon Brivic, "The Terror and Pity of Love: ALP's Soliloquy," *James Joyce Quarterly* 29 (Fall 1991):145–71.

11. For a detailed chronology of its composition, see David Hayman's *A First Draft Version of Finnegans Wake* (Austin: University of Texas Press, 1963), 329.

12. David Hayman, *The "Wake" in Transit* (Ithaca and London: Cornell University Press, 1990), 34, 62.

13. David Hayman, *A First-Draft Version of Finnegans Wake* (Austin: University of Texas Press, 1963), 329

14. Adaline Glasheen, *Third Census of Finnegans Wake: An Index of the Characters and Their Roles* (Berkeley: University of California Press, 1977). This is a revised version of *First Census* (1956) and the *Second Census* (1963).

15. The table that precedes the Census, "Who Is Who When Everybody Is Somebody Else," *Third Census of* Finnegans Wake, lxxii–lxxxiv, illustrates this concept quite clearly.

16. Robert Boyle, S.J., *James Joyce's Pauline Vision: A Catholic Exposition* (Carbondale: Southern Illinois University, 1978), 44–46, 54–55.

17. For an overview of the rise of complexity theory and of its relationship to literary criticism, see my "(Meta)physics and 'the portals of discovery': Literary Criticism and the New Physics," *James Joyce Quarterly* 34 (Summer 1997):597–612.

The Washerwomen Skit Adapted from *Finnegans Wake*

MARGARET ROGERS

ONE GLIMPSE AND SMITTEN! LIKE MANY, I FOUND THE ALP SECTION OF
Finnegans Wake irresistible, so I decided to try my hand at creating a
dramatic setting of the text James Joyce stated cost him twelve hundred hours of labor.[1] The elements of humor and pathos and the
rhythmic and linguistic devices are ideal for such an interpretation.
My objective was to separate and delineate the voices of the two
women, accentuate the powerful rhythms inherent in words and
sentence structure, highlight linguistic attributes and (when appropriate) set portions to music. In the actual dramatic presentation,
the rhythms are further accented through gestures such as scrubbing, folding, wringing, and shaking. (This setting is based on pages
196–205 of the 1976 Viking edition of *Finnegans Wake.*) Further exploration will be made of the remainder of the section for possible
dramatization.

Distinctive patterns emerge. The two women appear to have consistently different personalities. A, the first to speak, seems younger,
less experienced. B is older, a know-it-all. A asks questions. B sup-
plies all the answers and then some. A yearns to know the dirt but
becomes uncomfortable when B goes too far. "She was? Gota pot!
Yssel that the limmat?" (198.13). A becomes defensive on behalf of
Anna Liv when B sullies Anna's character by referring to her as a
"proxenete" (198.17). A exclaims and tsk-tsks ("tista suck" 198.27)
throughout. B bangs away at her "lavabibs" (203.19), rubbing and
scrubbing and topping her own story with increasingly more enthu-
siasm. B is more of a cynic, not given to nuance, reveling in the gossip, viscerally connected to the dirt she's wringing out of her
laundry. She joyously initiates A into the mysteries of sin, sex, and
scandal. A loves the gossip but registers or perhaps feigns shock at
the "trent" of it.

The dramatic technique for "The Washerwomen" is musical dialogue as the conversation between the two is sung as well as spoken. Rhythm and linguistic features are the most important elements of this musical dialogue. Both are key in evoking the multiple images of the sights and sounds of water[2] glistening, rippling, flowing, lapping, and, of equal importance, the sounds and images of two women doing laundry. The scrub rhythm is an up-down, down-up two-beat. The washerwomen scrub "in two," a continual one-two–beat rhythm primarily either in the 6/8 time of a well-known song "The Irish Washerwomen" or the 2/4 time of a familiar tune such as "The Kerry Dancers," both of which are used in the musical dialogue. Here the 6/8 rhythm is a modified trochaic (accent, unaccent) pattern with the accent falling on the one of the six-beat: ONE two three four five six, TWO two three four five six, and so forth. For example, in the opening "Tell me all about Anna Livia" (196.14, 15), which in the skit is sung to the tune of "The Irish Washerwomen," we hear *Te-el me all a-bout A-an-na Li-vi-a* with the accents on the first syllable of "tell' and of "Anna."

In adapting the ALP section of *Finnegans Wake* (*FW*) for performance, the cast gave special care to linguistic features of the text. When saying "How he used to hold his head as high as a howeth" (197.2,3), washerwoman B takes care to emphasize the glottal *h*. In singing "She was just a young thin pale soft shy slim slip of a thing then, sauntering, by silvamoonlake" (202.26,27,28), washerwoman A stresses the sibilants. In *Joyce Again's Wake,* Bernard Benstock wrote "*l* sounds couple with *s* sounds as the gossip crosses the river"[3]. The array of such combinations of letters reminds the performer that this is no ordinary script; every element of the linguistic arsenal has been employed so every part of vocal anatomy must be used to produce the liquid *l*'s and *r*'s, the voiced *b*'s and *d*'s, and nasal *m*'s and *n*'s. As Joyce intended, the ALP section is a veritable verbal feast.

Songs incorporated into the skit were chosen for rhythmic and narrative qualities and their ability to evoke images. For example, "The Irish Washerwoman" was a logical choice for the opening section both for its rhythmic construction (6/8 time) and subject matter: Irish washerwomen. Other songs included are "The Kerry Dancers," "The Moldau," "Loch Lomond," "The Volga Boatmen," "Villa," Schubert's "Ave Maria," "John Peele," "Di Provenza il Mar" from Verdi's "La Traviata," the love duet from Wagner's "Tristan und Isolde," ("Wasut? Izod? Are you sarthin suir?" 203.8,9), songs I composed especially for the skit, and, of special note, "Die Lorelei," composed by Friedrich Silcher from the German of Heinrich Heine.

The song opens with "O tell me what it meaneth" (*Ich weiss nicht was soll es bedeuten*) and continues in verse two with "Above the maiden sitteth, a wondrous form and fair" (*Die Schonste jungfrau sitzet dort oben wunderbar*). "O tell me" is a leitmotif in the ALP section of *FW* from which the skit was adapted. "O loreley" occurs in *FW* (page 210, line 5) and contains two central themes: the O for omega, the brook of life that is the opening syllable of the section, and the lorelei, nymphs sitting on the Lorelei rock above the rapids of the Rhine river luring boatmen to their destruction (shades of "The Sirens" from *Ulysses*).[4] Variations of this theme occur throughout the section: "O tell me all about Anna Livia" (196.14,15); "Tell me all, tell me now" (196.17); "Well, ptellomey soon" (198.2); "O, tell me all I want to hear" (198.14); "Tell us in *france langua*" (198.19,20); "Tell me moher. Tell me moatst" (198.28); "Tell me. Tell me. *Phoebe, dearest, tell, O tell me*" (200.10); "Tell me the trent of it" (200.33,34); "Onon! Onon! tell me more. Tell me every tiny teign" (201.21); "Tell me, tell me. how cam she camlin" (202.7); "Dell me where, the fairy ferse time!" (203.16); "Tell me quick and dongu so crould!" (206.8). The "tell me" questions are asked by washerwoman A of washerwoman B. They serve as leitmotif and punctuation throughout the section, and in the skit they are sung to the tune of "*Die Lorelei.*"

The text divides itself naturally into several distinct sections. In addition to the "Lorelei," I used a descending do sol mi do sol sol sol la ti do to signal changes in the narrative.

The following is a partial outline of the composition. The skit opens with washerwoman A trilling a long "O" and then singing text to the tune of "The Irish Washerwoman."

TUNE: "THE IRISH WASHER WOMAN"

O   te-ell   me   all   a-bout   A-an-na   Li-vi-a

(196.13,14)

B responds in spoken dialogue, "Well, you know Anna Livia"
A replies, "Yes, of course, we all know Anna Livia,"   then sings "Tell me all, tell me now, Tell me every tiny ting"   to music adapted from the song "The Lorelei."

TUNE: "DIE LORELEI"   by Friedrich Silcher

Oh,   tell   me what   it   mean- eth, This   gloom and tear - ful   eye.
FW   Oh,   te - ell me Phoe - be   dear- est, O   tell me tell   me   now.

(200.10)

B scrubs and sings,

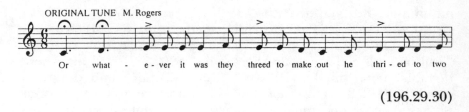

ORIGINAL TUNE M. Rogers

Or   what - e - ver it was   they   threed to make out   he   thri - ed to two

(196.29.30)

A replies on the same tune, and B says rhythmically

"Scorchin my hand and starvin my famine to make
his private linen public."

**The words are accented in a 6/8 trochaic rhythmic pattern.
B chants while A sings:**

TUNE: "THE MOLDAU"   by Bredrich Smetana

My   wrists are rus - ty   rub - bin   the   Mol - dau   stains

(196.29,30)

**The next section is spoken in iambic meter, "What was it he did a
tail at all on animal sendai?"**

A then sings:

And how long wa - as he un - der loch a - and neagh

(196.31,32)

More dialogue, then B speaks, "And the cut of him, and the strut of him, how he used to hold his head as high as a howeth . . ." (good example of alliteration). A replies in song:

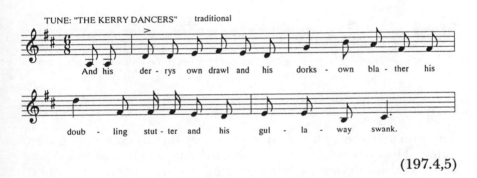

And his der - rys own drawl and his dorks - own bla - ther his

doub - ling stut - ter and his gul - la - way swank.

(197.4,5)

There is more rhythmic conversation punctuated by:

Don Dom Domb - domb and his wee fol - ly - o

(197.18)

The banter continues and A sings:

(197.15,16)

A slight narrative shift occurs signaled by A and B singing the "Dom dom" theme followed by A singing:

(197.21,22)

This preceding section has four verses, which both women sing alternately. The two continue to examine the lapses in Anna Livia's character. B then delivers a large load of dirt in the "old Humber" section, which is set (loosely) to the tune of the "Volga Boatmen."

(198.29)

The climax of the skit is reached with B telling the Michael Arklow story. B expounds while A sits, folding clothes and humming snatches of "It's a Long, Long Way to Tipperary," "*Di Provenza il Mar*," and the love duet from "Tristan and Isolde," all background for the great seduction scene. B's impassioned narration leaves A aroused, and she muses on the "Bold priest" and the "naughty Livvy" envisioning Anna Livia as:

TUNE: "VILIA" from the "Merry Widow" by Franz Lehar

She was just a young pale soft shy slip of a thing.

(202.26,27)

When considering her rape, she angrily sings:

> O Leada, laida, all unraidly,
> Too faint to buoy the fairiest rider,
> Too frail to flirt with a cygnet's plume,
> She was licked by a hound, Chirrup-Chirruta.
>
> O drop me the sound of the findhorn's name
> And why in the flenders was she frickled
> In fear to hear the dear so near
> Or longing ooth and loathing longing.

TUNE: "JOHN PEEL"   traditional

O   lea- da, lai- da, all un- rai- dy, too - faint to buoy the fai- riest ri- der

(204.10,11)

A and B return to their washing and gossiping, and the skit ends with a ricorso of the opening "Washerwoman" song.

A washboard was the only instrumentation used in this "singspiel." Formal accompaniment would seem to interrupt the flow, so no plans are made for adding other instruments. The constant alternation between singing and speaking moves the skit and energizes it. Communicating to the audience is made more difficult because of the obscurity of the language, but the rhythms, gestures, and music convey the story. Audience response has been enthusiastic.

Notes

1. Biographer Richard Ellmann quotes Joyce: "[B]ut I assure you that these twenty pages now before us cost me twelve hundred hours and an enormous expense of spirit." See Richard Ellmann, *James Joyce* (New York: Oxford University Press, 1982), 598.

2. Ellmann reports: "To a friend that complained it was just dada, he said, 'It is an attempt to subordinate words to the rhythm of water.' He felt some misgivings about it the night it was finished, and went down to the Seine to listen by one of the bridges to the waters. He came back content." (See Ellmann, 564.)

3. Bernard Benstock, *Joyce Again's Wake: An Analysis of Finnegans Wake* (Seattle: University of Washington Press, 1965), 149.

4. Other similarities between the washerwomen of *Finnegans Wake* and the "Sirens" of *Ulysses* occur in the following examples from the texts. "O gig goggle of gigguels" (*FW* 206.14) and "goggle" and gigglegold" (*U* 213.146, 159). "In fear to hear the dear so near" (*FW* 204.25, 26) and "Too dear to near to home" (*U* 238.1258). The texts used here are James Joyce, *Finnegans Wake* (New York: Viking Press, 1976) and James Joyce, *Ulysses,* ed. Hans W. Gabler, with Wolfhart Steppe and Klaus Melchior (New York: Random House, 1986).

Part IV
New Views of Samuel Beckett

Beckett's *Happy Days,* Burton, and Schopenhauer

JAMES ACHESON

IN *SAMUEL BECKETT'S HAPPY DAYS: A MANUSCRIPT STUDY,* S. E. GONTARSKI reveals that in his final typescript Beckett identified the sources of many of the play's allusions.[1] Some—the allusions to Shakespeare, Milton, and Gray, for example—are well-known passages whose sources did not need to be specified. Others, however—the echo of Browning's *Paracelsus,* and of Charles Wolfe's "Go! Forget Me," to give two examples—are less obvious, making Beckett's revelation of his sources welcome. Significantly, two important quotations play in the background of *Happy Days* (*HD*) that are not mentioned in the typescript. The first is from Beckett's favorite philosopher, Arthur Schopenhauer, and the second from a favorite text, Robert Burton's *The Anatomy of Melancholy.*[2] Only when we examine these quotations with care can we properly assess the significance of Beckett's listed allusions and reach a fuller understanding of the play.

In *Happy Days,* Beckett creates an artificial world, filled with arbitrary torments, and places at its center an absurdly optimistic female character, Winnie, who is determined to make the best of things. Beckett wants to demonstrate, satirically, that being as relentlessly optimistic as Winnie places limits on what one can expect to learn about oneself and the world.[3] Beckett's indictment of Winnie's optimism may derive from Leibniz, whose famous phrase, "the best of all possible worlds," the play repeatedly brings to mind. Or it may come from Voltaire, whose *Candide,* a satiric attack on Leibniz, Beckett echoes in other works.[4] Given the frequency with which he refers to Schopenhauer in his other works, however,[5] the following passage, in which the German philosopher heaps scorn on the confirmed optimist, seems a more probable point of departure for *Happy Days*:

> If . . . we should bring clearly to a man's sight the terrible sufferings and miseries to which his life is constantly exposed, he would be seized with

85

horror; and if we were to conduct the confirmed optimist through the hospitals, infirmaries, and surgical operating-rooms, through the prisons, torture-chambers and slave-kennels, over battlefields and places of execution; if we were to open to him all the dark abodes of misery, where it hides itself from the glance of cold curiosity, . . . he, too, would understand at last the nature of this "best of all possible worlds." For whence did Dante take the material for his hell but from this our actual world?[6]

Like Dante's hell, the world of *Happy Days* is a place based on the actual world, but clearly not part of it. The play provides us not with a fourth-wall view of someone's drawing room, but with a private hell of Beckett's own devising—a hell derived both from the world as we know it and from Dante's *Inferno,* another favorite text of Beckett's.[7] Its two main characters, Winnie and Willie, suffer varying degrees of torment: in the first act, Winnie is buried up to her waist in a mound of earth, and in the second, up to her neck. Her husband, Willie, lies behind her, sometimes retreating from the blazing sunlight into a hole in the mound, but for the most part remaining outside it. The sun is so hot that it can set a parasol alight, yet only one of the characters—Willie—is threatened with sunburn. The fair Winnie, whose shoulders and arms are exposed to the sun, remains arbitrarily unscathed. Similarly, though Winnie is sucked into the earth by the ever-increasing pull of gravity, Willie is free at all times to move about at will (which may shed light on Beckett's selection of his name).[8] Strangely, only Winnie is awakened, like a Pavlovian dog, by the sounding of the offstage bell; Willie always sleeps through it. That they do not suffer equally and in the same way in this unique afterworld is never explained, though various explanations suggest themselves.

The world of the play is a timeless world, where to use terms like "hours" and "days" is "to speak in the old style" (*HD* 19)—the style one would associate with life on earth, rather than with Beckett's unique afterlife.[9] That nothing ever changes—that Winnie can be sure that her parasol and other belongings will be restored to her "tomorrow" (and the next "day," and the next)—suggests that the play's two characters suffer endlessly, like Sisyphus, who is obliged to roll a rock repeatedly to the top of a hill, only to have it always roll down again. If a third act were added to *Happy Days,* it would probably return us to the situation in which Winnie finds herself at the beginning of act 1.[10]

While Winnie may not believe that hers is the "best of all possible worlds," she is nevertheless a "confirmed optimist" in the sense that she habitually makes the best of things. Despite the wretchedness of her situation, she is grateful to a merciful God for ensuring that it is not worse. At the beginning of act 2, for example, she says it is a "great mercy" (*HD* 38) to be spared knowing whether Willie has left her; more generally, she is glad to be spared full knowledge of her situation. Winnie can only guess why she suffers as she does, and she is glad that the reasons for her suffering have not been made clearer.

Beckett originally thought of calling *Happy Days* "Tender Mercies," "Many Mercies," or "Great Mercies," no doubt with various biblical sources in mind.[11] Any one of these titles would have been ironic (as the title *Happy Days* itself is), for in the final version of the play, it is clear that if God exists, he is a not altogether merciful figure. In Act II, when Winnie says "My neck is hurting me! *(Pause. With sudden violence.)* My neck is hurting me! *(Pause.)* Ah that's better" (*HD* 44), we have a momentary sense that God has intervened to alleviate her pain, and that Winnie is right to think that her prayers are "perhaps not for naught" (*HD* 12). Elsewhere, however, God appears to be cruel—as, for example, when Winnie complains that the bell that jolts her awake "hurts like a knife. . . . A gouge" (*HD* 40). Here the God of *Happy Days* not only refuses to help her feel better, but also makes it impossible for her to pray for mercy by having the bell ring every time she closes her eyes to do so.

Winnie is apparently being punished for her sins, though what she has done to merit her punishment is never made clear. By contrast, Willie's interest in obscene postcards and his many suggestive comments suggest that, like his namesake in Robert Burns's "Holy Willie's Prayer," he is guilty of the sin of lechery,[12] and is being punished by an arbitrary God like the one to whom Willie prays in the poem:

> O Thou, wha in the Heavens dost dwell,
> Wha, as it pleases best Thysel',
> Sends ane to Heaven and ten to Hell,
>   'A for thy glory,
> And no for any guid or ill
>   They've done afore Thee![13]

Similarly, in *Happy Days* Beckett implies that if God exists, He often punishes the innocent and spares the guilty: though capable of occasional mercies, He is for the most part arbitrary and cruel.

Winnie has occasional doubts about God's attitude toward His creatures, and remarks at one point on His apparent habit of playing unpleasant "little jokes" (*HD* 24) on them. One such joke arises from the unexpected appearance of an ant on the mound.[14] That Winnie uses the archaic term "emmet" (*HD* 23) for "ant," brings us to our second key passage, the one from *The Anatomy of Melancholy*, where Burton comments that

> Our villages are like mole-hills, and men as so many emmets, busy, busy still, going to and fro, in and out, and crossing one another's projects. . . . Some few amongst the rest, or perhaps one of a thousand, may be Jove's favourite, in the World's esteem, the white hen's chick, an happy and fortunate man, because rich, fair, well allied, in honour and office; yet peradventure ask himself, and he will say that, of all others, he is most miserable. . . . It is not another man's opinion can make me happy; but, as Seneca well hath it, *he is a miserable wretch, that doth not account himself happy; though he be Sovereign Lord of the world, he is not happy, if he think himself not to be so; for what availeth it what thine estate is, or seems to others, if thou thyself dislike it?*[15]

According to Burton, happiness is a function not of the individual's circumstances but of his (or her) state of mind, and this of course is entirely consistent with the situation in *Happy Days*, where Winnie is subjected to various forms of adversity, but remains cheerful throughout. She is less interested in discovering the truth about why she is suffering than in ensuring that she remains happy. As a deluded optimist who refuses to face the unpleasantness of her situation—who imposes her own limits on the extent of her knowledge about the world she inhabits—she earns our contempt, just as she would surely have earned Schopenhauer's. Yet she also elicits our sympathy for the efforts she makes to prevent herself from succumbing to despair.

Winnie's most obvious defense against despair is her daily routine, which includes praying, brushing her teeth, combing her hair, putting on makeup, and so on. She sustains herself partly through habit, the all-important "compromise" that Beckett refers to in his 1931 essay on Proust—the compromise that the individual effects between himself and his environment.[16] Like B in Beckett's *Act Without Words II*, Winnie has worked out a routine that fills her day and keeps at bay any melancholy thoughts she may have about her situation. In *Proust*, Beckett describes Habit as "the Goddess of Dullness" (*P* 33), and so dreary is much of what Winnie does and says that the phrase might be applied to her as well, though not to the play, whose comedy counters her dreariness.

One of Winnie's greatest fears is that she will be left with nothing more to say or do and hours to run before the bell for sleep sounds; in silence, without little tasks to perform, it would be very difficult for her to keep pessimistic thoughts at bay. She solves the problem of finding things to talk about by varying the subjects to which she addresses herself: at times she comments on her present situation, and at other times recalls various scenes from the past. For much of the play she talks to Willie, since she has no one else. Her incessant chatter keeps her occupied, and the presence of Willie is a source of comfort to her.

Another comfort is the literature of the past, though her recollection of specific passages is often faulty. It is "wonderful," she says, that "a part remains, of one's classics, to help one through the day" (*HD* 43). Winnie's imperfect quotations from (for example) Shakespeare, Milton, Gray, and Keats are such an important part of the play that when it was first performed, Beckett presented the director, Alan Schneider, with the same list of sources that appears on the final typescript.[17] Significantly, Winnie's use of these quotations divides our sympathies. As elsewhere in the play, we feel contempt for her "pernicious and incurable optimism" (*P* 15)—her unwillingness to face the horror of her situation—yet we also sympathize with her efforts to find solace in the wisdom of the past.

Two of Winnie's quotations are from Milton and are obviously religious in character. She opens act 2 with the first words of book III of *Paradise Lost*, "Hail, holy light" (*HD* 37), just as earlier she speaks of the "holy light . . . blaze of hellish light" (*HD* 11) that streams down on her from the blazing sun overhead.[18] While Winnie finds the light "hellish" in the sense of being uncomfortably bright and hot, she is glad it is not brighter and hotter, and feels grateful to God for His mercy.[19] Earlier she tries to remember a line from Book X of *Paradise Lost:* "What is that wonderful line? . . . Oh fleeting joys— . . . oh something lasting woe" (*HD* 13). Here she is alluding to Adam's "O fleeting joyes /Of Paradise, deare bought with lasting woes."[20] Though Adam laments the fact that he and Eve have been cast into the wilderness for eating the fruit of the forbidden tree, Milton makes it clear that the punishment is just, since God warned them that the fruit was not to be consumed. If it is the thought that God behaves fairly to man that makes this passage attractive to Winnie, however, her own situation suggests that His fairness is illusory, for no clear indication exists in the play as to why she is being punished. Since Winnie is not guilty of any obvious sin, it may simply be that the God of *Happy Days* takes pleasure in tormenting His creatures, or alternatively, that He enjoys punishing Winnie and all mankind for "the original sin of having been born."[21] Winnie, of course, is oblivious of such possibilities as these: she prefers to think that, in general, God is benignly disposed to man.

Some of Winnie's other quotations are from Shakespeare and have a bearing on her relationship with Willie. Her first Shakespearean allusion occurs in act 1, where she says, "What are those wonderful lines—*[wipes one eye]*—woe woe is me—*[wipes the other]*—to see what I see" (*HD* 11). This is an echo of the speech in *Hamlet* in which Ophelia gives voice to her distress over Hamlet's madness:

> O, what a noble mind is here o'erthrown!
> The courtier's, soldier's, scholar's, eye, tongue, sword;
> . . . .
> [And] I, of ladies most deject and wretched . . .
> Now see that noble and most sovereign reason,
> Like sweet bells jangled, out of tune and harsh;
> That unmatch'd form and feature of blown youth
> Blasted with ecstasy. O, woe is me,
> T' have seen what I have seen, see what I see![22]

Here Winnie takes pleasure in Ophelia's recollections of a handsome, accomplished prince, a man who, prior to his madness, forms a striking contrast to Willie. Winnie would like to think well of her husband, but is dismayed at his lack of interest in her: "Oh I know you were never one to talk, I worship you Winnie be mine and then nothing from that day forth only titbits from *Reynolds' News*" (*HD* 46).

That Winnie makes the best not only of a harsh environment, but also of an unsatisfactory marriage, is even clearer in the light of her brief allusions to *Romeo and Juliet* and *Twelfth Night*.[23] Her muttered "Ensign crimson . . . Pale flag" (*HD* 14) as she applies her makeup echoes Romeo's speech in Juliet's tomb: "[B]eauty's ensign yet / Is crimson in thy lips and in thy cheeks, / And death's pale flag is not advanced there."[24] Although Winnie is pleased that she still retains a certain youthful beauty (the stage directions tell us that, although fifty, she is *"well-preserved"* [*HD* 9]), the reader or theater-goer nevertheless is aware that she is past the first flush of youth, and that the hopes and dreams of young love will probably always be denied her. When she says in act 2 that "no damask" (*HD* 39) is in her cheeks, she echoes the passage in *Twelfth Night* in which Viola tells Orsino of a young woman who concealed her love for a man: "She never told her love, / But let concealment, like a worm i' the bud, / Feed on her damask cheek."[25] In contrast to the young woman referred to here (Viola is actually speaking of herself), Winnie has not wasted away because her love for Willie has been unrequited. She has always made the best of her situation; that "no damask" is in her cheeks is simply another indication that she is no longer young.

Further indication of the depth of Winnie's optimism can be found in act 1 when she echoes a line from Thomas Gray's "Ode on a Distant Prospect of Eton College": "what is that wonderful line . . . laughing wild . . . something laughing wild amid severest woe" (*HD* 25). In the poem, Gray gazes at some boys on the playing fields of Eton, and reflects on the misery that lies ahead of them in adult life:

> The stings of Falsehood those shall try,
> And hard Unkindness' altered eye,
> That mocks the tear it forced to flow;
> And keen Remorse with blood defiled,
> And moody Madness laughing wild
> Amid severest woe.[26]

"[M]oody Madness laughing wild / Amid severest woe" is not a state of mind we would ascribe to Winnie, for despite the unpleasantness of her situation, she remains cheerfully committed to making the best of things. It is impossible to imagine her in agreement with the epigraph to Gray's poem, a line from Menander reading: "I am [human], a sufficient excuse for being unhappy."[27] Much closer to Winnie's unremitting optimism are the Ode's closing lines: ". . . where ignorance is bliss, / 'Tis folly to be wise."[28] Winnie does not inquire too deeply into the cause of her suffering. In her allusion, elsewhere, to Browning's *Paracelsus,* a narrative poem about a sixteenth-century charlatan, and also to "The Lily of Killarney," a song referred to in both Joyce's *A Portrait of the Artist as a Young Man* and *Ulysses,* she simply accepts that what "cannot be cured" (*HD* 10) must be endured.[29]

The two remaining quotations of interest are from Yeats and Charles Wolfe. Winnie's "I call to the eye of the mind . . ." (*HD* 43) in act 2 echoes the opening line of Yeats's *At the Hawk's Well,* a play whose two main characters are denied the prospect of immortality offered by drinking water from a magic well. In *Happy Days* Beckett makes it clear that immortality (at least in the form in which Winnie and Willie experience it) is not—despite Winnie's insistent cheerfulness—something to be desired. Winnie accepts immortality as an unalterable condition of her existence, and turns repeatedly to the literature of the past for comfort. "What are those exquisite lines?" she asks near the end of the play. "Go forget me why should something o'er that something shadow fling . . ." (*HD* 43). The lines she is trying to remember are from Charles Wolfe's "Go! Forget Me":

> Go! Forget me, why should sorrow
> O'er that brow a shadow fling?

. . . .
May thy soul with pleasure shine,
Lasting as the gloom of mine.[30]

Winnie takes satisfaction in these lines, knowing that her soul is filled not with gloom but good cheer, and believing (perhaps mistakenly, though she is unaware of it) that she is a source of pleasure to her husband, rather than pain.

When not calling quotations to mind, Winnie busies herself by recalling scenes from the past, an activity in which Willie both helps and hinders her. Thus in Act I, for example, Willie prompts romantic memories of Charlie Hunter, only to undercut them:

WILLIE: *[reading from newspaper]* His Grace and Most Reverend
            Father in God Dr Carolus Hunter dead in tub.
            Pause.
WINNIE: *(gazing front, hat in hand, tone of fervent reminiscence)* Charlie
            Hunter! *(Pause.)* I close my eyes . . . and am sitting on his
            knees again, in the back garden at Borough Green, under
            the horse-beech. . . . Oh the happy memories! . . .
WILLIE: *(reading from newspaper)* Opening for smart youth.

                                                                (*HD* 14)

Winnie wants to make a romantic scene of her memory of Charlie Hunter, but the romance evaporates with Willie's "Opening for smart youth." He is implying, of course, that Charlie Hunter was no more than a smart youth bent on seduction.

Throughout the play, Winnie prefers not to acknowledge human sexuality too directly.[31] Yet it is also apparent that she takes pleasure in being sexually domineering, as for example in Act I, when she says:

Go back into your hole now, Willie, you've exposed yourself enough. . . . That's the man. *(She follows his progress with her eyes.)* . . . You have left your vaseline behind. . . . More to the right. *(Pause.)* The right, I said. *(Pause. Irritated.)* Keep your tail down, can't you! *(Pause.)* Now. *(Pause.)* There! (*HD* 20–21)

Clearly, this passage is not only a direction to Willie to get out of the sun, but is also (by way of various double entendres, as various critics have noted) a set of instructions as to how he should make love to her. Later in act 1, Winnie reminds Willie how he used to implore her to take his revolver away because he feared he might kill himself. Though it is not clear why Willie is suicidal, one possibility is that he has been driven to despair by a combination of Winnie's bullying and her unrelenting optimism.

At the end of the play, Willie emerges from behind the mound for the first time, *"dressed,"* as the stage directions tell us, *"fit to kill"* (*HD* 45). Whether this means that he intends to harm Winnie (assuming that is possible in an afterlife situation), or that he wishes to reaffirm their marriage vows (he is dressed as for a wedding) is ambiguous. Winnie, of course, takes the optimistic view, and in a transport of joy sings part of the "Merry Widow Waltz":

> Though I say not
> What I may not
> Let you hear,
> Yet the swaying
> Dance is saying
> Love me dear!
> Every touch of fingers
> Tells me what I know,
> Says for you,
> It's true, it's true,
> You love me so! (*HD* 47)

It may be that Willie's just audible "Win" (*HD* 47) is a prelude to a renewed declaration of love, in which case Winnie's song is entirely appropriate to the circumstances. Yet it is also possible that Willie is announcing his intention to "win"—to bring a victorious end the battle he has been fighting against her bullying and her irritatingly insistent optimism. He might do this by killing one or both of them with the revolver (assuming, again, that it is possible to do so). What he intends is not clear.[32] In the light of what has gone before, it seems possible that Willie's intentions are less than loving, and if that is so, we feel in the end, as earlier, both sympathy for Winnie's unhappy condition and contempt for her efforts to make everything seem for the best. For as Beckett makes clear in *Happy Days*, drawing on Burton, Schopenhauer, and various others, an optimistic attitude can be seriously misleading: it can place significant limitations on the extent of what we can hope to know about both ourselves and the world we inhabit.[33]

Notes

1. See S. E. Gontarski, *Beckett's Happy Days: A Manuscript Study* (Columbus: Ohio State University Press, 1977), 59–73, for the sources of the allusions.

2. In *Samuel Beckett* (London: Routledge and Kegan Paul, 1976), 7, John Pilling notes that Beckett began reading Schopenhauer in the thirties, and that "Schopenhauer is still a figure likely to call forth from Beckett such terms as 'wonderful' or 'extraordinary,' and he always stresses how fine his *writing* is." Beckett's interest in *The Anatomy of Melancholy* dates from at least the early forties, given the number of references to Burton in *Watt*, the novel he wrote at that time. According to Burton, "Milk, and all that comes of milk, as butter and cheese, curds, &c. increase melancholy . . ." (*The Anatomy of Melancholy*, ed. Floyd Dell and Paul Jordan-Smith [1621; New York: Tudor, 1948], 191); Watt, we are told, drinks "nothing but milk" (*Watt*, [London: Calder & Boyars, 1970], 21). An "inordinate diet" can give rise to melancholy, says Burton (186–87); in Part IV of *Watt*, a disembodied voice tells the main character: *"The only cure is diet"* (*W* 225). "[T]oo much solitariness" (Burton, 213) is another cause of melancholy: Arsene says that like Watt, Vincent and Walter had "big red noses, the result of too much solitude" (*W* 57). Beckett alludes to Burton not only in *Watt*, but also in various other works. See, for example, the opening stage directions to *Krapp's Last Tape* (1958), in Samuel Beckett, *Collected Shorter Plays* (London: Faber & Faber, 1984), 55, where Krapp is described as "a wearish old man." This is a direct echo of Burton's description of the pre-Socratic philosopher Democritus in *The Anatomy of Melancholy*, 12: "Democritus . . . was a little wearish old man, very melancholy by nature, averse from company in his latter days, and much given to solitariness. . . ." Allusions to Burton appear in other Beckett works as well, but are too numerous to list here.

3. All quotations from *Happy Days* are from the Faber & Faber edition of the play (1961; rpt. London, 1963); page numbers are given in the text, preceded by *HD*.

4. For information about Beckett's interest in Leibniz and Voltaire, see John Pilling, *Samuel Beckett* (London: Routledge & Kegan Paul, 1976), 32, 116, 119, 124, and 141. Pilling comments that "Voltaire provided the title of one of Beckett's earliest works," this being "Che Sciagura," in *TCD: A College Miscellany*, 36 (14 November 1929), 42. The same phrase, but in English, "What a Misfortune," appears as the title of one of the stories in Beckett's *More Pricks than Kicks*. The words "Che sciagura d'essere senza coglioni" ("What a misfortune it is to be without balls") are spoken by the eunuch in *Candide*, Chapter 11.

5. For a full discussion of Schopenhauer's influence on Beckett, see my *Samuel Beckett's Artistic Theory and Practice: Criticism, Drama and Early Fiction* (London: Macmillan, 1997), 6–7.

6. *The World as Will and Idea*, trans. R. B. Haldane and J. Kemp (London: Kegan Paul, Trench, Trübner & Co., 1909), I, 419. Subsequent references to this edition will be given in the text, preceded by the abbreviation *WWI*.

7. For discussion of Beckett's interest in Dante, see *The Novels of Samuel Beckett* (London: Chatto & Windus, 1964), 16–17. In *The Long Sonata of the Dead* (London: Rupert Hart-Davis, 1969), 290, Michael Robinson comments that the world of *Happy Days* is "the visual presentation of an isolated corner of Dante's Inferno. Like the Violent against God, Nature and Art [Winnie] is confined to a burning desert under a rain of perpetual fire, visible first from waist to head like the Heretics in their burning tombs, and then from forehead to neck like the Traitors Dante saw in the Lake of Cocytus."

8. See *Happy Days*, 26, where Winnie asks: "Is gravity what it was, Willie, I fancy not. . . . Don't you ever have that feeling, Willie, of being sucked up?"

9. In *Samuel Beckett: The Comic Gamut* (New Brunswick, N.J.: Rutgers University Press, 1962), 253, Ruby Cohn comments that "Winnie's 'old style' is implicitly contrasted with Dante's *dolce stil nuovo;* she even utters the phrase 'sweet old style.' "

10. In *Samuel Beckett* (London: Hutchinson University Library, 1971), 117, Francis Doherty comments that if a third act existed, there would be "silence, the burial of the head up to the eyes, no mouth to talk, no one to talk to, only the mind to think, to be made to think." That is also possible, though the daily return of Winnie's belongings makes it seem more probable that act 3 would return Winnie to the situation in which she finds herself in act 1.

11. See S. E. Gontarski, *Beckett's Happy Days: A Manuscript Study*, 13. In 2 Samuel 24.14, David says of God that "his mercies are great," and in Isaiah 54.7, God says, "For a small moment have I forsaken thee; but with great mercies will I gather thee." Reference to God's "tender mercies" is to be found in various Psalms, including 25.6, 40.11, 51.1, 77.9, 79.8, and 103.4.

12. In contrast to Winnie, Willie is presented in the play as a sexual animal. Thus in act 1 Winnie speaks of envying "the brute beast" only a moment before Willie's "hairy forearm" (*HD* 16) appears above the mound; throughout the play Willie never rises to his feet, but crawls on all fours; and when Winnie notes that the bristles on her toothbrush are "pure . . . hog's . . . setae," Willie gives this comment a sexual dimension by revealing that a hog is a "Castrated male swine" (*HD* 35). In context, this phrase seems to relate to Willie, since various hints are made that he has been metaphorically emasculated by his domineering wife.

13. Robert Burns, "Holy Willie's Prayer," in *English Romantic Poetry and Prose*, ed. Russell Noyes (New York: Oxford University Press, 1956), 143. It should also be borne in mind that "willie" is British/Irish slang for penis.

14. When Winnie says that the ant is carrying an egg, Willie utters the word "Formication" (*HD* 24) and laughs. Clearly he is amused at the resemblance between this word (which means the sensation of having ants crawl over the skin) and "fornication." Why Winnie laughs is less clear: she may think it funny that God sends ants to Hell and allows them to breed, so that He can punish successive generations of them for the original sin of having been born (see note 21); or she may be amused at the appropriateness of ants appearing in her world, given that human activity is to God like that of ants on an anthill.

15. Robert Burton, *The Anatomy of Melancholy*, ed. Floyd Dell and Paul Jordan-Smith (1621; rpt. New York: Tudor, 1948), 237–38.

16. Samuel Beckett, *Proust/Three Dialogues: Samuel Beckett and Georges Duthuit* (1931; rpt. London: Calder & Boyers, 1965), 18. All quotations are from this edition; page numbers will be given in the text.

17. S. E. Gontarski, *Beckett's Happy Days: A Manuscript Study*, 63. Like Gontarski, Anthony Brennan, in "Winnie's Golden Treasury: The Use of Quotation in *Happy Days*," *Arizona Quarterly* 35 (1979), 205–27, offers an interpretation of the significance of the allusions in *Happy Days* that differs in various ways from the one I offer here.

18. Gontarski comments that, "as Milton reminds us, 'God is light,' and light is eternal. . . . But the celebration of the eternity of light is a sharp contrast to the reality of Winnie's condition. What Winnie needs, in point of fact, is not a rhapsody on the divinity of light, but shade, a relief from oppressive reality" (69). Nevertheless, the line is a comfort to Winnie, who, despite her cynicism about some of God's poorer "little jokes" (*HD* 24), is nevertheless convinced that someone— presumably God—is "[c]aring for her still" (*HD* 37).

19. Elsewhere in act 1 Winnie echoes *Cymbeline* when she says to Willie "Fear no more the heat o' the sun" (*HD* 21) as he crawls into his hole behind her. This is the first line of the song that Guiderius and Arviragus sing over the body of a youth named Fidele, who is really their sister Imogen in disguise (*Cymbeline* IV.ii.258). Im-

ogen is not, as Guiderius and Arviragus assume, beyond the dangers posed by the heat of the sun, for she is drugged, not dead. Similarly, Willie is susceptible to sunburn, as we have seen, while Winnie is not: Winnie considers it a great mercy that she does not suffer as Willie does.

20. *Paradise Lost* X.741–42.

21. Two of Beckett's favorite lines of verse are: "The greatest crime [or sin] of man / Is that he ever was born." The lines, from Calderón, are quoted by Schopenhauer in *WWI*, I, 328 and 458, and *WWI*, II, 420.

22. *Hamlet* III.i.158–69.

23. Winnie echoes Edward FitzGerald's translation of *The Rubáiyát of Omar Khayyám* to the same effect in act 1, when she says to Willie, "just to know you are there within hearing and conceivably on the semi-alert is . . . er . . . paradise enow" (*HD* 25). The lines she is alluding to are the famous ones that speak of "A Book of Verses underneath the Bough, / A Jug of Wine, a Loaf of Bread—and Thou / Beside me singing in the Wilderness— / Oh, Wilderness were Paradise enow!" (*Rubáiyát* XII.45–48). In *Happy Days* Winnie's fragmented memories of the classics take the place of any book of verses: there is no wine or food, which reminds us that this is an afterlife situation. The wilderness is so extreme that Winnie's parasol catches on fire, and Willie is a less-than-ideal object of love.

24. *Romeo and Juliet* V.iii.94–96.

25. *Twelfth Night* II.iv.113–15.

26. Thomas Gray, "Ode on a Distant Prospect of Eton College" (1747), in *Eighteenth Century Poetry and Prose*, ed. Louis Bredvold et al. (New York: Ronald Press, 1956), 591.

27. *Ibid.* Gray's epigraph appears in the original Greek; the above is the translation furnished by the editors of *Eighteenth Century Poetry and Prose*.

28. *Ibid.*, 592.

29. The phrase "cannot be cured" is clearly an allusion to "The Lily of Killarney," a song Joyce alludes to in *A Portrait of the Artist as a Young Man* and *Ulysses*. For the words to the song see Zack Bowen, *Musical Allusions in the Works of James Joyce* (Albany: State University of New York Press, 1974), 37–38. See p. 369 for a list of the places in *Ulysses and Portrait* where Joyce alludes to this song. Beckett did not mention the song in the list of sources he supplied to Schneider.

30. Quoted in *Beckett's Happy Days: A Manuscript Study*, 71.

31. Winnie says she is disgusted by the obscene postcard Willie produces in act 1, but examines it carefully to see what the people pictured in it are doing (*HD* 16–17). Her story of the little girl she calls Mildred is interesting for its autobiographical implications: that Mildred resembles both Willie and herself in various respects suggests that the story of the mouse running up her leg may be Winnie's way of describing her own first experience at sex—her fright at its animality, and at the invasion of her person.

32. Cf. *Beckett's Happy Days: A Manuscript Study*, where Gontarski points out that in an early typescript of the play, Winnie says " 'Is it me you're after, Willie . . . or is it something else? . . . Is it a kiss you're after, Willie . . . ?' " He comments that "Although [the word] 'kiss' make[s] the scene more concrete, the incident is dominated by the vague phrase . . . 'or something else'. . . . Is Willie struggling toward Winnie, the revolver, or both? And to what end: to kiss or kill her?—or to end his own misery? . . . She may not even be aware that Willie is possibly struggling toward the gun" (37).

33. I would like to acknowledge the help of my good friend Melvin Friedman, who read an early draft of this essay and made many helpful suggestions, which I incorporated into the final draft.

Beckett [f]or Nothing

Raymond Federman

Wʜᴀᴛ ꜰᴏʀᴍ ᴄᴀɴ ꜰɪᴄᴛɪᴏɴ ᴛᴀᴋᴇ ᴡʜᴇɴ ɪᴛ ᴇɴᴄᴏᴜɴᴛᴇʀꜱ ᴇᴠᴇʀʏᴡʜᴇʀᴇ nothing but verbal dust? How can the being of fiction give himself a form, relate himself, if he constantly suppresses himself, if he **blots** out the words, the very words that *made him be possible?*

And yet, *Only the words break the silence.*

Strange paradox: *Blots, words can be blotted and the mad thoughts they invent, the nostalgia for that slime where the Eternal breathed and his son wrote, long after, with divine idiotic finger, at the feet of the adulteress, wipe it out, all you have to do is say you said nothing and so say nothing again.* **[Text 6]**

What will become then of the speaking/writing **I**, if he blots out, negates, cancels the words that have been him—his life?

That is the question raised by **Texts for Nothing.**

But that question could only be raised after the journey of Molloy, the reincarnation of Malone, the verbal agony of The Unnamable.

That is to say, after **The Trilogy** was written.

Suddenly, no, at last, long last, I couldn't any more, I couldn't go on. Someone said, You can't stay here. I couldn't stay there and I couldn't go on. **[Text 1]**

Here/There—in the space of writing/speaking—one is far from Murphy's garret in the insane asylum, far from Mr. Knott's house of deception, far from Molloy's room, far from Malone's bed.

Far also from the questions The Unnamable posed at the beginning of his verbal journey: *Where now? Who now? When now? Unquestioning. I, say, I.*

97

But close, very close to the end of **The Unnamable:** *You must go on, I can't go on, I'll go on.*

The text of **The Unnamable** attempted to answer the questions of *Where, When,* and *Who*—time, place, and being—by localizing the narrative voice into a fiction, *a kind of story,* but in the process discovered that the voice could not be named, could not speak itself, that in fact it was being spoken by the words that kept it/him unnamable, even though time and space had been inflicted on him.

. . . yes, they've inflicted the notion of time on me too . . . but it's entirely a matter of voices, no other metaphor is appropriate.

I see me, I see my place, there is nothing to show it, nothing to distinguish it, from all the other places, they are mine, all mine, if I wish, I wish none but mine, there is nothing to mark it, I am there so little, I see it, I feel it round me, it enfolds me, it covers me, if only this voice would stop, for a second. . . .

Who are these *They* who inflict time and space but not a name on The Unnamable?

First I'll say what I'm not, that's how they taught me to proceed, then what I am, it's already under way, I have only to resume at the point where I let myself be cowed. I am neither, I needn't say, Murphy, nor Watt, nor Mercier, nor—no, I can't even bring myself to name them, nor any of the others whose very names I forget, who told me I was they, who I must have tried to be, under duress, or through fear, or to avoid acknowledging me, not the slightest connexion.

In his search for a place to be, a time to be, in his search for being-ness, The Unnamable encounters only *silence and words,* nothing else. Silence that negates him. Words that fail to name him, to make him. But The Unnamable is not ready to admit, to accept that he is mere *wordness* or *wordlessness.* Therefore, he too, like his predecessors, in order to sustain himself, or give himself the illusion of being, invents fiction, stories, playmates—Mahood, Worm.

And why not, since, as he says, mocking the old cliché: *While there is life there is hope.*

Real or fictitious, life here gives the speaking voice only the illusion of being: *It's a question of voices, of voices to keep me going, in the right manner. . . . words pronouncing me alive, since that's how they want me to be. . . .*

But whose voices? And which pronouns? *. . . enough of this cursed first person, it is really too red a herring, I'll get out of my depth if I'm not careful. . . . Bah, any old pronoun will do, provide one sees through it. Matter of habit. To be adjusted later.*

In order to speak of **Texts for Nothing** one has to backtrack into **The Unnamable**, which gradually generates **Texts for Nothing.**

The Unnamable: Ultimate effort to BE—to BE somewhere, in time and place. But also ultimate failure to do so. Except in the illusion of story-telling. That's Mankind for you, or rather Mahoodness. To give oneself the illusion of being.

The metamorphosis of the pronoun **I** into **he** or **we**, or into the dynasty of the couple, doesn't negate the fact that it remains the story of **I**—*I the teller told.*

An **I** struggling with a growing ontological awareness of himself as he becomes the words, the very words that **I** speaks. The very words that **I** calls his life.

Words, mine was never more than that, than this pell-mell babel of silence and words, my viewless form described as ended, or to come, or still in progress, depending on the words. . . . **[Text 6]**

Again one must backtrack into **The Unnamable**, for it is not easy to arrive at the stage of pure word-beingness of **Texts for Nothing.** Or rather the stage of wordshit: *That's right, wordshit, bury me, avalanche, and let there be no more talk of any creature. . . .* **[Text 9]**

But to depersonify itself, to decharacterize itself, to become word-lessness, the **I** must undergo several transformations:

1. Transformation of the **I** narrator/hero, writer/written, teller/told into an unnamable being. Therefore, loss of nomination, loss of a name.
2. Transformation of the story. The sustaining process that situates the **I** in place and time, whether real or imaginary. Therefore, loss of the anecdote, the fable.
3. Transformation of the fictitious word-being into wordshit that

subsists only as residua beyond fictitiousness. Therefore, loss of beingness.

4. Transformation of the language of fiction that gave the I the illusion of progress. Reduction of discursive/descriptive language to a verbal delirium that leaves the voice stranded on the edge of the precipice of meaning, leaning against the wind of meaninglessness. A delirium that cannot go on and yet cannot stop going on. Therefore, loss of syntactical order, sense, direction.

Language becomes *A rumor transmissible ad infinitum in either direction* **[How It Is]**

This difficult, almost impossible undertaking, that qualifies itself as a *torture*, consists in seizing Mahoodness beyond all concepts of fiction or fabulation. Beyond the lies of fiction.

No, no souls, or bodies, or birth, or life, or death, you've got to go on without any of that junk, that's all dead with words, with excess of words, they can say nothing else, they say there is nothing else. . . . **[Text 10]**

The Unnamable puts it this way: *Agreed, agreed, I who am on my way, words bellying out my sails, am also that unthinkable ancestor of whom nothing can be said.*

Being on his way to nothingness, The Unnamable cannot render himself present—present to his own being, even though he realizes that one cannot exist outside of one's fictions.

The Unnamable, that miraculous work of fiction reveals that man manifests himself while demonstrating that he cannot be found without his fictions. Or rather without language. The language of fiction can no longer create beingness, **as** in the old fables of the past, it can only manifest a defect of being, expose the imposture of literature. Paradoxically then, even though there is still language there is no being.

Texts for Nothing: *. . . who is this raving now. . . . one who speaks saying, without ceasing to speak, Who's speaking?* And if someone is speaking, who hears him? Is Man/Mahood this being who speaks, but who doesn't know why he speaks? *Why, why this need to speak,* since to speak leads nowhere, fails to create being, *fails better.* Especially since the notion that someone is listening to whoever is speaking is a delusion.

. . . *qu'il ne vienne plus nous emmerder avec ces histoires d'objectivité et de choses vues. De toutes les choses que personne n'a jamais vues, ces cascades sont assurément les plus énormes.* [**La peinture des van Velde ou le monde et le pantalon**]

The fundamental implication of what can be called subjective literature (from Romanticism to Realism to Proust, Joyce, Sartre, and Camus) was precisely to assure the identity and continuity of being—of the self.

Even in the so-called realistic/objective novel of the 19th century, it was the world, society, reality that was vacillating in relation to the individual—the self of fiction, an **I** usually disguised as a **He** or a **She.**

For most characters (as they used to be called) of that novel, the world was an object of doubt. The subject doubted the object that made him what he (she as well) was.

The romantic hero (the realist hero, same thing) felt alienated from everything except himself. Always ready to undermine the basis, the grounding of others, but never his or hers.

Though the existentalist hero (anti-hero?)—Roquentin, Meursault, including The Dangling Man of Saul Bellow (that displaced neo-existentialist)—doubts the world, nonetheless he believes in the solidity of his own self, in the freedom of the self, even if it brings him to the edge of despair and nausea.

The romantic/realist/existentialist hero remains Cartesian, and like Descartes he doubts everything only to arrive at an absolute certitude of his own self, however mediocre, tormented, laughable that self may be.

Think of the Dostoevsky hero, the Balzac hero, and even the Proust sufferer. They all want to assert their being and beingness. Stephen Dedalus, that pompous self-impressed *artise-en-herbe*, goes further in asserting his being and his freedom of self, by declaring emphatically: *I will not serve that in which I no longer believe whether it calls itself my home, my fatherland or my church.* Down with the great social institu-

tions that have sustained the self for so long. Let the self go alone
. . . *to encounter for the millionth time the reality of experience and to forge
in the smithy of* [his] *soul the uncreated conscience of* [his] *race.*

The Beckett creature (what else can it be called?)—whether named
Molloy, Malone, The Unnamable, or simply **I**, generated by Belac-
qua, Murphy, Watt, Mercier, Camier, and all the others—is the first
to negate this assertion of being, the first to doubt and cancel his
self. The first to dare go beyond doubt, *as no other dare . . . fail.* As
such, **Texts for Nothing** is situated beyond the very idea of fiction,
beyond the kind of fiction that managed, even as a system of doubt,
to sustain beingness.

The central paradox of these short impossible texts is there in the
title if one brackets the **f** of **[f]or**—the paradox of writing texts for
nothing, into the void, into the abyss of the white page while writing
on, writing on to produce yet more words on the page, to write nothing. There is no way in, and no way out: *I couldn't stay there and I
couldn't go on.* But description is nonetheless necessary, even though
useless: *I'll describe the place, that's unimportant.*

There is then a description of place—*The top, very flat, of a mountain,
no, a hill, but so wild, so wild, enough.* But unimportant.

The Unnamable also attempted to describe his location: *This place,
if I could describe this place, portray it, I've tried, I feel no place, no place
around me, there's no end to me, I don't know what it is, it isn't flesh, it
doesn't end, it's like air. . . .*

Flesh . . . air . . . mountain . . . hill . . . doesn't matter, all the same.
Change a word in the text, change mountain or hill to flesh or air,
the place is different, but that's unimportant.

Change the **I** to **you** or **he**, the being changes, but that's unimportant. The same goes for time. Being and time are one and the same
textual movement here. The being hidden in words, the time of the
movement from one word to the next. Both these concepts collapse
into words, so that being and time implode to being-as-tense: *At first
I only had been there, now I'm still here, soon I won't be here yet.*

Time is tense: *now . . . soon . . . yet . . .* the past *had been,* the present
is, the future *will be*—*now soon yet* what kind of temporality is this?

As such, **Texts [f]or Nothing** raises the question of what is a text? What kind of texts are these that reject logical temporality? Are these sacred texts, biblical texts, texts without measure, texts without purpose. If so, then why not simply **For Nothing**, as a title? Why use the word text as part of this non-title work? Is it to suggest that these texts are without a story, without characters, without plot, without human verisimilitude, without time and place? If so, what are these texts about?

No, not about nothing or nothingness in the philosophical sense. These thirteen **Texts for Nothing** are nothing but themselves. There is no *about* here. No references to anything outside these texts, except of course, by necessity, to the texts that have generated them— Beckett's previous fiction, now reduced to **Texts [f]or Nothing.**

Nonetheless, one must ask: Who speaks here, and from where? Who says **I**, here, and what kind of **I** is it? Certainly no longer a human pretense or substitution.

These thirteen meditations, tales, sessions, break off the chain of the delirious flow of words of **The Trilogy.** They present the insularity of the short, brief text as a sign of the isolation, the detachment, the alienation of the wanderer of the preceding fiction. The speaking voice now functions without support, without staging, without crutches. They are like flares of lightning in the silence of language. Pure acts of farewell, through halts and silences, hesitations and false departures.

These thirteen texts must be read, heard rather, as one text, one sound that stops, starts again, overlaps, cancels out. Only language is heard, nothing else. The sound of language speaking from the other side of fiction—from *the reverse of farness.* [**Text 5**]

This language that speaks in the void, this *excess of words* can no longer create birth or death—that's *the junk* of old fiction. That's the old fable: . . . *that's all dead with words, with excess of words, they can say nothing else, they say there is nothing else, that here it's that and nothing else, but they won't say it eternally, they'll find some other nonsense, no matter what. . . .* [**Text 10**]

The writer who holds the pen, the scribe who scribbles with the old quill—*I'm the clerk, I'm the scribe, at the hearings of what cause I know not.* [**Text 5**]—is still present, somewhat, here, but outside the fable, outside the myth, beyond the pretense by which he hoped to create a fiction, invent someone. Or as he puts it: *I am far from that wrangle, I shouldn't bother with it, I need nothing, neither to go on nor to stay where I am. . . .* [**Text 1**]

Later he adds: *I'm making progress, it was time, I'll learn to keep my foul mouth shut before I'm done, if nothing foreseen crops up.* [**Text 4**]

While the scribe rants, the voice of fiction, or rather the voice of language watches the hand that is writing it: *Out of the corner of my eye I observe the writing hand, all dimmed and blurred by the—by the reverse of farness.* [**Text 5**]

Marvelous hesitation—this hyphenation that allows the language of these texts to locate itself in its own paradox—*the reverse of farness.*

Strange reversal of roles, crucial, however, to an understanding—hearing?—of these texts. This voice of fiction that speaks from inside the page, this voice locked inside language is telling us that it's all words, only words, the words that come out of this mouth to organize themselves on the paper to mean nothing. That voice, and the otherness of that voice—the **I** who speaks—are at the same time the voice of fiction and the mental voice of the fictioneer—the clerk, the scribe.

I'm not in his head, nowhere in his old body, and yet I'm here, for him I'm there, with him, hence all the confusion. [**Text 4**]

Whereas in **The Trilogy** the text was attempting to establish, to install the writer as the central figure of the text, here in **Texts for Nothing**, the language mocks that figure, because finally it is all **wordshit.** Wordshit: language and excrement packaged into one sound.

*Wretched acoustics this evening, the merest s[**crap**]s, literally,* laments the voice from within the page [**Text 6**]. One can barely hear what remains to be said and heard—*ill-said ill-heard ill-recaptured ill-murmured in the mud.* The mud, the muck, the merde, the wordshit, that's what remains now. The last element, the final residence, the ultimate abode of the word-being that looms ahead—the reptilian creature of **How It Is.**

Wordshit, the final production of the writer. While demolishing the kind of fiction that could only function on an intention and a pretension, Beckett denounces the inefficacy of language.

The **Texts for Nothing** are not fall-outs, left-overs from **The Trilogy**, as some critics have claimed, but important traces that the Beckettian creature leaves behind—as one leaves one's excrement behind in nature while on an outing—before undergoing yet another mutation.

But there is more to these **Texts for Nothing.** One must be careful not to fall into the trap of a title apparently without ambiguity. **Texts for Nothing** are not for nothing. True, they have nothing, that is to say the word *nothing* as their subject. Le **rien** of the French title—**Textes pour rien**—but this nothing, this **rien** should be read as a little something. In French **rien, un rien** really means a little something, a minor thing. *Nothing* here is both the subject and the object of these texts. Or, rather, language, the meaninglessness, the nothingness of language is the subject here.

The spectacular research, searching, probing, groping of the preceding fiction has led to this. The Unnamable has exhausted himself in search of himself, in search of his own self as language. Here, in **Texts for Nothing**, language is on the verge of becoming the result, the end product, the wordshit—the testimony of the search. After having attempted to designate the being of the protagonist: the wandering of Molloy, the dying of Malone, the speaking and the unspeakability of The Unnamable, language now designates itself as **Texts [f]or nothing.**

Therefore, these thirteen texts are not about nothing, they are about the nothingness of fiction, thus affirming the absoluteness of language, language deprived of fiction. A language without stories, without people: *And yet*—the voice tells us—*I have high hopes, I give you my word, high hopes, that one day I may tell a story, hear a story, yet another, with men, kinds of men as in the days when I played all regardless or nearly, worked and played.* [**Text 6**]

But of course, Beckett cannot, will not tell another story. Once committed to language as pure language, one cannot retreat into storytelling. The rest of us can do that, but Beckett will not do that, cannot do that, as he goes on **Worstward Ho.**

These thirteen meditations on language—language as writing, language as voice—not in a philosophical or linguistic sense, and certainly not as fable, declare words as supreme, and it becomes clear that this supremacy of words has no need of order, that is to say form. Impossible to speak here, as one could for the other Beckett works, of a form, or of a narrative structure. Yes, even form and structure have disappeared from **Texts for Nothing.**

How then, one must wonder, are these text constituted? How are they made possible as—here one must hesitate to find the right word, but there is no other word—as fiction? For they are, after all, fiction, and not essays, or philosophical treatises, or whatever. Unclassifiable fiction, and yet fiction, even though the words now lead nowhere, achieve nothing: *The words too, slow, slow, the subject dies before it comes to the verb, words are stopping too. Better off then than when life was babble?* [**Text 2**]

. . . *when life was babble:* babbling, with all its implications and connotations of birth, growth, development toward being, toward character, toward maturity, death, and inevitably toward narrative structure, is no longer necessary here. Here, the text no longer needs to seek growth and form. Here, language does not accumulate upon itself to create a narrative whole that moves towards a resolution, or a final solution. Here, words merely belong to themselves, to their own formlessness and meaninglessness.

Where am I? . . . who is this clot who doesn't know where to go, who can't stop, who takes himself for me and for whom I take myself, anything at all, the old jangle. Those evenings then, but what is this evening made of, this evening now that never ends, in whose shadows I'm alone. . . .[**Text 11**]

The *where am I?* and especially the word *evening* set up a series of terms that accumulate around *this evening,* that gather like grapes, not to construct a story or an anecdote, but simply to fill the gap of *this evening now*—the writing *session.*

That is the process here. One word sets up a movement of words without direction, without destination, without shape, until there is nothing more to write. Words follow their course so well toward nothingness that ultimately they cancel out: *I recapitulate,* says the **I-voice,** and then adds, *impossible.*

The words of **Texts for Nothing** postulate a fictitious being that remains neutral and remote, a being who cannot become another, as

Molloy, Malone, and even The Unnamable became the playmates they invented.

Will they succeed in slipping me into him, the memory and dream of me, into him still living, amn't I there already, wasn't I always there, like a stain of remorse. . . . Pah there are voices everywhere, ears everywhere, one who speaks saying without ceasing to speak, who's speaking?

If the voice can no longer incarnate itself into another body, another character, another self, into fictitious beingness, how can it exist? How can it be? It exists because it is heard—*pah there are voices everywhere, ears everywhere. . . .*

In **Malone Dies** spoken language (spoken-ness) becomes written language (written-ness) when Malone corrects himself: *. . . it must be over a week since I said, I shall soon be quite dead at last, etc. Wrong again. That is not what I said, I could swear to it, that is what I wrote.* In so doing Malone escapes his own death as a spoken/speaking protagonist, or rather resurrects himself as the writer of his own undying. Malone does not die, he writes himself out of death, as he emerges backward out of the *great cunt of existence.*

In **Texts for Nothing**, the words are made possible, the words become their own fiction because there is, inscribed in the texts themselves, a listening presence (an implied reader?), an ear that hears these words.

That is the crucial step that Beckett's fiction will take beyond **Texts for Nothing**. Starting with **How It Is** until the final words, the last testament **Stirrings Still**, language will listen to itself talk in the vacuum of fiction, language will invent a listener for itself to hear its own logocentricity.

It is no longer a question of the teller/told dichotomy, or the teller/told juxtaposition or superimposition, it is now the coming together of the speaker and the listener, the verbal and the oral: *fallen in the mud from our mouths innumerable and ascending to where there is an ear . . . an ear to hear even ill these scraps of other scraps of an antique rigamarole* [**How It Is**].

The French says *s'entendre* when they mean to hear oneself, to understand oneself. The existence of one who speaks is made possible because he is heard, or hears himself talk. It it's a question of *acoustics* we are told. [**Text 6**]

If in the fiction that led to **Texts for Nothing** it was a question of telling and writing, now it is a question of saying and listening: . . . *so given am I to thinking with my breath. . . . And personally, I hear it said, personally I have no more time to lose. . . .* [**Text 7**]

Ultimately, it is the presence of human breath that sustains and co-ordinates these texts, this oral adventure of words. With **Murphy** and **Watt**, we were in the zone of seeing. With **The Trilogy**, we were in the zone of telling. With **Texts for Nothing**, we enter the zone of listening. Beckett does not write for nothing, he writes for all the senses.

Beckett Briefly on the Nature of Everything: A Reading of *Texts for Nothing* in the Half-Light of Greek Philosophy

LIVIO DOBREZ

COMING FROM BECKETT, EVEN MODEST PROPOSALS TEND TO BE RATHER ambitious, and this is particularly true of *Texts for Nothing*. While "for nothing" would not seem an auspicious start, the option of transforming it into a "from nothing," an *ex nihilo,* exists with maximum possibilities. Certainly this move is explicitly blocked: "Here . . . no talk of a creator, and nothing very definite in the way of a creation."[1] But since the impossible route is the one Beckett habitually chooses, we may read the statement as Socratic *eironeia,* a truly false and falsely true profession of ignorance. *Texts for Nothing* consists of (unlucky) thirteen prose fragments. With the witty weariness expected of Beckett, it begins at the end: "Suddenly, no, at last, long last. . . . I couldn't go on" (71). Naturally the admission functions as a spring that, wound to unbearable stasis, can only unwind at a speed, often breathless, that will propel the narrative forward for some seventy pages before its energy is triumphantly exhausted.

The situation is that of a tramp of sorts lying face down in the mud, amid surroundings, possibly Irish, which are described with a lurid sweep of imagination, undermined by irony. The subject seems to be dead or dying, though he admits he gave up the ghost, provisionally, on numerous occasions ("I've given myself up for dead all over the place . . . nothing like breathing your last to put new life in you" 74). All this suggests identification with other Beckett characters, those of the more-or-less contemporary novellas and the trilogy in particular. As the first Text approaches its elegiac close, comforting thoughts of finality bring up the image of a child lulled to sleep by a father's story. In this context, the subject, now alone and therefore both father and son, teller of and listener to the tale, slips, like Leopold Bloom home after his Dublin odyssey, into peaceful oblivion, release laced with the gentlest sarcasm: "I'm holding myself in my arms. . . . Sleep now . . . tired out with so much talking, so much listening, so much toil and play" (75). The second Text is closely linked to this one. It too suggests the situation of the tramp; it too brings stray memories—if they are that—to the surface. As in the previous segment, everything appears to be slowing down. Time has become "one enormous second, as in Paradise, and the mind slow, slow, nearly stopped" (78). Absurdly, the thought occurs that one might reach the desired end of speech *too soon* as it were, die before one is ready. In that case—exquisite logic—it might be as well to *ration* speech by being silent for the time being: "Jesus, better ration yourself, watch out for the genuine deathpangs, some are deceptive, you think you're home, start howling and revive" (78–79). Like the first Text, this one closes with a touchingly understated evocation of human vulnerability. The subject is moving through a wild, somber landscape, expressionist in its obsessive, almost demented vitality. Eventually he passes the lighted window of a house. That's all. The point, which is the enormity of human solitude and desire for comfort and company, is left unstated. If a comment exists, it can only be in the form of sarcasm at the other enormity, that of human hope, a light inevitably extinguished: "How one hoped above, on and off. With what diversity" (80).

So far the narrative appears straightforward enough. But a problem exists from the start: the subject who is talking insists all along that the talking voice is not *his,* the formula being "*Someone* said" (71). By the third Text, the tramp has disappeared, only a narrative voice remains. What is its connection with the dying or dead character? Apparently none, as with nice irony and a deal of bitterness, the voice sets out to insert itself forcibly into a character, *any* character: "It's enough to will it . . . will me a body, will me a head" (81). Of course all this amounts to a glorious parody of the realist tradition, in the novel in particular. But it is not a facile parody, rather an anguished one, since this text simply *can't* go along the old path. It *tries*. It *constructs* a creature: "There you are now on your feet, I give you my word, I swear they're yours, I swear it's mine, get to work with your hands, palp your skull, seat of the understanding, without which nix" (82).

Where will this human sine qua non of narrative emerge? Possibly in the Gobi desert. He'll need a nanny. Let's call her Bibby. "She'll say to me, Come doty, it's time for bye bye" (82). Moving ahead in a fit of wild optimism, let's have our hero in the prime of senility. Let's give him a friend: "I'll have a crony, my own vintage, my own bog, a fellow warrior, we'll relive our campaigns and compare our scratches" (83). No sooner said than done: "We spend our life, it's ours, trying to bring together in the same instant a ray of sunshine and a free bench. . . . In a choking murmur he reads out to me from the paper of the day before, he had far far better been the blind one. The sport of kings is our passion, the dogs too. . . . Nothing human is foreign to us, once we have digested the racing news" (84).

At this point this bitterly farcical version of Terence's *nihil humanum* theme is overwhelmed by its own implausibility. The voice in any case is denied all association with it from the start. It was just an exercise. So just as the tramp of Texts One and Two denied identity with the narrative voice, so, here, the voice denies identity with any character. The real difficulty is that it also denies identity with *itself*. In a few lines it makes a statement, withdraws it with the claim "I was *going* to say," promptly adds that it makes no difference *who* is speaking, then concludes "*someone* said what matter who's speaking" (81). Zestfully it looks forward, tongue-in-cheek, to further developments, a real narrative start, plot and character and everything else as it were: "There's going to be a departure, I'll be there, I won't miss it, it won't be me, I'll be here, I'll *say* I'm far from here, it won't be me, I won't say anything, there's going to be a story, someone's going to try and tell a story" (81). Who then is the speaker of the Texts? It is not the dying creature, nor the prattling narrative voice. Of course the text consists of nothing other *than* this voice. More precisely, we can isolate three modalities of the narrative voice. First, the voice speaks for a given character, say the dying tramp. Then the voice is heard *as* voice, and, finally, the voice speaks neither for the tramp nor for itself. In practice, these distinctions are constantly being blurred, for the simple reason that the text is made up of the utterances of the voice. But it is possible to discern a three-fold protagonist, a trinity, no less: "There's a pretty three in one, and what a one, what a no one" (130). That one and no one, disembodied, Other to the voice of the text, remote, obscure, may be termed Beckett's Unnamable, the problematical center round which all else turns.

At any rate we have established the pattern of Beckett's Texts, a pattern that remains constant from the third to the thirteenth. An unnamable thing, speaking through a voice it will not acknowledge as its own, tries repeatedly to concretize itself, to embody itself in a character, a story, always without success. Again, even as it does so, and fails, it refuses to admit it is doing anything, being anything. The pattern then is that of a dynamic absence, a gaping hole in the middle of the narrative, thirteen times patching itself up, thirteen times reopening. *Texts for Nothing* is a thirteen-fold abortion, a false start repeated thirteen times. The text *is* precisely this failure to be, a distinguished and witty failure. On occasion, though, the comic metamorphoses into tragedy, and Beckett's rhetoric becomes very powerful indeed. The superb opening of the fourth Text, for example, with its unashamedly Romantic breadth of gesture—"Where would I go if I could go, who would I be if I could be, what would I say if I had a voice?"—invites comparison with the "who, if I cried, would hear me" of Rilke's opening Duino elegy.

This comparison leads to the main point of the present article. Beckett's writing, like Rilke's, is philosophical not because in it we find references to philosophy and philosophers, but because it philosophizes. It is with this in mind that I approach *Texts for Nothing* as an argument, one in the literary form of a *livre composé*. I propose to examine the pattern outlined above from the standpoint of Greek philosophy. Of course Beckett's interest in the philosophers of antiquity is well known and has been commented upon. But the present approach is rather different. Since the theme is Greek, I divide my material as the Greeks would have done. It was Diogenes Laertius who noted of the Stoics: "Philosophy, they say, is like . . . an egg: the shell is Logic, next comes the white, Ethics, and the yolk in the center is Physics."[2] So I begin with the shell.

The opening of Text Eleven is as good an example as any of the logic operative in *Texts for Nothing*. The narrative voice sets out to make a statement, rejects it, tries again, elaborates, then collapses: "When I think, no, that won't work, when come those who knew me, perhaps even know me still . . . it's as though, it's as if, come on, I don't know, I shouldn't have begun." Attempts at precision peter out and we find we've gone nowhere: "[I]t's still the same old road I'm trudging, up yes and down no, towards one yet to be named. . . . Name, no, nothing is nameable, tell, no, nothing can be told, what then, I don't know, I shouldn't have begun" (123). We are back at the beginning. If this is an argument, it is a truncated one. Yet argument of this kind has an illustrious pedigree. After all, the classical Socratic dialectic proceeds toward a definition, whether of virtue or knowledge or justice, by means of refutation of inadequate definitions, the method of *elenchos,* and, characteristically, it never gets there but stops short at a point of *aporia.* Beckett's text also sets out to define—its Unnamable—rejects its definitions and comes up short. The road is up Yes and down No, and its terminus is Socratic nescience. In fact, the entire logic of the Texts is aporetic: "I don't know, I can't know beforehand, nor after, nor during" (113). If the voice could say anything with conviction, it would be on the way to Socratic knowledge. *Any* truth grasped would grasp, or begin to grasp, the Unnamable, the absent key to the entire performance. But the title of the performance says it all: *Texts for Nothing.* The voice cannot get beyond aporetic impasse, the dialectic of affirmation and negation, affirmation generating negation, negation in turn generating affirmation. So Beckett's logic is a form of wrestling, Yes pinned down by No in turn pinned down by Yes, or something more violent still: "The screaming silence of no's knife in yes's wound" (135).

This is a terrifying parody of the elenchic method, and moreover it is a one-way dialectic because those "same old questions and answers" (74) are addressed *to* the speaker by the speaker. Socratic dialogue has become short-circuit monologue. In the process, the classical principles of Greek logic, of Identity, Contradiction, and the Excluded Middle, are also short-circuited. If the voice could, in all truth, say "A is A" or "not both A and not A" or again "either A or not A," then it would be well on the way to solving its problem. But it is stuck in contradiction: "There's going to be a departure, I'll be there, I won't miss it, it won't be me, I'll be here" (81); "How many hours to go, before the next silence, they are not hours, it will not be silence" (101); "It's not me, yes, it's me" (116); "It's not true, yes it's true, it's true and it's not true" (135). Paraphrasing the Dantean *maestro di color che sanno,* Beckett pays ironic homage to "Aristotle, who knew everything" (110) in the eighth Text. But he systematically breaks Aristotle's rules.

Where all else fails in a Platonic dialogue, when you cannot *reason* your way to something, you can always fall back on a myth, like the story of Er or of the Cave in *The Republic,* or the myth of the afterlife in the *Phaedo,* or of the Charioteer or the invention of writing in the *Phaedrus,* or Aristophanes' story in *The Symposium.* Beckett's voice follows just this trajectory, from *logos* to *mythos.* It tells a children's story, technically a comedy, since it begins unhappily and ends happily, in Text One. In Text Two it introduces the stories of Mother Calvet and Mr. Joly; then there is the twelve-year-old boy of the sixth Text, the man at the station of the seventh, the Parisian beggar of the eighth, the Humanities student of the eleventh. The stories are inevitably rejected, however, sometimes in a fury of frustration ("enough vile parrot I'll kill you." 104), sometimes with light sarcasm ("I have high hopes, a little story, with living creatures coming and going on a habitable earth crammed with the dead, a brief story, with night and day coming and going" 101).

Where does this leave us? Everything we hear is a lie: "all is false. . . . it's only voices, only lies" (81). But it is the *voice* that tells us this, like the Cretan who proclaims all Cretans liars and with the same result. "All you have to do is say you said nothing and so say nothing again" (99). But the trouble is that in saying nothing you've said *something,* in lying you've told *a* truth, if not *the* truth. "So many lies, so many times the same lie lyingly denied" (135): is it or isn't it a lie? Descartes saw that doubt itself constitutes affirmation. The dilemma of Beckett's voice is the ultimate dilemma of the—classical or modern—sceptic. You can't say that you don't believe in *anything* without contradicting yourself, since you presumably believe your own statement. No negative is so negative as to contain no positive. The voice looks for this paradigmatic No: "a new no, to cancel all the others . . . a new no, that none says twice" (126–27). It knows it won't find it because the No that undermines Yes undermines itself as well: "ah if no were content to cut yes's throat and never cut its own" (109). We must conclude then that something *is* rescued from failure by the aporetic logic of the Texts. But what is it, exactly?

To answer we must proceed from logic to ontology, from the methodology of the text to its elusive subject. In the terminology proposed above, we turn to Physics, the yolk at the center of the egg. For the Greeks, physics related to that activity that constituted things as they were or brought about things as they were. It investigated the nature of things, *phusis,* the *rerum natura.* Its question encompassed the universe—*kosmos*—including the gods. Heidegger, who like Beckett pondered the Greeks, formulated it as follows: "Why beings instead of nothing?," which amounts to "Why beings instead of being?," that is, "Why multiplicity, why differentiation?" Because for the Greeks it was a matter of explaining the coexistence of the One and the Many, Sameness and Difference. Lots of horses exist, but as horses these are one, that's to say, horses are both same and different in relation to each other. If only one horse existed, would it be a horse? Can you have a category of one? Presumably, that one horse would be unknowable, since knowledge presupposes connections. A horse is a horse by virtue of its sameness with other horses. Something absolutely particular could scarcely be said to be, except as a potential (in Aristotle's terms) or as chaos, a raw material waiting to be used, the negative end of being. Mind naturally brings things together; it organizes and groups, making things one. Having prioritized unity, it wonders how the many come to be; how, given being, becoming is possible; how change, motion, in other words, the varied, transient world we experience is actualized.

In what follows, I focus on philosophical systems that seem especially relevant to Beckett, emphasizing the Greek obsession with the One and a number of models for the construction of the *kosmos.* The earliest philosophers, the original Milesian *phusikoi,* postulated some kind of ur-substance, an *arche* that might function as origin for all the rest. Thales who, according to the gossip of antiquity, Diogenes Laertius, was something of a Beckettian (he had no children out of love for children and when asked to marry used to say "too early, too early" until one day he said "too late, too late"),[3] proclaimed his *arche* to be water—for reasons already obscure to Aristotle. The mechanism of the Milesians and others like them was to generate all substances from the original, say by the action of heat and cold, rarefying, compressing until they had the four elements. The Pythagorean version was numerical. Archetypal contraries of odd and even generated the hearth of the universe, the creative number 1, the *point* from which proceeds *line* (as Beckett notes in his novel *Murphy*), from which proceeds two-dimensional *surface*, from which proceeds three-dimensional *solid*, the mystical *tetractys*, the number 4: in other words, the world.

Now an obsessive mind like Beckett's might well be attracted to the radical Eleatic solution to the question of the One and the Many. *Texts for Nothing*, after all, cannot get beyond its archaic starting point. I quote from Parmenides' famous poem: "Only one story, one road, now / is left: that it is. And on this there are signs / in plenty that being, it is ungenerated and indestructible, / whole, of one kind and unwavering, and complete. / Nor was it, nor will it be, since now it is, all together, / one, continuous."[4] Nothing comes from nothing, *ex nihilo*. Nothing comes from being: being just *is*. So becoming is impossible. Static being is the only thinkable, for, in Heidegger's rendering of Parmenides, "thinking and being are the same." Yet one wonders how it might be possible to think, in fact, to do anything, in a context in which no change occurs, no Many, only the One. We are in that situation of fixity Beckett parodies sympathetically in *Waiting for Godot*, with its opening sally "nothing to be done" and its close "let's go" / stage direction: "they do not move"; or in *Happy Days*, whose protagonist is buried in sand throughout the play; or in *Endgame*, whose characters are stuck in wheelchairs or in bins. (These last also recall the tub or funerary vessel inhabited by the Cynic Diogenes, the one who, when asked by Alexander the Great whether he wanted anything, replied, "[O]nly for you to get out of my light." In Zeno's famous riddles, movement bogs down and founders: Achilles never overtakes the tortoise, the man crossing the stadium never gets to the other side—because he has an affinity of Pythagorean points to negotiate. Beckett loves this self-cannibalizing logic: "Softer, every year a little softer. . . . Slower too, every year a little slower" (107); "as if to grow less could help, ever less and less and never quite be gone" (108). It is the principle of action in *Waiting for Godot,* which runs down in the second act, as well as in other plays. The reply to Zeno is nicely articulated by Socrates in the *Parmenides,* where Socrates, with his usual gentle mockery, puts it something like this: "So what you're saying Zeno is that there's no such thing as Many? And you offer *many* proofs of this in the *many* books you've written?" To which Zeno replies, presumably with a smile: "you've grasped it perfectly Socrates."[5]

Alternatives to the bald Eleatic assertion of "One and One only" are themselves legion. One could counter the radical argument that everything *is* with the equally radical view of the Sophist Gorgias that *nothing* is. One could accept the argument that "all things are one" with the understanding that one is itself *many,* that "in differing, it agrees with itself" in the way that the bow agrees with the lyre: without contraries is no progression. The original unity now appears as finely strung to a pitch of tension, not static but liable to spring. That means a world ruled by war, by the element of fire: "the thunderbolt steers all things."[6] Everything is one, but one constantly metamorphosing and remetamorphosing into itself: *panta rei.* Whereas the Eleatic world simply *was,* this one generates itself without pause, down the elements from fire to earth and up again from earth to fire. The Stoics who took over this system elaborated from it a complex dynamism of creation. The original Heracleitian *logos* took on the attributes of mind while remaining in some sense fire. This *logos,* like the one in John's gospel, became flesh—by virtue of its own instability, expanding, cooling, condensing—until a countermovement, like the recoil of a spring, returned the world it had become to the original flame. Everything was consumed in the cosmic conflagration, only to repeat itself by a process of eternal recurrence: an oscillating universe, one and many by turns.

This is an elegant model of multiplicity. Another model, and one that on the evidence of many texts clearly fascinates Beckett, is that of the Atomists, the enemies of the Stoics. In this case, the logic is simply to deny the oneness of being by the assertion of the Many. Or, looking at it another way, to *multiply* the Eleatic One. Instead of a single, indivisible whole, infinite numbers of minuscule indivisible wholes exist. The monad units, solipsistic, self-sufficient, appear in Beckett in the form of despairingly solitary characters. Sometimes the atomic theory comes by way of Leibniz, as in the novel *Murphy,* sometimes directly from Democritus. Beckett quotes the Greek philosopher in the trilogy: "[N]othing is more real than nothing." This is because, if you postulate moving particles, you must allow for empty space, the birth of the void—which is anathema to the Parmenideans. As Lucretius puts it, "[R]emember that the universe is bottomless."[7] In *Texts for Nothing*, as in other texts, not least *Godot*, Beckett acknowledges the Atomists in many references to one of his favorite substances: sand. The motion of sand is classically atomic, through action exerted mechanically from without. In the Epicurean version of the generation of the universe, seed-particles tumble in space as a result of weight. Without cause, that is, freely, they "swerve" a fraction. This indeterminacy of movement provokes chains of collisions, out of which the universe is constructed. You could call it creation by mistake, an erratic failure to collapse in a straight line. (I shall return to this interpretation, as well as to the Epicurean *metakosmia* or *intermundia*.) Once atomic aggregates have produced worlds, these worlds are separated by spaces—the *intermundia*—and it's here Epicurus banished the gods he really had no room for in his system.

I here offer a final model for the generation of the Many from the One. For Plato the dialectic of sameness and difference is, of course, that of the changeless, paradigmatic Ideas on one hand, and the world of change on the other. Becoming is separated from being in which it participates (*methexis*) or which it imitates (*mimesis*). The dynamics of nature are explained by the "likely story" in the *Timaeus* of the demiurge who constructs the universe using raw chaos, principle of difference and disorder, and the exemplary Ideas, principle of sameness, order, and unity. This produces soul, which is both cosmic and ultimately human and individual, and in both cases operates by the mechanism of sameness and difference, distinguishing, uniting, bringing things together, setting them apart, affirming, negating. Equally relevant for the present argument, it produces a hierarchy of creation from the cosmic to the individual soul, from gods to matter. The Neo-Platonists added complexities and gradations to this model, beginning with a supreme, godlike *arche*, then moving down the scale. That of Plotinus was a supremely Other, a One without predicates, neither thinking nor willing nor acting, something of which one could say "it *is*" without actually admitting existence in the normal sense of the word. This brings us, as Plotinus says, to "the problem endlessly debated by the most ancient philosophers: from such a unity as we have declared the One to be, how does anything at all come into substantial existence, any multiplicity . . . ? Why has the Primal not remained self-gathered so that there be none of this profusion of the manifold which we observe in existence and yet are compelled to trace to that absolute unity?"[8] It appears that like fire, which, being fire, must give out heat, so the One, even in its archetypal solitude, must give out something of itself. Like an eye turned in on itself, it *sees*, and this seeing of itself produces the first emanation, that of *Nous* or Mind. Mind then speaks Soul, an image of itself, mediating between Soul and the original One. And so on, all the way to the material. Creation is a contemplative act, rather than one of *techne,* as in the *Timaeus.* It amounts to a fall, as in Plato, from light to darkness. As in earlier philosophic systems, a ladder leads back to the origin, a return *Odyssey* corresponding to the *Iliad* journey out. This is the ecstatic movement of the alone to the alone, the individual soul in its solitude reaching back to the solitude from which it came, in the concluding words of the *Enneads* "the passing of solitary to solitary."[9] Proclus added further refinements and more intermediaries to the Plotinian series, as if one might bridge the unbridgeable gap from One to Many by means of endless gradations. In the pseudo-Dionysius, the hierarchy of being takes on a Christian coloring. Undifferentiated Godhead, transcendent, totally Other, "overflows" into the Many,[10] first into a three-fold manifestation and a trinitarian movement of circles and spirals. As the streams of sameness and difference, Universal and Particular, revolve, they intersect, and the point of intersection generates in order: matter, vegetable, animal, human, angelic—then, by a counterthrust, returns, after the manner of Plotinus, to the original source. From the philosophic question "Why things?," we have progressed historically to a graduated, stepladder universe of motion whose key is an unmoved mover, God who has no need of the universe but brings it into being anyway, just by being God, or by a *fiat.*

I have already suggested that one may identify three protagonists, or at least three modes of the speaking subject in *Texts for Nothing.* Also I have argued that the principle of action in the text is one of affirmation and negation. This requires reconsideration in the context of a physics, the construction of a *kosmos.* Clearly an initial building block is available in the dying or dead protagonist of the first two Texts, as well as in the characters who make sporadic appearances throughout, only to be dismissed as implausible fictions. If *Texts for Nothing* is to construct a world, it has some ready-made creatures available. These are not very promising, admittedly: a protagonist dead or dying on page 1, a couple of decaying cronies, a Parisian beggar, a Humanities graduate (university of life, like Leopold Bloom) pissing with great difficulty in a urinal in the Rue d'Assas. Still, it constitutes a world, having all the necessary ingredients: process or mutability, space and time, motion, multiplicity, materiality. Once we have body, we have action, even if we just have a head on two legs or on one, or even just a head, the perfect Greek shape and suited to the perfect movement—more or less: "Just the head and the two legs, or one, in the middle, I'd go hopping. Or just the head, nice and round, nice and smooth, no need of lineaments, I'd go rolling, downhill" (85). From here we can progress to questions about space/time ("Where am I, to mention only space . . . and since when, to mention also time" 125), or we can progress to perambulating tramps, pissing in Paris en route to an Irish bog in which they'll breathe their last, or even to what Beckett acidly and with some pathos termed "company" in the novel of that name: here the two cronies, or the short-circuit of the lighted window one passes on the outside. Like the featureless head, the decrepit, always changing, always one, character of the Texts exists as a *solitary* particle, at best colliding briefly with another monad, never able to share in otherness. If it *moves,* it does so minimally, since Beckett's world inevitably comes into being at a point of near collapse. If it *is,* it is minimally, since its becoming always tends to nonbeing. Its status in the Texts is that of the lowest order of being, particular, like the raw matter of chaos, impenetrable to knowledge, contemptuously dismissed by the voice as contingent. Matter is irrational, like the Pythagorean square root of the hypotenuse. But it is there, ineluctably: "peekaboo here I come again, just when most needed, like the square root of minus one, having terminated my humanities" (124). Let's call the creature X, as Beckett does in a passage that sums it all up: "X, that paradigm of human kind, moving at will, complete with joys and sorrows, perhaps even a wife and brats, forbears most certainly, a carcass in God's image and a contemporary skull" (104).

If matter, the subject "bedded in . . . flesh" as Text Three has it, is too passive to function as Beckett's *arche,* we must look elsewhere for the originator of this textual universe. Certainly the next building block, the narrative voice, is anything but passive. It simply can't stop, like a demented Socratic *daimon* endlessly whispering or screaming its commentary on the proceedings. Even dying won't shut it up, as if for it, as for Thales, death and life were no different. (Incidentally, when the philosopher made that claim, someone asked "Then why don't *you* die?" to which he answered, logically, "Because it makes no difference.")[11] Looking at it another way, we could say the Beckettian voice, like the Pythagorean and Platonic souls, it is immortal. It runs down like Zeno's Achilles but never quite claps out. And when it is on the verge of expiring, it revives ("nothing like breathing your last to put new life in you" 74). In fact, many indications of a cyclical movement can be found in the Texts: a transmigration of souls, body to body, "met-him-pike-hoses," as Molly Bloom puts it in *Ulysses.* The voice speaks of itself as dead or as unborn, or both. More precisely, it finds itself unable to do either, an Achilles paralyzed before the initial as before the last step: "here are my tomb and mother. . . . I'm dead and getting born, without having ended, helpless to begin" (115). Readers of the *Timaeus* will recall the options of reincarnation offered by Plato: cowardly or immoral males return as females, materialist astronomers as birds, unphilosophical types go down on all fours next time round—and the worst, not meriting to breathe air, become fish. The best, presumably, return as Guardians in the ideal Republic. For Beckett it's a question of different/sameness: "What variety and at the same time what monotony, how varied it is and at the same time how, what's the word, how monotonous" (114). The voice, endowed with Platonic *anamnesis,* recalls its past, imaginary or real (129), the boy of twelve who looked into his mirrored eyes and believed in what he saw, the down-and-out in Paris. Why not go further, beyond this text? As Pythagoras recalled other lives, it recalls characters from other books, Molloy, Malone, (88), even Pozzo from *Godot* (92). And when it refuses to identify with this decrepit crew, it is refusing *reincarnation,* sometimes with flippant irony ("But what is this I see . . . where, Place de la République, at pernod time . . . it's perhaps me at last" 110), sometimes with majestic, somber despair, as elevated in its tone as the *na iti na iti* of the *Upanishads:* "I would know [this of a Parisian beggar] it was not me, I would know I was here, begging in another dark, another silence, for another alm" (111). The hatred of embodiment, understood Pythagorean and Orphic fashion as entombment, imprisonment in "the dungeons of this moribund" (130), is immense. It echoes more or less negative views of physical love and procreation from Thales to Parmenides to Democritus to Epicurus, and finds expression in other Beckett texts: "Scoundrel? Why did you engender me?" from *Endgame,* and, from *Molloy:* "My mother. I don't think too harshly of her. I know she did all she could not to have me, except of course the one thing" (35 and 19).

At the start of the twelfth Text, the cycle of metempsychosis is described as follows: "It's a winter night, where I was, where I'm going, remembered, imagined . . . but on earth, beyond all doubt on earth, for as long as it takes to die again, wake again, long enough for . . . something to change, to make possible a deeper birth, a deeper death, or resurrection in and out of this murmur of memory and dream. A winter night . . . this impossible night, this impossible body . . . remembering the true night, dreaming of the night without morning" (129). Clearly the great desire of Beckett's creature is to get off the Pythagorean merry-go-round so vividly described in the *Phaedrus,* to escape "earth" and all its incarnations; to evade past and future, as well as life, death, and rebirth, memory of "where I was" and dream of "where I'm going." The wish is for the true night, the terminal death, the terminal birth, the final resurrection. Into what? Not into another constructed being nor into the narrative voice; in other words, the wish is to enter neither into Body nor into Mind. Only one other option exists in the text: the Unnamable who denies identity with the characters and with the voice. If an *arche* or first principle exists in Beckett's physics, it is this obscure subject, the one speaking through the voice, the one moving in the tramps.

What can be said about this subject? Not much. Its time is no-time, "end . . . of being past, passing and to be" (135). That implies no-change. Its space is no-space, "this infinite here" (98). Its movement is no-movement: "There's going to be a departure I'll be there. . . . it won't be me" (81). Its multiplicity is one, solitary: "I'm alone, I alone am" (82). Its activity is no-activity, no demiurgic "making": "the end of the farce of making" (135). Its utterance is no-utterance: "nothing has stirred, no one has spoken" (86). So when the voice tries to speak, to act, to be, it is speaking, acting, being for itself, not for the subject. In the words of the subject: "That should have been enough for him [for the voice and its incarnations], to have found me absent, but it's not, he wants me there, with a form and a world like him . . . me who am everything like him who is nothing. And when he feels me void of existence, it's of his existence he would have me void. . . . The truth is he's looking for me to kill me, to have me dead like him, dead like the living. He knows all that, but it's no help his knowing it, I don't know it. I know nothing. . . . He thinks words fail him, he thinks because words fail him, he's on his way to my speechlessness, to being speechless with my speechlessness. . . . He tells his story every five minutes, saying it's not his, there's cleverness for you. . . . of course he has no story, that's no reason for trying to foist one on me. . . . He has me say things saying it's not me, there's profundity for you, he has me who say nothing say it's not me" (87–88). Nothing the text states of its subject is true of its subject. The subject accepts no predicates, not even negative ones. If it is *not,* it is not not as the voice is not; if it is speechless, it is not speechless as the voice is speechless; if it has no story, it has no story as the voice has no story. But no way, other than a paradoxical one, exists of putting all this, since whatever the subject denies is denied through the *voice* and so becomes the *voice's* denial. And the voice's denial cannot be the subject's denial because the subject is not the voice. The subject is silent.

We have reached another merry-go-round corresponding to the cycle of Yes and No in what I termed Beckett's Logic. Everything

must be negated, even the negation, so that we may reach, as Beckett puts it, "the silencing of silence" (135). Then at last it will be the
Unnamable's silence, "a voice of silence, the voice of my silence"
(121). But that voice will never speak a text or texts, not even a text
for nothing. So there is no transcending the problematics of naming
the Unnamable, the *arche,* the thing presupposed by everything else,
including the act of naming. At this point, if the subject of the Texts
appears to owe something of its nature to the Eleatic One, still with
the perfection of indivisible being; or to the Neo-Platonic One, or
the Godhead of the pseudo-Dionysius, without attributes, totally sufficient unto itself, the unmanifested, that's to say the *un*speaking,
then the whole painful process of the Texts can be regarded as an
exercise in the *via negativa.* Beckett's subject, "knowing none,
known of none" (127), "this unnamable thing that I name and
name and never wear out" (100), cannot be the object of a positive
epistemology. It can only be apprehended negatively. Not even that
is true, as we have seen. Required is an affirmation, followed by a
denial of that affirmation, followed by a denial of the denial, ad infinitum. We are in the Socratic and Platonic tradition, seeking
knowledge, and achieving, like Socrates, nescience, *un*knowing. The
No will always stifle the Yes. But no No will so stifle it as to inhibit a
further Yes—followed by a further No—an epistemological variation
of the Pythagorean series of reincarnations, or of the *logical* short-
circuit previously discussed. Again, Beckett's model is Neo-Platonic.
It follows the pattern of the doctrines of the pseudo-Dionysius, the
originator of Negative Theology: "[F]or while applying affirmations
or negations to those of being that come next to It, we apply not
unto It either affirmation or negation, inasmuch as It transcends all
affirmation by being the . . . Cause of all things, and transcends all
negation by the pre-eminence of Its simple and absolute nature."[12]
If you make a positive statement about this god, you must follow it
by a negative, then deny that too by saying that God transcends both
attributes: the method of Affirmative, Negative, and Superlative
Theology. Beckett is tantalized by this concept of seeking "by the
excessive light of night" (77). He returns to it parodically in many
works, and most explicitly in *Murphy* and *Watt:* "What we know partakes in no small measure of the nature of what has so happily been
called the unutterable or ineffable, so that any attempt to utter or
eff it is doomed to fail."[13]

We return to Beckett's Physics. Everything begins, must begin,
with the subject of the voice, "voice . . . that can be none but mine,
since there is none but me" (126). This is the absent key to the puz-
zle of things, to the being and activities of voices and their incarna-

tions and the worlds they traverse. It is a *deus absconditus* or sine qua nix of which nix can be predicated, and like the pseudo-Dionysian deity, it must be regarded as Cause of things, the *ex nihilo* of Beckett's genesis. "It" initiates nothing. Only the voice initiates. But since voice is referrable to it, it must be the source of motion, speech-in-silence, "the voice of my silence." Beckett's world now acquires its Aristotelian unmoved mover or Final Cause (in fact, twisting philosophy a little, we could term it an *in*efficient cause). Once utterance is a fact, the subject has only to scream "it's not me, it's not true" (83) to be caught up in the merry-go-round of procreation, or rather parthenogensis. The subject, by opening its unopenable mouth has, God is trapped in speech, the One enmeshed in the Many—through the mechanism of an inverted *via negativa*. In saying "not me," the subject, refusing to name anything other than itself— the only real in an otherwise fictional *kosmos* filled with shadowy copies and copies of copies—names everything anyway, constituting it negatively, as *not itself*. Beckett's *rerum natura* is thus a product not of the deity's *fiat* but its frustrated No, creation by unwilling, as knowledge was by unknowing. The more you say "not me" to wipe the slate clean, the more you repeat the original *fiat*. *Saying* you said nothing, you say nothing *twice*. So Yes and No generate each other and, as in the *Timaeus*, logic and physics are one, the affirmation/ negation pattern constituting the motion of thought as much as the motion of the *kosmos*.

Everything emerges from the primal dynamism, voices, decrepit avatars one after another, in procession, emanating through an act of intellect, as in the Neo-Platonic systems, One to Many, in hierarchic order. Beckett's theophany, like the Greek one, constitutes a graduated series, "number one and his pale imitations" (120). The obsession with series of all kinds, mind-produced, as here, or mechanically or atomistically contrived, as in the novel *How it is,* or simply farcical, parodic of all logic after the manner of the Sceptics' Infinite Regress, in the novel *Watt,* recurs in Beckett's writing. How could the ghastly business of generation be stopped? If the source could name itself, it would not need to continue. But no name serves the purpose, since once spoken, *no* name is the right name. So divinity is a prisoner of its own nature. As in the pseudo-Dionysius, it simply overflows. The Texts speak of Chance and Fate (73), offer recurring models of compulsion, state that things *must* be, since they *are* (113). This is a version of the Necessity of the Greeks (*ananke*) colored by an element of Graeco-Roman Stoicism. Certainly no rightness exists in Beckett's creation. It proceeds by *theological error*, more like that unpredictable atomic "swerve" from the vertical than the fine logic of Plotinian contemplation. The pattern of issue and return, a rewrite of the master's dynamism in *Ulysses,* Bloom orbiting the still center of Molly, remains Beckett's grotesque, parodic, yet anguishedly serious gloss on the Greek problem of the One and the Many and his answer to the question: Why are there things? Beckett's One is absent; his Many are ridiculous. The two oscillate, destroyed, renewed by turns, like the Stoic universe, and, also like it, they give every indication of eternal recurrence. Beckett's physics, like his logic, operates as a short-circuit. One breeding Many in a series of abortions. It represents Beckett's aporetic failure to name things as they are and, like the Yes coiled inside the Sceptic's No, it demands constant resurrection from the ashes of previous attempts.

Here I offer a comment on the implications of this for Ethics, the white in philosophy's egg. If Beckett's universe exists as the embodiment of a failure, it may also be seen as a Fall in the Platonic tradition. Indeed a reference is made to a fall from a cliff in the Texts—shades of Leopold Bloom's 32-feet-per-second. The fifth Text takes up the question in the form of a parodic theodicy. We are in "that obscure assize where to be is to be guilty" (91) and punishment is coterminous with being. It is an idea Beckett returns to elsewhere, including *Godot,* often with Schopenhauerian or Dantean overtones. *Texts for Nothing* mentions the Purgatorio and Inferno (100). Given a universe botched into being, the reverse of that is the best of all possible, which obtains in the *Timaeus*—dissatisfaction is built into the system. This means that, like its Logic and its Physics, the Ethics of the Texts has a dual face. It is the Stephen Dedalus situation of stasis and kinesis, after a fashion, with the supreme *maker* standing aloof, paring his fingernails, while the *made* writhes in agony. Beckett's creation inevitably suffers. The voice is constantly on the brink of shrieks (92), its speaking is a form of weeping (107). And the tramps are either in pain or too close to death to care. All this while the ur-subject of the Texts feels nothing, like an eye of the cyclone, "deadly calm at the heart of my frenzies" (103), commencing drily "What agitation and at the same time what calm, what vicissitudes within what changelessness" (114); "what calm and silence, which nothing has ever broken, nothing will ever break, which saying I don't break" (121). Such impassibility derives from that of the inaccessible Neo-Platonic One. Or rather it has complex origins, borrowing something from the Pythagorean *theorein,* the spectators at the games of life; from the unfeeling Eleatic One as described by Melissus;[14] from the imperturbability advocated by Democritus;[15] from Socratic detachment; from the indifference practiced by the disciples of the Dog, perambulating ascetics and beggars in whom we find a major prototype for all Beckett's tramps; from the ataraxic serenity of the Sceptics; from Epicurean *ataraxia;* above all, from the *apatheia* of the Stoics. Like the gods of Epicurus, far removed in the *intermundia* where they converse ethereally in a language much like Greek, Beckett's Unnamable is detached from what goes on below. A specifically Beckettian twist occurs, suggested by the references of the sixth Text to what appears to be an asylum, housing the subject. Of course, this is simply another *mythos,* but it implies not merely an impassible but a catatonic/schizophrenic god, one who hears voices, his own of course, a deity reminiscent of the tragically ludicrous Mr. Endon of *Watt,* round whose stillness generations of servants and nurses revolve. At any rate, the ethics of this being and of the Texts as a whole must be something like the ethic of Epictetus: desire what you get, will what is already the case, travel east, as Beckett (echoing seventeenth-century Stoicism) puts it elsewhere, on a ship sailing west. The ship is the body, what Epictetus, long before Francis of Assisi, very nearly called brother ass: "You ought to possess your whole body as a poor ass loaded . . . as long as you are allowed. But if there be a press, and a soldier should lay hold of it, let it go, do not resist, nor murmur; if you do, you will receive blows, and nevertheless you will also lose the ass. . . . When the body is an ass, all the other things are bits belonging to the ass, pack-saddles, shoes, barley, fodder. Let these also go: get rid of them quicker and more readily than of the ass."[16] This reference to ready detachment from care brings us to a Beckettian motif extrapolated from Democritus. Before a world like this one, we can weep, like the narrative voice of the Texts or the lachrymose philosopher Heraclitus, or we can emulate the uncaring, unmoved mover, insofar as is possible, by laughing the laugh Beckett ascribes to the advocate of good cheer, Democritus. This is the mirthless laugh in the face of misery mentioned in *Watt* and the trilogy. It makes several appearances in the Texts, as "the long silent guffaw of the knowing non-exister" (130), the laugh that, as Beckett says, was never very droll (79).

As postscript, I offer a Poetics to round off discussion of *Texts for Nothing.* I have described Beckett's physics as a building from the ground up, from first principles, however difficult these may be to uncover. But of course the construction is a textual one. To ask "why things?" must in this context be to ask "why *this* thing, this text, this aggregate of words?" The question must be concrete, it must question its own present activity. Beckett therefore reproduces the affirm/negate pattern of his Logic and his Physics at the textual level. Or, looking at it from the other end, the pattern of Yes and No indicates, first of all, the *textual* dynamics of Beckett's writing. Only in this case it takes the form of an interplay of silence and words. For silence, read the One—principle of stasis, sameness, the unwritten unwritable text; for words, read the multiple *logoi*—differentiation, kinesis, the written. Beckett assigns to his text the same ambiguous status as to his physics. It cannot really get off the ground. But with that Not it *has* got off the ground, the inconceivable start has been made. Thus the text exists as a by-product of its own problematics, starting with its inability to start. This is because Beckett has no comfortable reply to the teasing questions of beginning or ending—or what happens in between, namely the constant dying into the end that operates as a further beginning. This textual tension never lets up, making for immense exhilaration in the midst of textual ruins. Beckett writes his book like Achilles chasing his tortoise. However slow the quarry, Beckett is slower still, stuck on the step before the first step. It is a bulldog methodology. Beckett won't let go of the nagging issue of the textual principle, the *arche* of the text. Every writing must be *ab initio*—as if no one had ever written before. After the achievements of Proust and Joyce, one either imitates or begins from scratch. He begins where? With the impossibility of a new beginning, tackling the absence of new forms, turning this very absence into a new form.

Whatever else it may be, the process is methodical. It may at any point be ready to give up the ghost, either in despairing scepticism or farcical despair. But nothing is random about it. If it is play, it is not play in the relativist sense of Post-Structuralist *jeu*. Far from opening out on the plane of surface, it digs in, uncovering depth. In the words of Beckett's commentary on Proust, "the only fertile research is excavatory, immensive."[17] Certainly self-parody is in the text's own comment on its regressive hunt after first principles, a comment that echoes Aristotle's celebrated Third Man argument against Plato, though its language is that of Berkeley: "That's the accountants' chorus. . . . all the peoples of the earth would not suffice, at the end of the billions you'd need a god, unwitnessed witness of witnesses" (130–31). Precisely—and in the Texts such a process and such a goal can only be envisaged parodically. But the function of parody here is not dismissive. For a start, parody heightens tragedy. Nor does it negate the textual hunt after an elusive Origin, in Derrida's terminology, a hunt that is theological. One *could* choose an anti-theological reading, interpreting the Texts as an admission of the *non*existence of the founding, grounding subject, the *un*availability of Origins. That would be Beckett as Michel Focault reads him in the celebrated essay "What Is an Author?," which opens and closes with a quotation from the third Text. However, such a reading weakens the dialectic stress and counterstress of the text. Even if you try to get around that, by preserving Beckett's dialectic in the form of a deconstructive process, one that denies the reality of the subject in language that has no choice but to affirm it, you will still be insisting that the subject is merely a theological/linguistic construct, however inescapable. For the toughness of Beckett's text relies on the *genuine* possibility of uncovering that impossible textual ground. In short, it seems that an anti-theological reading requires Beckett's text to mock its own dogged process. My reading, which I put forward as a Likely Story in the Platonic sense, emphasizes that if Beckett's subject dies, it does so not into power-discourse or deconstructive free play or linguistic codes—all the contemporary variants of a philosophy of *différance,* i.e., the Many—but into its own aboriginal ground. If textuality disperses into shifting combinations of signifier, it does so to contract to the point of the signified. The *logoi* are emptied of meaning so that *the* original, founding meaning may be teased out. I do not say that that meaning is *grasped* by the text— that would be *too* theological a reading—but it is not ruled out. On the contrary, it continually activates the text, there being no question of foreclosure. At this point Beckett's ambition appears outrageous. Socrates turns into Faust—and vice versa. Then the see-saw begins all over again.

Notes

1. *Texts for Nothing* in *No's Knife: Collected Shorter Prose, 1945–1966,* trans. Samuel Beckett and Richard Seaver (London: Calder and Boyars, 1967), 71. Subsequent references in the text.

2. *Lives of Eminent Philosophers,* 7.40, trans. R. D. Hicks (London: Heinemann, 1925), vol. 2, 151.

3. In Jonathan Barnes, ed., *Early Greek Philosophy* (Harmondsworth: Penguin, 1987), 66.

4. *Ibid.,* 134.

5. In H. N. Fowler, *Plato with an English Translation: Cratylus, Parmenides, Greater Hippias, Lesser Hippias* (London: Heinemann, 1963), 203–4.

6. Heraclitus in *Early Greek Philosophy,* 104.

7. *On the Nature of the Universe,* trans. R. E. Latham (London: Penguin, 1951), 62.

8. *The Six Enneads,* trans. Stephen MacKenna and B. S. Page (Chicago: Encyclopaedia Britannica, 1952), 5.1.6, 211.

9. *Ibid.,* 6.9.11, 360.

10. *Dionysius the Areopagite on the Divine Names and the Mystical Theology,* trans. C. E. Rolt (London: Macmillan, 1940), 185.

11. *Early Greek Philosophy,* 68.

12. *Dionysius the Areopagite*, 201.
13. London: Calder and Boyars, 1963, 61.
14. *Early Greek Philosophy*, 147.
15. *Ibid.*, 271.
16. *The Discourses of Epictetus*, trans. George Long in *Lucretius, Epictetus, Marcus Aurelius* (Chicago: Encyclopaedia Britannica, 1952), 4.1, 217.
17. *Proust and Three Dialogues* (London: Calder, 1965), 65.

"A Sup of the Hawk's, or the Saints": Beckett and Irish Theater

JAMES LIDDY

As A CHILD I WAS HYPNOTIZED BY A LINE OF THOMAS DAVIS SO REDOLENT of our private despairs churned into public, historical calamity, the line about "From Dunkirk to Belgrade" lie the officers and soldiers of the Irish Brigade. As adults then, some of us crossed over into modernism, and now we have our soldiers scattered in the earth of European capitals: Joyce in the Fluntern at Zurich and Samuel Beckett in Montparnasse. In a book about Switzerland, by the Wisconsin writer Herbert Kubly, I am quoted as remarking about Joyce's grave, which, as many readers may remember, portrays a studious man reading a book; I observed that "a bottle and a glass would be more appropriate." I cannot imagine Beckett's resting place, but I know that the symbolic, historical writing of the Abbey dramatic tradition both leads into him and proceeds from him. That small but great stage was where much of twentieth-century Irish literature was fought for or over, indulged in, or spat out.

We knew a great playwright when we came to town in the 1950s. In Alan Simpson and Carolyn Swift's Pike Theatre, down an alluring lane, we saw a modern "miracle play." The following is how the poet Patrick Kavanagh saw that first Irish production of *Waiting for Godot*: "Part of this play's importance is that it both holds a mirror up to life and keeps reminding you, if you are interested in sincerity, that the reason you couldn't endure the theatre hitherto was that it was tenth rate escapism, not your dish at all." Now there was somewhere to go in the evening in addition to the pub. Apart from where it stands in world literature, *Godot* trumpeted a new phase of Irish theater.

We knew that the tree in *Godot* was the tree of Yeats's *Purgatory*, the tree that had been fat, "greasy," with life and is now lifeless except for an illusion of illumination. The quotation from Beckett that is the title of this essay, written during the 1950s by him to the actor Cyril Cusack, comes as no surprise. We saw an Anglo-Irish tree of life

129

reduced to its roots, to its idea; this minimalism was of the essence
of the literary connection between them—as if Beckett were Yeats
without the supernaturalism, and Yeats were Beckett without the realism. It seems to me that the plays of Yeats are as assimilated to the
core of Irish theater in the same ways as Beckett's; they are present
and within the possibilities of the Irish drama of the 1960s and
thereafter, but this joint influence is not up front or immediately
visible. Their major contribution to contemporary Dublin theater is
most obviously poetry: specialized emotional language, repeated extension of the image, and an elaborate naming of catastrophe. Yeats,
of course, inclines to aristocratic relations, while Beckett endures
human relations.

I cannot agree with Professor Nicholas Grene that the consciousness of Beckett in recent Irish playwrights constitutes an "uneasy
awareness." My sense is that phrase should read something like "in-
tense familiarity," a condition that could give rise to uneasiness.
James Stephens described Yeats's plays as "masked" and
"shrouded," terms that could refer to aspects of Beckett and also
encapsule some of the thematic and technical developments in the
work of Frank McGuinness and Brian Friel. Perhaps the historical
and cultural subject demands such apparent obscurity.

I am sure Beckett used the common Hibernianism "sup" deliber-
ately; apart from supping from the curing water of the Hawk's well,
it would imply, in local code, desire and excess. In fact, Beckett must
mean here's a "partaking" in some kind of magic substance, a belief
that urges me to use another Celtic phrase, "second sight." I have
wanted to apply this term for some time to Yeats, Beckett, Friel, Mc-
Guinness, and others such as Tom Murphy and Tom Kilroy. It suggests a kind of psychic overview of history, folklore, victimization
(race and culture memory), pain, and the varieties of a syntax and
rhythm not found elsewhere in English. Some will not see Beckett
in this line, but I think a "native" edge can be detected in him, a
resonance, a far seeing, hearing, and listening that come from having lived in Dublin, or Ireland, and having used that living aestheti-
cally. Indeed, I discern a great postcolonial gift here: Beckett as the
second patron of a great missed inheritance, an articulate voice
speaking out of both sides of its mouth (Gaelic and Anglo). I refer
to a condition of mind and speech that rejects both parochialism
and provincialism, something priceless for the younger generations
of dramatists. I am suggesting voice(s) that modify, enrich, and distance the Catholic tribal cultus that Friel and the younger dramatists
have been deconstructing and remaking.

Beckett's contribution can be framed in Thomas Kilroy's terms:

"The world of the Beckett plays is pre-social, pre-tribal, pre-commu-
nal, but one might as easily describe it as post-social, post-tribal, post-
communal." I think Kilroy has, *inter alia,* the local context in mind.
Beckett's closeness to the Irish tribe must arise primarily from participation as a young man in the Abbey's romantic rituals of Irish-
ness; it is well attested critically that the closest Beckett gets to this
in his texts are the homeless wanderers of Synge's *art nouveau* coun-
tryside. Beckett is the most private of Irish-born writers, a quality that
led to his elaborations of silence on the stage. This dimming of exuberance is balanced by the singing and joking of his characters. It is
noteworthy that Beckett eschews dancing, including Yeats's Salomé-
like "Noh," a tradition Friel restores with a vengeance in *Dancing at
Lughneasa.* Friel, the next dramatist of importance after Beckett, and
the father of the Young Turks of the 1980s, got what Yeats developed: salutory seasons of recuperating and retheorizing and a post-
masters stage, in part divergent from Beckett, but related to him.
Donegal has depths of the mind different from Dublin's. *Godot* and
the other plays of Beckett's great middle period mushroom into moments in the later playwrights and sometimes become their stage devices and verbal ticks. While McGuinness and Friel adopt varying
strategies, their sense of theatrical artifice primarily descends from
Beckett.

This younger generation has perhaps the perverse luck of possess-
ing political and cultural subjects that Beckett missed seemingly as
a matter of chance; thus their connection with the older writer is
conveniently veiled. Yeats had the "phantasmagoria" of 1916 and
the subsequent Anglo-Irish conflict with which to work; Friel,
McGuinness, and others are presented with the long-running Northern Ireland "troubles" to confront.

Beckett seems minimal in this political context, but he expresses
harrowing descriptions of personal crisis in "West British," genteel
Foxrock. That wealthy suburb and the National Theatre in down-
town Dublin could hold cosy hands. Beckett, though politically remote by comparison, partakes of cultural "native" Irish procedures:
he coats his birth and neocolonial upbringing with techniques borrowed in part from Gaelic sources. In particular, one notes Beckett's
use of sarcasm and parody, and his adherence to singing and quotation. Beckett and Friel have a common need for some sort of ear-
nestness at the heart of their drama: they trim their craft to its finest
point, and they both insist on being in control of the text and timing
of plays in production. In a sense, the spontaneity of their writing
leaves nothing to the spontaneous.

A summary of what I am saying might read as follows: The "before" relationship within the Irish Dramatic Movement of Synge and Yeats to Beckett can be paralleled by the later adoption of Beckett by the group associated with Friel. As Beckett added an extra isolated voice to Synge's original characters (Martin Doul in *The Well of the Saints* is a fearsome pre-Beckett presence), so Friel and the younger playwrights take from Beckett tactical silence, pauses in monologue and duet, and abrupt and rhetorical philosophical discourses. Thus the last great Anglo-Irish writer is delivered into the hands of that other island of folklore and nationalist politics, and closer to that fated island's soil ambivalence. Friel, in the final expansions of his creative career, leads his characters in a descent into the shades in a manner similar to Beckett's. The characters are evicted from their past and from familiar occasions. Molly in Friel's *Molly Sweeney* is an example. In her isolated consciousness, every shape becomes an apparition; any person Molly remembers must undergo a fragmentation dance in her mind. Sometimes the voices in the two dramatists' work collapse from incessant reminiscing. In the background of both these writers is apparent a core idea of necessary self-sacrifice, some sort of breakdown of the hero's survival. This is another indication that Beckett did not get his "sup" from his Church-of-Ireland family who had no holy wells, no monastic saints, and no priest's jug of whiskey. There, the idea of self-sacrifice was not the paradigm of collective action.

Recent Irish drama abounds in Beckettian epiphanies, especially in devising a series of silence adjacent to an important or complete statement. Friel's handling of this approach sometimes includes "the speech from the dock." The best-known illustration of this is in *The Freedom of the City*, where Lilly, Skinner, and Michael speak to the audience as they exit to be shot. The verbalization, highlighted by silence, is not a technique confined to ideological drama; it is often a sign of closure. Perhaps *The Faith Healer* provides Friel's most absolute command of this device. The curtain speech, ending with "At long last I was renouncing chance" and the direction "Pause for about four seconds. Then quick black," is the last unraveling of the protagonist, Francis Harvey, as man, artist, and conman. Beckettian focus and dissolution are everywhere in these dramatists: McGuinness, for instance, in *Observe the Sons of Ulster Marching towards the Somme,* inserts such a pause and silence in Pyper's crammed monologue in act 1. A new Irish stage liturgy has materialized, and it hails from Beckett's repertoire. These instances can appear as "sanitized" Beckett or "poor man's" Beckett. Of Pyper, in his first appearance, one may be tempted to remark, "Krapp's son speaketh." Friel takes Beckett's thorny dissolutions over the line: the major personae in *Freedom of the City, Faith Healer,* and *Aristocrats* are dead at the onset of the action; in the older writer they remain on the verge, one and a half feet from the grave. Friel's recent masterpiece, *Wonderful Tennessee,* a rich, appealing compilation of history, folk religion, apocalypse, apologetics, and music, incorporates Beckett's range of language and theatrical suggestions and asides. Entwined family and friends meet on a remote pier with the intention of making a turas (pilgrimage) to an island that is variously a saint's place, the home of people of enchantment (fairies), and a place of ritual murder.

The pivotal moment—and the pure Beckettian catharsis—occurs when the group waits all night for the boatman Carlin (intimations of Charon, but the name might also be McGodot) to ferry them over. It must be Friel's intention for the theatergoers to be seized by nostalgia, for the reference is unmistakable. The characters see the boatman's house in the distance, they see a possible light in it, and of course Carlin never comes. The people on the pier sing, "Beyond the sand dunes / You will find the boat" (incidentally from "Abide with Me," one of Beckett's hymns). And so it goes on here and in later parts of the play. This question and answer, this hope and dismal echo, both reject and reanswer the small pandemonium sand the endless vistas of locations already known in the theatre. In short, Synge's descendants are partying again, and their resolutions are just as wild and impossible.

David Richards, in his review of McGuinness's *Someone Who'll Watch over Me* in *The New York Times,* grasps the Beckett analogies. "Stripped of its political underpinnings [the play] calls instantly to mind the work of another Irish playwright, Samuel Beckett, equally preoccupied with waiting rituals in bleak places. . . . For no reason they can fathom, three people have been incarcerated, possibly forever, by unseen captors who may be vengeful madmen or irrational children, but in either instance exercise power quixotically. As the Irishman notes, two words sum up their plight: 'ridiculous, ridiculous.' " McGuinness's plays, especially his innovatingly brilliant *Carthaginians,* echo, mime, and even copy Beckett (with gales of Wildean wit added). The characters in *Carthaginians,* in particular the males, search for transformation, or change for change's sake, in their impossible habitations. They are Vladimir and Estragon as new Carthaginians waiting to be saved from Rome (England); in addition, Dido, the transsexual main role, magnifies the routines until he/she becomes a Godot older than Godot. The cemetery in the play is as claustrophobic as the room at the end of the world in *Endgame,* and here the resemblance is how McGuinness's characters rack each other with impossible and poetic demands. They are, in their pairings, Ham and Clov, an alternative community in an apocalyptic glow. As in Beckett, definitions become increasingly uncertain as they grow extreme and beautiful. The homoerotic tone of some Beckett stage characters is often renewed in these scripts. As Anthony Roche notes, in his *Contemporary Irish Drama: From Beckett to McGuinness,* many more more explicit passages can be read including, in *Observe the Sons of Ulster Marching Towards the Somme,* the line "I keep hearing the Dead." Roche points out convincingly that this is an echo of the refrain between Didi and Gogo ("Like all the dead voices").

These cross-currents are common to the après-Beckett Irish theater. In *Carthaginians,* McGuinness offers a play within a play, which becomes a comic and grueling satire on the gods of this theater: Yeats, O'Casey, Behan, and others. Despite all the borrowings, never a verbal hand is laid on Samuel Beckett. He is our perfect knight of the stage. He is in the text but not of the text. He is the Irish theater but not of it. He is us, not one of us. I call on Yeats to add the last word to this small celebration of influence: "the heart of a phantom is beating."

Part V
Perspectives Ethnic and Cultural

Virginia Woolf's Construction of Masculinity: A Narrative Model—A Reading of *Mrs. Dalloway*

RICHARD PEARCE

AT THE END OF *MRS. DALLOWAY,* AFTER LADY ROSSETER LEAVES, PETER Walsh sits for a moment. "What is this terror? what is this ecstasy?" he thinks to himself. "What is it that fills me with extraordinary excitement?" He then looks up to see Clarissa.

Clarissa's story reaches its climax and conclusion with her being framed in Peter's gaze. She is also framed in his sentence: "It is Clarissa." And his sentence is authorized by the narrator's "For there she was" (194). By Peter's sentence the narrator would seem to authorize his transcendent view. However, his view does not include her private realization just moments before—which Peter could never imagine—when she identified with Septimus. She "felt somehow very like him—the young man who had killed himself. She felt glad that he had done it; thrown it away. . . . He made her feel the beauty; made her feel the fun. But she must go back. She must assemble. She must find Sally and Peter" (186). But Peter finds *her*. The narrator repositions her climactic realization within the frame of Peter's story. His story—which began when he left her drawing room, followed him through the streets to his hotel, and then took him and us to her party—takes the form of a male quest.

What disturbs me about the narrator's move is that, up to the end of her story about Mrs. Dalloway, she has abrogated and appropriated the traditional narrative role, which, like the "male sentence," had evolved to express male experience.[1] Peter's climactic view and the narrator's authorization do not of course deny Clarissa's climactic realization. The narrator nonetheless concludes in a way that frames Clarissa within *his* story, and leaves us with *his* final word, view, and judgment.

Does Peter colonize Clarissa at the end of *Mrs. Dalloway*? I answer this question by examining the way this male character is con-

137

structed and develops, the kind of narrative power he wields, the social forces that provide that power, and the way Woolf resists, exposes, and undermines, but cannot fully escape its power.[2] Moreover, I hope to demonstrate that Woolf's innovative narrative explores and from time to time gets beyond the social power system, especially as it is reflected in the dominant system of narrative. Woolf's narrative innovations, designed to represent experiences and voices of women ignored or silenced in traditional (male) forms of narrative, were what Michel de Certeau defines as "tactics": the practices that enable disenfranchised and oppressed people to realize their variety of voices, maintain communities, and achieve practical kinds of power. "Tactics" are opportunities seized "on the wing," fragmentary and fragile "victories of the 'weak' over the 'strong' (whether the strength be that of powerful people or the violence of things or of an imposed order, etc.), clever tricks, knowing how to get away with things, 'hunter's cunning,' maneuvers, polymorphic simulations, joyful discoveries, poetic as well as warlike." But the weak cannot keep what they win; rather they appropriate spaces of the dominant culture for their own uses—or make them "habitable, like a rented apartment . . . transform another person's property into a space borrowed for a moment" (xxi).

Woolf uses a variety of narrative strategies to position us in a fictional world predominantly framed by a woman's experience and focalized from a woman's perspective. Nor do we simply experience Woolf's world from a woman's perspective passively as voyeurs, for she makes us into active readers, or leads us to collaborate in constructing a present and a past, weaving them together with women's experiences and perspectives. She not only develops a female sentence to counteract the sentence used by "all great novelists like Thackeray and Dickens, and Balzac" (*Room* 76), but also ways of undermining traditional male story conventions.[3] This doesn't mean that, as a male reader, I read *as* a woman. And I should acknowledge my uncomfortable, indeed anxious, position as a male claiming to discover a new way of reading Virginia Woolf. I can't overcome my anxiety, but I can at least explain that I am a constellation of positions, the most powerful of which are constructed by social and historical frames that have positioned me as male, some of which I've tried to resist or negotiate. But the choices I make as a reader are limited by my position within a predominantly female frame.

Mrs. Dalloway begins (her story frame) in Clarissa's mind as she opens the window thinking of flowers and of the happiest time of her life, when she was kissed by Sally Seton. We are positioned as female readers—not only because we are in a predominantly female frame, but also because Woolf has developed a female narrator who abrogates and appropriates the traditional male narrative. We are also positioned very close to Clarissa, since her thoughts are barely mediated, and in a woman's world that Clarissa constructs as she leads us from the private domain of her home to the public domain of the street where women shop, shopping being the domain of women. In the closing set of overlapping frames of the novel, Clarissa withdraws from the public world of her party to a private revelation that links her to a suicidal, lower-class young man who has repressed his homosexual desires[4] (but whom Peter mistook for a lover quarreling earlier in the day). It also links her to Sally Seton, with whom she had a relationship that parallels that between Septimus and Evans, and an anonymous old woman. Peter's affirmation recuperates and colonizes Clarissa because it is focalized from his point of view and positions her within the climactic frame of his storyline.

But that is not quite all. For we must consider that the final narrative frame is situated within Clarissa's *sphere of influence*. Peter has led us to her party: "The brain must wake now. The body must contract now, entering the house, the lighted house, where the door stood open, where the motor cars were standing, and bright women descending: the soul must be brave to itself endure. He opened the big blade of his pocket-knife" (165). But, as his opening of his pocket-knife suggests, he will be repositioned in the next paragraph, when Lucy comes running down the stairs.

Even more important, Peter has been positioned in a storyline where his power varies—largely in relation to the narrator's moves. He begins in an apparently dominant position as he leaves Clarissa that morning, making condescending judgments about her parties and about her growing hard but sentimental, and reflecting on his fortune to be in love as well as on his administrative success in India. But the narrator mediates enough to puncture subtly Peter's pretension, or to reveal how his power and his reflections are constructed: "There he was, this fortunate man, himself, reflected in the plate-glass window of a motor car manufacturer in Victoria Street." "This fortunate man" is gently mocked by the narrator, when she captures his self-congratulatory glance. But she then extends her frame to include the material reflector of his self-image, the plate glass window of a motor car manufacturer in Victoria Street. Indeed, she superimposes his reflection on a motor car that recalls the one that backfired that morning, and that carried a man "of the very greatest importance" (14). She then extends the frame of his reflection even further to include its imperialist grounding: "All India lay behind him; plains, mountains; epidemics of cholera; a district twice as big as Ireland" (48).

Following his thoughts as they turn from triumph to rejection by Clarissa, the narrator now shifts the ideological frame of public power from male (the motor car manufacturer) to female, not by a shift in perspective but by mockingly mediating with her own voice: "Ah, said St. Margaret's, like a hostess who comes into her drawing-room on the very stroke of the hour and finds her guests there already" (49). And it is within this frame that Peter recalls Clarissa with deep emotion ("coming down the stairs on the stroke of the hour in white" [50]), realizing (as his thoughts turn to the present) that she has been ill, and pictures her dying. He also recalls that "he had been sent down from Oxford—true. He had been a Socialist, in some sense a failure—true" (50).

Our view of Peter changes as his position shifts between masculine and feminine frames of power. He feels optimistic as he begins to keep step with the "boys in uniform, carrying guns, [marching] with their eyes ahead of them" (51) and indeed superior to "the weedy . . . boys of sixteen, who might, to-morrow, stand behind bowls of rice, cakes of soap on counters" (51). Indeed, he is able to position the young woman walking across Trafalgar Square within the masculine frame of his fantasy. He is a reckless adventurer, a romantic buccaneer. And the young woman would "shed veil after veil, until she became the very woman he had always had in mind; young, but stately; merry, but discreet; black, but enchanting" (52).

But then the narrator mediates parodically to reposition him within her frame and bring into focus the ideology of the romantic adventure that shapes his fantasy and singles him out:

> Straightening himself and stealthily fingering his pocket-knife he started after her to follow this woman, this excitement which seemed even with its back turned to shed on him a light which connected them, which singled him out, as if the random uproar of the traffic had whispered through hallowed hands his name, not Peter, but the name which he called himself in his own thoughts. "You," she said, "only you," saying it with her white gloves and her shoulders. (52–53)

According to Louis Althusser, when the policeman calls, " 'Hey, you there!' . . . One individual (nine times out of ten it is the right one) turns round. By this mere one-hundred-and-eighty-degree physical conversion, he becomes a *subject*. Why? Because he has recognized that the hail was 'really' addressed to him, and that 'it was *really him* who was hailed' (and not someone else)." In the same way a culture's ideology hails, calls an individual "*subject*" into being—though the recognition testifies to his having already been one (Althusser, 1971 #261, 174). Peter misrecognizes himself as the subject his fantasized woman has hailed, interpellated, constituted as an individual. For the fantasized woman, a product of his ideology, hails him as the self he would like to be. But the narrator focuses what he cannot imagine, the psychological and social dimensions of the ideology that shapes his fantasy and hails him. First, she shifts her focal point from sympathetically close to mockingly far and pictures him "straightening himself and stealthily fingering his pocket-knife." Then, though a mixed metaphor that calls attention to itself, she highlights the illogic of psychological projection. The ideological source of his fantasy is the commercial center of the empire that hails him and gives him his identity: the "random uproar of the traffic had whispered through hollowed hands his name." And the narrator's mixed metaphor reveals how the ideological power is projected onto the young woman: " 'You,' she said, only 'you,' saying it with her white gloves and her shoulders" (53).

Once the adventure is over, Peter can recognize that "it was half made up . . . invented" (54), but he is no more able to reflect on the ideology that hailed him as a concrete individual, or shaped his fantasy, than he was to understand how the motorcar in the plate glass window on Victoria Street shaped the reflected image he saw there. This is not to say that he doesn't sometimes resist the ideology, or recognize his ambivalence: "disliking India, and empire, and army as he did," there were still "moments when civilization . . . seemed dear to him as a personal possession" (55). Only that, like all of us, he cannot get beyond the ideology, just as he cannot think of the individual "private name which he called himself in his own thoughts (53)," or an identity prior to ideology.

The "grey nurse," who sits "indefatigably" knitting beside Peter on the hot park bench and frames Peter's later thoughts, adds a complementary frame to that of the seductive woman who hailed him on the street. The narrator mediates his dozing stream of thoughts to picture the grey nurse ambiguously as "the champion of the rights of sleepers, like one of those spectral presences which rise in twilight in woods made of sky and branches" (56)—that is, as both mother and witch. Mediating his dreams, the narrator also frames Peter parodically to focus another way he is hailed and constituted as an individual by the ideology of romantic adventure. He is "the solitary traveller, haunter of lanes, disturber of ferns, and devastator of great hemlock plants." He endows the branches with womanhood, now grave, now majestic, now dispensing charity, comprehension, and absolution, proffering "great cornucopias full of fruit to the solitary traveller," or murmuring "in his ear like sirens" (57). And then, beyond the wood, the solitary traveler returns to the "elderly woman" with "hands raised, with white apron blowing . . . who seems . . . to seek . . . a lost son" (58). But the mother figure who hails him is of no avail, for Peter wakes suddenly saying, "The death of the soul," and realizes he had been dreaming of Clarissa's decision to marry Dalloway.

Septimus, as well as Peter, is in the vicinity of the grey nurse. And the ambivalent mother figure also appears in Septimus's day-dreams—the story frame shifts—which go back to his youth in London and his relation to Evans, who died in battle, lead up to his present violent quarrel with Rezia, and lead forward to his suicide. As a result, Peter is positioned within Septimus's (feminized) story frame. And within this frame the narrator shifts back for a while to Peter. At this point Peter provides what we accept as the most positive and detailed judgment of Clarissa—as not only intelligent but also well read and quite radical in her youth, who "had a perfectly clear notion of what she wanted" (75), who "enjoyed life immensely. It was her nature to enjoy" (78), who "had a sense of comedy that was really exquisite" (78), and who had "that extraordinary gift, that woman's gift, of making a world her own wherever she happened to be. She came into a room; she stood . . . in a doorway with lots of people round her. But it was Clarissa one remembered. Not that she was striking; not beautiful at all; there was nothing picturesque about her; she never said anything specially clever; there she was, however; there she was" (76).

But how are we to judge this view of Clarissa—which the narrator reinforces in the last sentence of the novel? For Peter had intruded into Septimus's story to mistake the distraught couple for quarreling lovers, and this misframing may lead us to be suspicious of his judgments. Moreover, very soon his thoughts will be interrupted by a "frail quivering sound, a voice bubbling up without direction . . . with an absence of all human meaning into 'ee um fah um so / foo swee too eem oo'—the voice of no age or sex, the voice of an ancient spring spouting from the earth" (80). This voice, we discover, comes from a battered woman. She may be singing of love; indeed, as J. Hillis Miller points out, she echoes Richard Strauss's "*Allerseelen.*" But Miller fails to consider how our view of the battered woman is mediated through Peter. Can she be singing the way Peter hears it—of the "love which has lasted a million years . . . which prevails" (81)?[5] Isn't Peter romanticizing the battered woman as he did Septimus and Rezia when he saw them as lovers quarreling—and as he will be when, hearing the siren of the ambulance carrying Septimus to the hospital, he proclaims, "one of the triumphs of civilization" (151)? If he romanticizes the underclass and the products of civilization, what are we to make of his view of Clarissa?

Peter is positioned within two overlapping frames; moreover, he is reframed from time to time within each of them. First he is positioned within the ideological frame of English imperial power—the frame of a traditional male narrative that takes the shape of a romantic quest. While he does not get Clarissa physically, emotionally, or dramatically, he nonetheless appears first in Clarissa's thoughts on that splendid spring morning, intrudes into her sitting room and causes her "to hide her dress, like a virgin protecting chastity" (40), is still found "enchanting" (41)—and leads us along a major narrative line through the novel. He walks through the park past Septimus and Rezia, takes us through the London streets first away from Clarissa and then back, and becomes a major focal point at her party. Most important, he has the culminating vision, indeed the last word. Peter Walsh literally gets Mrs. Dalloway into his sentence, which—being the final sentence in the diegesis, or story proper, and then being author-ized by the narrator—becomes the point toward which a strong narrative line, the romance plot, has been leading.

Within the frame of the traditional male narrative, Peter is most often viewed, and therefore positioned, parodically—to illuminate the power structure that frames him. He is also viewed—or reframed and therefore repositioned—sympathetically within that frame—as being victimized by the ideology that hails him, mocked by the models of manhood that made him attractive only "to women who liked the sense that he was not altogether manly" (156), limited by the opportunities open to him for thought as well as action. But, despite the parody and the sympathy that expose and undermine the power of the ideological frame of imperial power, this frame has a residual narrative power, accumulated from centuries of tradition. For readers have been positioned by the traditional narrator to admire if not identify with the questor and desire a victorious, happy ending. As a result, this narrative frame has the potential to appropriate or recuperate Clarissa in Peter's final vision, especially as it is reframed by the narrator.

Peter is positioned not only within the frame of the traditional male narrative, though. He is positioned also within a second narrative frame, presided over by the grey nurse, and shared by Septimus and Evans. This makes him part of a (feminized) homosocial community at odds with what Eve Sedgwick defines, and what in *The Waves* Woolf reflects, as the homosocial community in power. From within this frame Peter sees strengths in Clarissa that cannot be seen by the other male figures in the novel—Richard, Hugh, Dr. Bradshaw, or the Prime Minister—or even by Clarissa herself. She pictures herself only as birdlike, nunlike, and shriveled—nor does she see the positive potential in any of these images.

The dual positioning of Peter Walsh results from and contributes to the instability of the novel. And it leads us to understand that we cannot ask questions of dominance, but only of hegemony—who or what force has power at a given moment. Peter's dual positioning also helps answer the question of how to judge Peter's framing of the most positive view we have of Clarissa and of the climactic image. But a further question can be asked: We know what Peter thinks and feels—but what does he actually see? For the frame of Peter Walsh's gaze is empty—"There she is." Clarissa is absent from the narration. We know that she is in the room, of course; the narrator told us this before shifting from Clarissa's climactic frame to Peter's. But we are now limited to Peter's frame, and, though we are made to feel Clarissa's presence through his exclamation, there is nothing for us to see.

And this is Virginia Woolf's ultimate—if fragile—subversion of traditional male construction, framing, and positioning. She leads *us* to fill the frame of Peter's vision with images that come from what Woolf called the "beautiful caves" behind her character: Clarissa's own thoughts stem from her memories of Bourton and her relation to Sally and come to fruition in her identification with Septimus (whose relation to Evans leads us back to Sally) and with the old woman across the way. What we see need not be what Peter sees, nor need we all see the same image. Woolf positions the reader as female—in a fictional world predominantly framed by a woman's experience, focalized from a woman's perspective, and centered at its deepest level on a lesbian relationship. The centrality of Sally in Clarissa's thoughts is an affirmation of women's relationships and the female frame, denying the hegemony of male power, and reducing Peter's power over her life as well as her story.

Moreover, Peter's vision and frame must be contextualized: he had been talking about Clarissa to Sally Seton, now Lady Rosseter. Looking at Clarissa after talking to Sally, he is in the company of women. And he is not dominating—his pocket-knife is in his pocket. The male frame may dominate the story space and ultimately frame Clarissa, but her story becomes hegemonic because the reader is positioned within a female frame: We begin by entering Clarissa's mind, because the "beautiful caves" Woolf digs behind her characters form the story's main interconnections and undermine the traditional storyline and the romance quest. We return to the female

frame at the end of the novel—and finally *we* fill in the empty frame
that Peter sets before us on the final page with Clarissa's thoughts.[6]
Woolf exploits the multiple possibilities of free indirect discourse—a
narrative tactic—in the very sense meant by Michel de Certeau. It is
a practice that enables her, like other disenfranchised and oppressed people, to realize a variety of voices, maintain a community,
and achieve a kind of power. Her narrative becomes a series of "opportunities seized 'on the wing,' " fragmentary and fragile "victories
of the 'weak' over the 'strong' " (xxi). As a result she can both explore and get beyond the simple binary of dominance and lead us
to understand the way strong middle-class women in London at the
turn of the century could make themselves seen and heard.

On the final page of the novel are two story frames: the predominant frame is Clarissa's, since the main storyline has been leading
up to her party, but Peter has led us to the party with a storyline that
began when he left her that morning. At this point, then, the story
frames overlap, and each character is in the other's sphere of influence. Clarissa's climactic appearance is framed by Peter's narrative
frame. Indeed it is framed by his sentence—"It is Clarissa"—which
is then refocalized by the narrator's supportive "For there she was."
And this clause, it is important to recall, echoes his earlier thoughts.
The narrative and story frames, therefore, may be multiple and need
not always coincide. They may add to, but also limit, the number of
positions available to the character. And they may also compete with
one another, as they do on the last page to determine Clarissa's most
memorable position. But the competition among shifting, overlapping, and conflicting frames should lead us to understand that characters are never finally positioned—for positionality is a way of
describing the self as a constellation of positions.

Appendix

I have adapted some familiar concepts and invented others to illuminate and analyze the continual power struggle in Woolf's sophisticated narrative, to get beyond easy notions of dominance, and to
extend our understanding of the novel. And I use these terms with
as much narrative precision as possible.

DEFINING TERMS

CONSTRUCT

"Construct" is the largest unit of characterization, which includes
"frame," "position," and "sphere of influence." It highlights the

social forces that Woolf exposes, judges, negotiates, and undermines.

FRAME

A unit of the storyline (story or diegetic frame), the narrative strategy, or, more generally, the ideology.

STORY FRAME

The stories of Woolf's main characters—Clarissa, Peter, and Septimus—are *shaped* through a series of *story* (diegetic) *frames,* or frames within the storyline.[7] Clarissa is introduced within the frame of her present drawing room, which gives way to the frame of her drawing room at Burton, eighteen years ago. But story frames overlap: her story ends in both her story frame and Peter's, since a large part of the novel traces his steps and thoughts from the time he leaves her in the morning to the time he returns to her party.

NARRATIVE FRAMES

The stories are *told* through a series of *narrative frames,* which result from the narrator's choice of perspective, or focalization.[8] Clarissa is introduced within the third-person narrator's frame, or focalization, until she stiffens on the curb and she enters the narrative frame of Scrope Purvis, who thinks, "A charming woman" (4).

POSITIONING CHARACTERS

Story and narrative frames *position* characters, establishing the limits within which we are allowed to see them act and think. A story frame positions a character as the main character (if it is her or his story), or as a subordinate character (if she or he is introduced in or enters the frame of another character's story). Woolf complicates her novel by overlapping story frames so that a character may have two simultaneous positions, and the reader must deal with this complication.

I use the term "position" for two reasons. First, it is precise: we can examine how and where the narrator positions her characters and reader (see following definition) in both shaping and telling the story. Second—and I am adapting Linda Alcoff's argument— positionality is a way of describing the self of the reader as well as the character as a constellation of positions—some of which are overlapping, some contradictory. Moreover, as Alcoff argues, the concept of construction is usually deterministic, whereas the concept of positionality enables the narrator's choice of this or that position from moment to moment. Positions are formed by changing historical and personal relations.[9] And in the act of reading a novel, these would include the relations among narrator, characters, and reader.

POSITIONING THE READER

We come to a book positioned by gender, class, race, education, age, sexuality, and so forth. We are then positioned from moment to moment by the narrator, who shapes and tells the story. The narrator also *positions the reader* by choosing a focal point. Woolf's narrator positions the reader anywhere on the continuum between sympathetically close to critically distant by representing his or her thoughts in a very flexible free indirect discourse. But Woolf does not maintain a focal point for very long; indeed what distinguishes her style is her continual, and often rapidly shifting, focal point.

MEDIATION

While positioning determines the narrator's and reader's emotional distance from a character, mediation determines our judgment. Free indirect discourse represents a character's thoughts in her or his speech patterns if not the direct words, while maintaining the third person and past tense. This is a form of *mediation*. When the mediation is just grammatical, it is effectively transparent. ("What a lark! What a plunge! For so it had always seemed to her, when, with a little squeak of the hinges, which she could hear now, she had burst open the French windows and plunged at Bourton into the open air" [3].) But free indirect discourse also allows the narrator to intervene further by mediating with her own voice. The narrator can mediate ironically and/or judgmentally with her own voice, and Woolf sometimes does so with metaphors and similes that call attention to themselves. As a result the narrative frame can distance, expose, and/or judge the characters' thoughts. When we first meet Peter Walsh in *Mrs. Dalloway*, he is positioned within the frame of Clarissa's story: she has opened the window, thought of Sally and Peter at Bourton, gone out to buy flowers, and returned home when Peter comes to visit. He is also positioned in Clarissa's narrative frame: the story at this point is being told from her point of view, or focalized within her mind, and this focalization provides the dominant narrative frame for the scene of Peter's visit. During this scene the narrative focus is continually reframed as it shifts back and forth between Clarissa and Peter. It also shifts between close and distant, as it is mediated by the narrator—now barely with a simple attribution ("She's grown older, he thought" [40]). It can do so now heavily with a romantic simile ("Then, just as happens on a terrace in the moon light, when one person begins to feel ashamed that he is already bored, and yet as the other sits silent, very quiet, sadly looking at the moon, does not like to speak, moves his foot, clears his throat, notices some iron scroll on a table leg, stirs a leaf, but says nothing—so Peter did now" [42]). It can now also do so parodically with a mock-epic simile ("So before a battle begins, the horses paw the ground; toss their heads; the light shines on their flanks; their necks curve. So Peter Walsh and Clarissa, sitting side by side on the blue sofa, challenged each other" [44]).

SPHERE OF INFLUENCE

When a character is introduced or enters another character's story frame—as when Peter is introduced in Clarissa's drawing room—our view of them is affected by that character's *sphere of influence,* even after the frame shifts. When Peter Walsh leaves Clarissa and starts walking through the streets of London, he is still in Clarissa's *sphere of influence,* even though he is thinking his own thoughts.

Notes

Melvin J. Friedman's *Stream of Consciousness* started me thinking first about the psychological novel, then about the way Virginia Woolf developed her own form of narrative. While our approaches grew further apart in the later years of his life, Mel continued to be a source of encouragement, and I acknowledge this important debt to him. I would also like to thank Robyn Warhol for her help while developing my narrative model and reading of Woolf.

1. In *The Politics of Narration,* I argue that Woolf creates a female narrator who builds on Woolf's discussion of the "male sentence" (*A Room of One's Own,* 76–77 [Woolf, #196]). "Abrogate" and "appropriate" come from the postcolonial model described so clearly by Bill Ascroft, Gareth Griffiths, and Helen Tiffin. "Abrogation is the refusal of categories of the imperial culture, its aesthetic, its illusionary standard of normative or 'correct' usage [or, I would add, conventions], and its assumption of traditional and fixed meaning inscribed in the words. . . . Appropriation is the process by which the language is taken and made to 'bear the burden' of one's own cultural experience" (38). I do not intend to appropriate the postcolonial model that evolved to give voice to the debased or marginalized experience of colonized people. But I feel that the model can be extended, given the way Woolf exposed the inseparability of British patriarchy and imperialism.

2. In my *Politics of Narration,* I argued that Woolf, wishing to tell women's stories, developed a narrative that intervened, exposed, judged, negotiated, countered, and undermined the social forces driving the traditional novel. But traditional forms retain a residual power. This essay revises my conclusion.

3. See my *Politics of Narration.*

4. See Jensen, 162–79.

5. Miller's discovery of the old woman's enigmatic song is a remarkable piece of scholarship, but his interpretation takes the free indirect discourse as direct authorial comment, rather than a reflection of Peter's thoughts, which tell us more about Peter than about the battered old woman. Granted, Peter is, as Miller says, resurrecting the ghosts of his past. Nonetheless, Miller fails to account for the discrepancy between the battered woman, whose present condition is so bad that her gender requires (Peter's?) confirmation—"for she wore a skirt" (81)—and the way Peter hears her voice as that of "an ancient spring spouting from the earth," singing of "love which has lasted a million years" (81).

6. My argument about Woolf's leading us to fill the empty frame of Peter's vision with images from Clarissa's own story was developed in a different context in my "Who Comes First, Joyce or Woolf?"

7. While "diegetic" is more precise, I will use "story frame" for the large number of readers for whom narratology is limited by its universal, structuralist claims. This is power utilizing historical forces and counterforces.

8. "Focalization" is preferable to "perspective" or "point of view" because, as Mieke Bal argues, it allows us to distinguish between visualization and verbalization, or between the narrative eye and the narrative voice.

9. I have adapted Linda Alcoff's argument that positionality is the logical step for feminists to take after cultural feminism and poststructuralism. Cultural feminism celebrates, appropriates, and transvalues the devalued values of women's culture, so that passivity becomes a form of peacefulness; subjectivism and narcissism become ways of being in touch with oneself; and sentimentality becomes caring and nurturing. But cultural feminism tends toward essentialism, identifies women with their bodies, and perpetuates biological determinism. Conversely, poststructuralism exposes "essence" and "femininity" as social and linguistic constructs. But in showing these constructs to be overdetermined by a wide range of social institutions and forces, it denies women agency, choice, and the possibility of change—and it renders gender invisible.

Teresa de Lauretis, Bal points out, shows us a way out of the bind between cultural feminism and poststructural determinism by arguing that we are constructed through a continuous and ongoing interaction with the practices, discourses, and institutions that shape value, meaning, and feeling. Alcoff extends this to the notion of positionality. The self, rather than having an essence or being overdetermined, is a constellation of positions, formed by changing historical and personal relations. Agency is a matter of choosing to take this or that position or negotiating among them.

I developed the notion of positionality to deal with the problem of male feminists in " 'Nausicaa': Monologue as Monologic."

Works Cited

Abel, Elizabeth. *Virginia Woolf and the Fictions of Psychoanalysis.* Chicago: University of Chicago Press, 1989.

Alcoff, Linda. "Cultural Feminism Versus Post-Structuralism: The Identity Crisis in Feminist Theory." *Signs: Journal of Women in Culture and Society* 3.13: 1998, 405–36.

Althusser, Louis. "Ideology and the Ideological State Apparatuses," in Louis Althusser, ed., *Lenin and Philosophy*. New York: Monthly Review Press, 1971.

Bal, Mieke. *Narratology: Introduction to the Theory of Narrative*. Christine van Boheemen, trans. Toronto: University of Toronto Press, 1985.

Butler, Judith. *Gender Trouble: Feminism and the Subversion of Identity*. New York and London: Routledge, 1990.

Friedman, Melvin J. *Stream of Consciousness: A Study in Literary Method*. New Haven: Yale University Press, 1955.

Jensen, Emily. "Clarissa Dalloway's Respectable Suicide," in Jane Marcus, ed., *Virginia Woolf: A Feminist Slant*. Lincoln: University of Nebraska Press, 1984, 162–79.

Miller, J. Hillis. *Fictions and Repetition: Seven English Novels*. Cambridge: Harvard University Press, 1982.

Pearce, Richard. " 'Nausicaa': Monologue as Monologic," in Beja Morris and David Norris, eds., *Joyce in Dublin*. Columbus: Ohio State University Press, 1996.

———. *The Politics of Narration: James Joyce, William Faulkner, and Virginia Woolf*. New Brunswick, N.J.: Rutgers University Press, 1991.

———. "Who Comes First, Joyce or Woolf?," in Vara Neverow-Turk and Mark Hussey, eds., *Virginia Woolf: Themes and Variations. Selected Papers from the Second Annual Conference on Virginia Woolf*. New York: Pace University Press, 1993.

Sedgwick, Eve Kosofsky. *Between Men: English Literature and Male Homosocial Desire*. New York: Columbia University Press, 1985.

Zangwill's *The Melting Pot* and Nichols's *Abie's Irish Rose*

OWEN ALDRIDGE

MOST AMERICANS INTERESTED IN THE CURRENT CONCEPT OF MULTI-culturalism recognize the name of Israel Zangwill and his 1908 play, *The Melting Pot*. Many assume that the play concerns ethnic assimilation in America and that its author was a citizen of the United States. In this they are only half correct. The play is indeed about ethnic amalgamation in the United States, but its author was born in England of Jewish immigrant parents (his mother Polish, his father Latvian), and he spent most of his life in the country of his birth. The best of Zangwill's extensive literary work, moreover, concerns the London ghetto.

Today, the major themes of Zangwill's play, immigration and assimilation, are both much less popular than they were at the beginning of the century. At that time, a Jewish American, Emma Lazarus, hailed immigration ecstatically in a sonnet inscribed on the Statue of Liberty in New York Harbor, the opening lines of which Zangwill quoted in his appendix to the 1914 edition of *The Melting Pot*.

> Give me your tired, your poor,
> Your huddled masses yearning to breathe free,
> The wretched refuse of your teeming shore,
> Send these, the homeless, tempest-tost to me,
> I lift my lamp beside the golden door.

Zangwill's personal connection with America grew out of an article he published in the British *Jewish Quarterly Review* in 1889. In it he contrasted faith in Judaism with modern developments tending to weaken that faith: skepticism, Jewish emancipation, and destruction of the ghettos. As a consequence of this article, Zangwill was invited to write a novel for the Jewish Publication Society of Philadelphia, the genesis of his *Children of the Ghetto* (1892).[1] Zangwill himself traced the origins of *The Melting Pot* to a change in his political-reli-

151

gious thought, not to any emotional or moral awakening arising from personal contact with the process of assimilation in America. This change in ideology came from his abandonment of Zionism. Losing faith in the possibility of the attainment in his lifetime of its goal, the creation of a Jewish homeland in Palestine, he shifted his efforts to promoting the settlement of ten thousand Russian Jews in the western United States. He cited as the "concrete experience" that led directly to his writing of *The Melting Pot* his work as president of the Emigration Regulation Department of the [Jewish] Territorial Organization.[2] The immediate theme of the play, therefore, was immigration, and the associated one of assimilation in the New World developed as the play was being written.

The process of naturalization or acquiring official citizenship does not appear at all in the play. When one character asks, "What true understanding can there be between a Russian Jew and a Russian Christian?," another character replies, "Aren't we both Americans?," an identity apparently acquired without official action or recognition. The play, moreover, does not reflect ethnic diversity. The male and female protagonists are both Russian born, David a Jew and Vera a Christian. Apart from a single native-born American, the only other nationalities represented are Irish, by a maid Kathleen, and German, by a musical conductor, Herr Pappelmeister, both of whom are standard comic types.

The storyline of *The Melting Pot* is simple and straightforward. David Quixano, a young Jewish immigrant from Russia with exceptional musical talent, lives with his uncle in a non-Jewish section of New York City. His career is fostered by Vera Revendal. She is also an immigrant from Russia, but Christian and a member of a patrician family from which she is temporarily separated because of her idealistic political sentiments. As David and Vera fall in love, David exalts the values of a "new secular Republic" over the "nightmare of religions and races." His uncle interprets this attitude as a desertion of his Jewish faith, and turns David out of his house (97). When David subsequently meets Vera's father, Baron Revendal, who is honeymooning with a second wife, he discovers that Revendal is the man who had been in charge of a notorious slaughter of innocent Jews, including David's own family, at Kishineff in Russia. For audiences of the early twentieth century, Kishineff inspired pain and horror equivalent to that evoked today by the Holocaust. The revelation of her father's guilt causes Vera to reject Christianity and convert to Judaism. David, nevertheless, turns away from her because of the "river of blood" separating them. Vera curses the day she was born Revendal's daughter, and Revendal gives David a pistol and cries "Shoot me." David takes the gun, then drops it on a table, where he exchanges it for a violin string, symbolizing his renunciation of force and destruction in favor of art. To say the least, this scene lacks realism. As Mark Slobin has noted, the "cold-hearted anti-Semite . . . relinquishes his pistol to the Jew and asks to be shot. David merely walks off the stage, mumbling, and the only dramatic moment of the play fizzles like a wet furnace."[3] David realizes that his rejection of Vera represents his rejection of God's crucible in both its divine and human manifestations. It had proved powerless to melt his hate. Although Vera understands that "the shadow of Kishineff" must keep them apart, she extends the metaphor of the cup to embrace David's music and prophetic visions, praying that his art may fill his life to the brim. Almost immediately, David pleads for a kiss of reconciliation, which she grants. With the strains of "My Country 'tis of Thee" emanating from the orchestral pit, the two young people look out upon "the great Melting Pot," where Jew and Gentile, "the palm and the pine, the pole and the equator, the crescent and the cross" are melted and fused by the great Alchemist "to build the Republic of Man and the Kingdom of God."

The multicultural theme is introduced early in the play by David's attending a meeting of the Peoples' Alliance, a Jewish social and cultural club, where the sight of a thousand children saluting the flag inspires him. He hears "the roaring fires of God" and sees "the souls melting in the Crucible," as he realizes that all these "little Jews will grow up Americans."[4] One must not assume, however, that Zangwill was oblivious to the less attractive aspects of American life that might have been expected to have decreased David's faith in the United States as a land of equal opportunity. The only American-born character in the work is an obnoxious playboy, whose main pleasure in life consists in squandering large amounts of money. Zangwill also includes a reference to American children dying of hunger (85) and allows Baron Revendal to put the question, "Don't you lynch and roast your niggers?" (111). The Irish maid is overtly anti-Semitic in the first act, although she speaks some Yiddish in the fourth. David, moreover, affirms that the assimilation process that is advantageous for some inevitably causes suffering for others. "It is live things, not dead metals, that are being melted in the Crucible" (146). This realization is linked to one of the subordinate themes of the play—that Jews always look to the past rather than to the future (164). Vera retains her faith in the crucible, but David loses it by adhering to the old message of blood and revenge rather than accepting the vision of brotherhood and peace (179–80). Despite the sentimental and intellectual reconciliation at the play's end, it is not apparent whether the relationship between David and Vera will ever be consummated. Most interpretations of the play assume that it advocates intermarriage between ethnic groups and religions, but this is by no means clear in the text. In giving David a kiss of reconciliation, Vera says, "I will kiss you as we Russians kiss at Easter—the three kisses of peace." The stage directions indicate that this be done "as in ritual solemnity."

In the appendix to the 1914 edition of the play, Zangwill retreats from advocating Jewish intermarriage. He declares that the melting process is not necessarily a physical one and that this should be a consideration of particular relevance to Jews. He defines the process of immigration not as assimilation, but as a give-and-take, which may lead to either enrichment or impoverishment. Although opposing interfaith marriage, Zangwill affirms that individuals not held apart by theological differences, including David and Vera in this category, will encounter no obstacles. "There will be neither Jew nor Greek" (209). But "when the parties stand in opposite religious camps," family division and dissension will arise over the rearing of children. He cites as example the antiquated doctrinal differences leading to discord "which keep even Catholic and Protestants widely apart." These divisions, along with anti-Semitism and ingrained conservativism, "tend to preserve the Jew even in the 'Melting Pot,' so that his dissolution must be necessarily slower than that of the similar aggregations of Germans, Italians, or Poles." Zangwill predicts, however, that even among the slowest ethnic groups to be assimilated, children of the third generation will be ashamed of both their parents and the latters' language and that ethnic newspapers and theaters will eventually die out. Continued immigration will slow this homogenizing process, but should it come to an end, "the crucible will roar like a closed furnace" (210).

Zangwill even argues that America does not have the right to exclude people from other parts of the world. "Exclusiveness may have some justification in countries, especially when old and well-populated; but for continents like the United States . . . to mistake themselves for mere countries is an intolerable injustice to the rest of the human race" (210). He does not, however, have a single word to say specifically about immigration from Asia, particularly China and Japan, although hotly debated Exclusion Acts had been passed as early as 1882.

Zangwill concludes by acknowledging with gratitude the universal acclamation by which *The Melting Pot* had been received by Americans "as a revelation of Americanism, despite that it contains only one native-born American character, and that a bad one" (214). He adds that it "played throughout the length and breadth of the States," that it "passed through edition after edition in book form," and that it contributed "its title to current thought." No question exists about the truth of the last claim, but the former two are somewhat exaggerated. Prior to the 1914 edition of the play, only three others—Macmillan (New York, 1909 and 1911) and Heinemann (London, 1909)—had been issued, and these are still the only ones. The stage career of the play was even less sensational. It was presented for the first time in Washington, D.C., on 5 October 1908, and then ran briefly in New York in 1909. One of Zangwill's biographers follows him verbally in affirming that the play "was produced throughout the length and breadth of the United States," and adds with equal flight of fancy[5] "to vast and appreciative audiences" (170). Even more of a hyperbole, the *Dictionary of National Biography* (Supplement 1922–1930) affirms that the play "created a sensation" in the United States "and ran for many years."

Theodore Roosevelt, who attended the opening performance in Washington, shouted across the theater, "That's a great play, Mr. Zangwill."[6] As a result, Zangwill dedicated with permission the 1914 edition to the American president. But Roosevelt was almost the only contemporary to say much good about the play. The following excerpt from *The Literary Digest* (39; Sept. 1909: 440) summarizes the critical response to the New York production.

> The New York *Herald*, it is true, describes it as "a big play," gloomy but strong," and *The Sun* calls it "unmistakably a man's size effort." *The Times*, however, sees in it only "a big and vital subject handled in a cheap and tawdry way," and asserts that "as drama it is hardly second rate." *The Tribune* complains that "it is a Zangwill story staged rather than dramatized," while *The Evening Post* remarks irreverently that "the product which came out of Mr. Zangwill's dramatic melting-pot might irresistibly suggest an Irish stew."

The last comment is probably the first published appearance of the culinary metaphor. Even a favorable critical response was headed in *Munsey's Magazine* (42; Nov. 1909: 258), "New York Scorns 'The Melting Pot,' " because the play failed to fill even the smallest auditorium in the city. A film version, however, was produced in 1915 in the United States in which Vera and David marry at the end.[7]

The play fared no better in London. After a preliminary performance at the Yiddish People's Theatre, 5 June 1912, it played at the Court Theatre on 25 and 26 January 1914, at the Queens from 7 February to 11 April, and at the Comedy from 13 April to 22 May—

for a total of 118 performances.[8] Zangwill's biographer says that the Foreign Office restricted performance of the play because it could be deemed as insulting to England's ally Russia.[9]

A few years later, a purely comic play, *Abie's Irish Rose* (1922), also designed to promote cultural assimilation, dazzled the Broadway stage. This play, by Anne Nichols, strongly advocates assimilation through intermarriage with no restrictions whatsoever. While *The Melting Pot* treats religion as a vital element of Jewish culture, *Abie's Irish Rose* considers religion as in itself an undesirable obstacle to assimilation. Although one play is serious drama and the other popular entertainment, both use essentially the same ingredients of plot and character.[10] The male and female leads of *Abie's Irish Rose* are lovers, both of whom had lost their mothers during infancy. Abie is the only son of a prosperous German Jewish merchant; Rose is the daughter of a wealthy Irish Catholic contractor. They had become acquainted in Europe during the war, where Abie was a wounded soldier and Rose a musical entertainer for the troops. Abie's father, Solomon Levy, is the counterpart of David's uncle, both rigid in their religious belief and practice. Rose's father, Patrick Murphy, is the counterpart of Vera's father, Baron Revendal, although he is a purely comic type in contrast to the sinister Baron. As in *The Melting Pot*, music is the catalyst that brings the lovers together. Solomon is prejudiced against all Irish people because he had been bested in a deal with an Irish contractor, a comic situation equivalent in structure to David's revulsion against Vera's father for his participation in the racial massacre of Kishineff. Both plays have stock ethnic character types: in *The Melting Pot*, the German orchestra conductor, Herr Pappelmeister, and the Irish maid, Kathleen O'Reilly; in *Abie's Irish Rose*, the parsimonious Jewish businessman, Solomon Levy; the blustering Irish contractor, Patrick Murphy; and a Jiggs-and-Maggie couple (a small husband dominated by a burly wife, Mr. and Mrs. Cohen.) The stage German and stage Irish characters in Zangwill's play figure as comic relief; in Nichols's play the type characters blend with the farcical action and are essential to it.

Abie's Irish Rose has three acts, in contrast to *The Melting Pot*, which is a "four decker." As the play opens, Abie and Rose have been married for only one and a half hours, the ceremony having been performed by a Methodist minister. Abie takes Rose home to meet his father, who gives her a frosty reception, assuming she is not the "nice Jewish girl" he had hoped Abie would select as a bride. Abie, anxious to placate his father, passes off Rose as a Jewish girl whose family name is Murpheski. Solomon now is delighted, particularly when he learns they are in love. The entrance of Rabbi Samuels on a social call stimulates Solomon to arrange for a wedding to take place within a week's time. In the next act, Solomon has decorated his living room profusely with orange leaves and fruit, a gesture to remind Rose of her native state of California. She has arranged for her father to arrive for the wedding ceremony just after its completion so that he will accept the marriage as a *fait accompli*. While the wedding is taking place offstage, Rose's father, accompanied by Father Whalen, enters and is confronted by Solomon. Upon seeing him and the orange decorations, Patrick expresses consternation, assuming that Rose is marrying a Protestant. During the animated conversation, Solomon discovers that Patrick is an Irish contractor and in his rage calls Rose a "little — Irish A.P.A." The rabbi and the priest, temporarily left alone on the stage, recount their war experiences, each having administered comfort to dying men of the other's faith. The logic of this stage theology suggests that, if their words are valid for death, they are equally valid for marriage.

This scene of conciliation balances the preceding one of bigotry between the two parents. Father Whalen then agrees to perform a Catholic wedding ceremony. He telephones the archbishop for authorization, and, presumably having received it, performs the ceremony offstage while the fathers continue ranting and insulting each other. As the act ends, the voice of Father Whalen is heard pronouncing the words, "Those whom God hath joined together, let no man put asunder."

The final act takes place a year later on Christmas Eve. As Abie and Rose are entertaining Mr. and Mrs. Cohen in their modest apartment, Father Whalen enters; he is followed soon after by Patrick Murphy laden with presents for a girl baby. Rabbi Samuels and Solomon appear subsequently, the latter with presents for a grandson. The two grandparents are finally reconciled when they learn that Rose has twins, one boy and one girl.

Jewish characters, dialect, and symbols predominate in this play, and nearly all the comedy derives from its two Jewish families. Rose, Patrick Murphy, and Father Whalen are the only non-Jewish characters, and Patrick is not portrayed sympathetically. The play cannot, however, be described as entirely a Jewish play. Ham is served at the festive dinner after the joyful climax, and Christmas bells ring out as the curtain descends. The ultimate message conveyed is that religion either does not count, or that it is a nuisance to be overcome. Father Whalen remarks about American soldiers in Europe, "Shure they all had the same God above them" (78), an echo of Vera's "all religions must serve the same God—since there is only one God to serve" (124). Both plays affirm that all creeds and faiths are essentially the same.

The form of religious bigotry introduced in *Abie's Irish Rose* is not anti-Semitism but anti-Catholicism. Solomon calls Rose a "little — Irish A.P.A." without knowing the exact principles of that organization, the American Protection Association, an Anglo-American group, something like the Ku Klux Klan, with Catholics, including Irish Catholics, as its main target. On the surface, this taunt is an example of Solomon's own ignorance, but it may have been intended as a subtle reminder that the Irish, the main opponents of Jews in New York City, were themselves victims of religious prejudice.

The notion of a melting pot is not overtly expressed in the play, and absolutely no patriotic allusions are made to America as a land of freedom or opportunity for the oppressed of the world. The nation is, nevertheless, portrayed as a place conducive to the intermarriage of people of historically antagonistic cultures and religions. In carrying out this theme of assimilation, the play defies the facts of real life as well as dramatic versimilitude.

Originally called *Marriage in Triplicate*, the play is based upon the experience of one of Nichols's friends "who found himself in the hero's predicament."[11] *Abie's Irish Rose* was first performed in Stamford, Connecticut, 6 March 1922.[12] It opened at the Fulton Theater on 23 May of the same year and played continuously until 1927 for a record-breaking total of 2,327 performances. It ran also in London from 11 April 1927 to 30 July for a total of 128 performances, slightly more than the total number attained by *The Melting Pot*.[13] It appears that straight comedy had a greater appeal to American audiences than Zangwill's mixture of comedy and social prophecy.[14]

As might be expected, drama critics were not kind to *Abie's Irish Rose*, considering it mainly a drawn-out vaudeville sketch. Public opinion, as frequently happens, ran contrary to contemporary critical appraisal. Arthur Hobson Quinn, a later historian of the American theater, however, has given the play serious consideration. Attributing its phenomenal success to its broad human appeal, without recourse to salaciousness or violence, he observes that it portrays "practically every form of love known to human beings: that of boy and girl, of fathers for their children, that sanctified by the dead mothers of the couple, and finally that of the grandparents for their children."[15] The only kind of love represented in *The Melting Pot*, except for the music-inspired attraction between David and Vera, is the abstract benevolence toward all peoples of the world, and even the love of the two young people does not seem to have had a happy outcome. Although *Abie's Irish Rose* is not a thesis play, it deals with the same social circumstances as *The Melting Pot* but arrives at more optimistic conclusions. As a contemporary Jewish scholar has observed, "the inflexibilities of Jewish tradition and Irish Catholicism have been eliminated and the goal of total assimilation achieved."[16]

Zangwill's notion of the melting pot aroused little opposition until 1924, when Jewish sociologist Horace Kallen expressed a competing theory, now known as cultural pluralism. He argued that American society should develop as a federation of various nationalities rather than as a homogeneous mass. Devising his own metaphor, Kallen described this ideal as "a multiplicity in a unity, an orchestration of mankind" (121). An even more radical opponent of assimilation, Henry Pratt Fairchild, in a book entitled *The Melting Pot Mistake* (1926), took the position that further immigration was in itself undesirable. Adopting the racist perspective that cultural traits or characteristics are genetic and "exclusively hereditary," he argued that racial separation and discrimination are "inherent in biological fact and human nature" (239).

Zangwill deals briefly and somewhat inconsistently with this genetic or racist argument in the afterword to *The Melting Pot*. He unequivocally rejects the notion of racial purity in regard to England, adopting essentially the same reasoning used two centuries earlier in Daniel Defoe's satirical poem "The True-Born Englishman." Zangwill reasons that "there is hardly an ethnic element that has not entered into the Englishman." Mark Slobin, however, has leveled the charge of racism because of Zangwill's opinion that, in view of all the unpleasantness attached "to the blending of colours, only heroic souls on either side should dare the adventures of intermarriage." Slobin interprets this to mean that "somehow the Jew, though distinctive, will indeed melt positively, as opposed to the Afro-American. . . . In short, only Euro-Americans can successfully dissolve."[17] Zangwill concludes his remarks on American immigration, however, with the admonition that "the action of the crucible is . . . not exclusively physical. . . . The Jew may be Americanized and the American Judaized without any gamic interaction." Zangwill, moreover, expounded a clear antiracist biological principle in an address, "The Jewish Race," delivered in London in 1911.

> Not only is every race akin to every other, but every people is a hotchpotch of race. The Jews, though mainly a white people, are not even devoid of a colored fringe, black, brown or yellow. There are the Bnei-Israel of India, the Falashas of Abyssinia, the disappearing Chinese colony of Kai-Fung-Foo, the Judaeos of Loango, the black Jews of Cochin, the negro warlike nomads of the North African deserts, who remind us what the conquerors of the Philistines were like.[18]

The "true race theory" for Zangwill is that no pure human race exists. In his *The Voice of Jerusalem* (1924), he quoted H. G. Wells to the same effect: "That men form one universal brotherhood, that they spring from one common origin, that their individual lives, their nations and races, interbreed and blend and go on to merge again at last in one common human destiny upon this little planet amidst stars."[19]

At present the public policy of the United States is that of amalgamation, which is apparent also in privately sponsored movements such as that to make English the official language. Assimilation is a policy contrary to that of England and Canada, both of which have officially adopted cultural pluralism. The current notion of multiculturalism, now widespread in the United States, rests upon the notion of separate racial, ethnic, and cultural identities, each seeking self-expression, often in competitive or antagonistic attitudes toward other groups or toward the mainstream.

Two distinguished Americans, one Jewish, Nathan Glazer, the other with an Irish background, Daniel Patrick Moynihan, have collaborated on a sociological study, *Beyond the Melting Pot* (1973), in which they describe Zangwill's play as "quite a bad one," both in its execution and its thesis.[20] They charge that it "is little involved with American reality. It is a drama about Jewish separation and Russian anti-semitism, with a German concertmaster and an Irish maid thrown in for comic relief. Both protagonists are New Model Europeans of the time. Free-thinkers and revolutionaries, it was doubtless in the power of such to merge. But neither of these doctrines was dominant among the ethnic groups of New York City in the 1900's. . . . The point about the melting pot is that it did not happen." In regard to the Jewish community of New York, the authors affirm that there is no reason to think that any considerable portion of it "ever subscribed to Israel Zangwill's version of a nonreligious, intermarried homogeneous population, but it surely does not do so today" (293).

Despite the somewhat negative attitude toward Zangwill's concept of the melting pot expressed by these authors, one might take the position that they in themselves represent a fine example of the actual working out of the concept. Two nationally recognized intellectuals, with Jewish and Irish roots, have collaborated in the writing of a major work of social philosophy. Their partnership certainly suggests amalgamation rather than a conflict of cultural identities, and it is in this sense a vindication of Zangwill's dream of the melting pot. Amalgamation, he insisted, "is not assimilation or simple surrender to the dominant type, as is popularly supposed, but an all-round give-and-take by which the final type may be enriched or impoverished."[21]

Notes

1. Maurice Wohlgelernter. *Israel Zangwill* (New York: Columbia University Press, 1964), 136.

2. "Afterword" in Israel Zangwill, *The Melting Pot* (London: William Heinemann, 1914), 199.

3. "Some Intersections of Jews, Music, and Theater" in Sarah Blacher Cohen (ed.), *From Hester Street to Hollywood: The Jewish-American Stage and Screen* (Bloomington: Indiana University Press, 1983), 33.

4. *The Melting Pot*, 53.

5. Wohlgelernter, *Zangwill*, 178.

6. *Ibid.*, 177.

7. *Variety* 1915, 4, 6; cited in *Jewish Film Directory*, (Westport, Conn.: Greenwood Press, 1992).

8. J. P. Wearing, *The London Stage 1910–1919* (Metuchen, NJ: Scarecrow Press, 1982), 11, 29.

9. Joseph Leftwich, *Israel Zangwill* (New York: Thomas Yoseloff, 1957), 255.

10. Although Nichols was not Jewish, her play was appreciated for its amiable comedy and engaging humor. A silent cinematic version of 1929 is listed in the *Jewish Film Directory*.

11. Gerald Bordman, *Oxford Companion to the American Theatre* 2d ed. (New York: Oxford University Press, 1992), 5.

12. *Who Was Who in the Theatre 1912–1976*. (Detroit, MI: Gale Research, 1978), III, 1802.

13. Wearing, *The London Stage 1910–1919*, II, 849–50.

14. *Abie's Irish Rose* was produced as a silent film in 1929 and as a talking picture in 1946. Nichols also wrote a novel version (Harpers 1927), which went through several editions. The novel has opening chapters describing the experiences of Abie, Rose, and the two clergymen during the war in Europe. Otherwise, it follows the play faithfully and frequently verbally.

15. *A History of the American Drama From the Civil War to the Present* (New York: Appleton-Century-Crofts, 1936), II, 121.

16. Sarah Blacher Cohen, "Yiddish Origins and Jewish-American Transformations" in *From Hester Street to Hollywood*, 5.

17. "Some Intersections of Jews," 107.

18. Wohlgelernter, *Zangwill*, 180.

19. *Ibid.*, 14.

20. Second ed. (Cambridge, Mass. MIT Press, 1973), 290.

21. *The Melting Pot*, 203.

Céline's Ultimate Focalization, or the Two Faces of Paranoia in *Bagatelles pour un massacre* and *Féerie pour une autre fois:* Toward a Theory of Paranoid Writing

David Hayman

Even without consulting the biographies and letters, we find in Louis-Ferdinand Céline's novels evidence of a persistent persecution complex, together with conspiracy theories. These are reinforced by the paranoid behavior of others as a way to make the fantasies of his first-person protagonists seem relatively mild. At the same time, they dramatize Céline's own need to purge himself of personal demons. (The biographies reinforce this aspect of his character by disclosing how badly he coped in his own life.) The questions remain, however: How was this self-acknowledged disposition voiced in the fiction? What does that voicing tell us about the reactions of other writers to similar personality problems? Why is his particular solution so exemplary?

I have long felt that a paranoid disposition (as opposed to a paranoid condition) provides the fuel for a good deal of our best fiction, to say nothing of other art forms. And even before I began to formulate my theory, I received remarkable confirmation from an author. Twenty years ago, at Iowa, I happened to mention my view quite casually in class. One of my auditors, Jane Vonnegut, repeated my remark to her husband, who was sufficiently impressed to write the following inscription in my copy of his novel, *Player Piano:* "For David Hayman, my only academic buddy, Kurt Vonnegut Jr., Paranoid under control." (I might add that he is very much under control, but his work reflects his effort to maintain such control with wonderful effect.)

Years later, at Wisconsin, I taught my first seminar in "Paranoid Discourse," where I formulated the idea that two polar paranoid personalities are available in literature. The first I called the "Mars paranoid," designating by that term the belligerent voice that woos

162

readers by the force of an intimidating rhetoric functioning as a charm against the force of the expected attack. That is, the speaker/ writer uses attack diction at once to inoculate himself and to seduce the reader enchanted by the fire directed at others through him. Such writing, though rendered difficult by the demands put on the reader's sympathies and by a variety of screening and masking tactics, is generally straightforward and accessible. Still, as we shall see, it is seldom pure.

As examples of writers using this tactic, I chose Ezra Pound, Wyndham Lewis, and Louis-Ferdinand Céline. I felt that such figures, and there are many more, had a radical need to vent their anxiety on ready and relatively powerless targets, double targets in fact, comprised of the exoriated enemy or enemies and the willing reader. It may be pure coincidence that they all found one of their most convenient antagonists to be the Jew, long a popular scapegoat and, until recently, relatively defenseless. All of them, in their most extreme utterance, attempted through innuendo and charged language to invest Jews with exceptional, if largely fictive, resources. That venting was clearly cathartic in a pre-Holocaust Europe, but it should be noted that anti-Semitism was by no means the only outlet—it was simply the easiest and rhetorically the most powerful.

Even today, though less effectively, the reader is drawn into becoming a collaborator by being placed on the positive side of the equation as at once covictim of, vicarious participant in, and beneficiary of the attack on the dark force. Conversely, the writer relieved himself with the aid of powerful vituperation, pointed sarcasm, and the massed force of accumulated, and often spurious, logic. Thus, each had his own tactics, but all found in the myths of Jewish power the necessary channel for a language that draws energy from them and gives pleasure with its sheer exuberance and frequently comic violence. In a sense, their language, while perhaps serious in its intent, performs a harlequinade complete with noisy slapsticks and verbal acrobatics. Although they may all have nourished a preexisting hatred or distrust, their discourse was unlikely, by virtue of its sheer excess, to instigate or even justify action. This does not make this aspect of their work appealing, but it permits us to enjoy other, less venomous components.

On the opposite end of the paranoid spectrum is what I shall call the "St. Sebastian." If Mars is the god of offensive behavior, St. Sebastian, the gatherer of wounds, is the emblem of the willing victim, the figure who draws pain on himself. (In other terms, we can speak of the sadist as opposed to the masochist or, more figuratively, of the Harlequin vs. the Pierrot figures in farce.) Writers in this group depict themselves as trapped in a world that inflicts damage, or rather they position themselves through their fictional tactics and fictional persona as targets or victims of opprobrium, ostracism, disapproval, and risk. Such writers tend not to need targets, although they can find ways to attack with disarming meekness those who offend them. Representative of this class are Joyce, Kafka, and Beckett, artists with radically different strategies but surprisingly similar profiles. Victims abound in their work, but, paradoxically, the work itself affronts the reader with its demands for ingenuity, patience, and intelligence. It does so by erecting a barrier to understanding through style and procedure, a barrier pierced by the challenged (or attacked) reader, who, through that conquest, becomes a collaborator. In effect, this is the mirror image of the Mars procedure, although it results in a very different sort of product.

A pair of offsetting traits can be found in the work of both figures, however. Not only are both mentalities products of a more or less powerful distress, but, despite the different manifestations, both are also controlling potentially devastating personal threats, even terrors. Furthermore, both seem to find ways to disguise or sublimate their most powerful exhibitions of disorder. The "defenseless" Joyce, always willing to discern betrayal, typically cast his and his protagonists' betrayers in a negative light; he did so even while making them superficially attractive in relation to their, in many ways unappealing, protagonists. To cite only two of many instances: in the "Telemachus" chapter of *Ulysses,* Buck Mulligan is presented as outwardly seductive even when he mocks the louse-eaten and impoverished Stephen Dedalus. But it is Stephen who wins our affection and support by virtue of his proximity to the reader who is engaged by his development and thought processes. Similarly, the vituperative Shaun the post, like his counterpart, the nameless dun of *Ulysses*'s "Cyclops" chapter, effectively buttresses the support of the long-suffering and vulnerable Shem the pen by overstating his case in Chapter I.7 of *Finnegans Wake.* Ultimately, he caricatures himself even while giving a surprisingly accurate picture of his brother's weaknesses and vices. The result is a disarming self-critique and a remarkably on-target portrait of the Mars paranoid models, all of whom are modeled after quondam friends. (Joyce had in mind Wyndham Lewis, Stanislaus Joyce, and Dr. Joseph Collins [the author of an early diatribe], and perhaps Ezra Pound, to whom he was otherwise beholden.)

The Sebastian writers, as a by-product of their stylistic and formal excesses, and perhaps of a seemingly paradoxical reluctance to expose their vulnerable person/persona to the incomprehension that they court, tend to produce very few well-crafted works. I suggest it is the process of writing that induces the subconsciously courted or avoided pain, obviating or postponing display. Exhibition is thus rendered less necessary. By contrast, the Mars figures, even as they launch their poisoned arrows, tend to find ever more strident instances of paranoid behavior to buffer their excesses. This means that, however powerful an utterance has been, however efficient in alleviating the angst, arrows must continuously be fabricated and launched. The mindset or condition will not vanish. Like a tapeworm it will continue to gnaw at the gut of its victim, urging him/her on to fresh statements, generally in the same vein.

As opposed to the St. Sebastians, who are prone to endless meditations and a radical sort of procrastination, Mars writers are generally very productive. But this is not always a risk-free procedure. Sometimes, as may be expected, society strikes back. This is because at times the bile is too bitter or the behavior of the offender hits too close to the bone.

Céline's is a case in point, but Ezra Pound, whose exhilarating bombast cannot be gainsaid, is also a good example. As we know, in the aftermath of his post-war incarceration, he became pathologically silent. (Compare his behavior with the shift in Oscar Wilde from the irreverent and antisocial, if much less strident and less gifted, Harlequin casting himself as a version of Christ in his prison letter, *De Profundus*. After his imprisonment, he took on the persona of Sebastian Melmoth, a disturbingly touching Pierrot.) The novelist Céline, as opposed to the pamphleteer, mimed this behavior even before he suffered retribution for his prewar and wartime excesses. One has only to compare his self-portrayal as the surprisingly meek victim of his situation and its torments to the strident and energetic voice of his narrating persona, the older and more experienced Ferdinand. Here, the generally voiceless protagonist plays Sebastian to his own Mars. All this suggests that both manifestations are tactics for assuaging essentially the same angst—that within every Mars lurks a closeted Sebastian, and vice versa.

Both manifestations cry out to the reader for acceptance, both find means to seduce. To these ends, each must draw the reader into a net of complicity. In this, as in the essential nature of their drive, they are equal-opposites, achieving their goal through an offensive act. The Sebastian typically hides weakness behind a wall of ambiguity and difficulty, inviting the reader to make an entry through wit and skill while denying anything like full access. The result is a sort of initiation that leaves the initiate both content and chronically ill informed. This is certainly the case with Joyce, Beckett, and Kafka, whose various tactics bear witness to the creative potential of their drive to expose and conceal.

The Mars may erect similar obstacles, but the lure is of a different facture. Verbal facility, especially that for vituperation, has an immense appeal, spiced as it often is with comic energy. For the Mars, conspiratorial laughter is a balm, while language becomes a mask for a power capable of demolishing sympathy while raising admiration. Though doubtless an efficient way to banish anxiety, the attack mode carries with it enormous risks, which the risk-taker attempts to diminish by projecting a dual image and by focusing his arrows on a limited and vulnerable target, his secret other. This tactic is in turn matched by the behavior of the St. Sebastian, who also employs the image of the antagonist in full attack regalia, but he manages to diminish the latter by presenting himself as unworthy of and somehow ennobled by the attack.

To illustrate in more detail the complex mechanics of this dual syndrome, I now turn to Céline and the radical shift illustrated by one of the most violent of his neglected prewar anti-Semitic pamphlets as it relates to the least-read of his postwar novels. Together, these texts reveal the writer's practice at the peak and the nadir of his public life, moments of perceived strength and weakness for anyone so afflicted. I should add that, true to the Sebastian mode, *Féerie pour une autre fois* is the most advanced formally and the most demanding of all the books, and that the pamphlets are as accomplished (and off-putting) as the Mars's most virulent diatribes. Coming as they did in the wake of his first successes and his unmasking as a public person, the anti-Communist and anti-Semitic pamphlets of the mid 1930s constituted in their way a major stylistic and perhaps a therapeutic breakthrough. It is in these non-anti-meta-literary performances that he discovered a cathartic voice so profoundly satisfying that it seems ultimately to have frightened even him. It was that voice that certainly put him at risk after the war and contributed to the accusations of treason and his confinement ("on death row") in a Danish prison.[1]

Of the four pamphlets published in the wake of *Mort à crédit*, in 1936, 1937, 1938, 1941, the most devastating and interesting is surely *Bagatelles pour un massacre* (1937), in which Céline established his polemic/propagandistic manner. Thanks to the work of Milton Hindus, Bettina Knapp, and, above all, François Gibault and Philippe Alméras, we have a fair understanding of the context of *Bagatelles* and the pathology of its writer. We can speak of the disposition inherited from his father, the petit bourgeois mentality, the political climate of the 1930s, the exposure to Henry Ford's theories, the reinforcement provided by friends, pressures felt at his workplace, and an apparently genuine and well-motivated fear of war. In *Bagatelles,* the Jew provided what a successful paranoia generally demands: a limited but vulnerable, socially convenient, and seemingly inexhaustible enemy. Our concern, however, will be with the rhetorical quality, the narrative substance, and the formal strategies devised to reshape the pamphlet form, that characteristically paranoid convention, into a balm capable of stilling the writer's unassuageable and previously unfocused angst.

For our purposes, *Bagatelles,* in conjunction with the *Féerie* sequence, constitutes a watershed between the more popular and accessible early and late manners. Together, they mark a radical shift in emphasis, a reification and redefinition of Céline's themes and tactics. Nowhere else do we see such a mini-maximizing of his devices: the radical paratactics, the diatribe, the clown act, paranoia as a presence and a trope, and the rhetorical catastrophe. Already in *Voyage,* he developed Robinson as Ferdinand's more paranoid alterego. Just about every page of *Mort à crédit* employs some rhetorical discontinuity, achieving its coherence against the grain of its transitionless and unhierarchical rhetorical procedures. The hysterical sequences spreading catastrophe across several pages of highly charged affective prose are only the most disturbingly delightful instances of its farcical overkill. The same may be said for the wartime *Guignol* novels and even the fragmentary and posthumously published "Cassepipe."

Still, it is in the *Bagatelles* that Céline's hyperparatactic style seems closest to being an integral mimesis of an unnamable outrage and despair, a mimesis and perhaps momentarily a cure. How else can we explain not only the embarrassment of the anti-Semitic ideologues of the time but also the most extreme of the discursive paratactics of the pamphlet, its small-arms chatter of sardonic tautologies? So powerful is the delineation of the anti-Semitic obsession that, when reading *Bagatelles,* one is reminded of Bruegel's splendidly macabre Triumph of Death in the Prado. There we see animated skeletons in every conceivable position and action, even in the act of half-shielding themselves with a mask of life. Like Bruegel's proliferating metaphor, Céline's associatively generated anti-Semitic assertions explode into discrete units of meaning, all pointing up the same message: the omnipresent and universal Jewish conspiracy, the Jew as the root of all social evils. Consistently, and with great rhetorical energy, they anatomize their topic before adding up to nothing more than their own tautological selves.

As previously mentioned, the pamphlet contributes several new

ingredients to a great tradition of pamphleteering. (It was a tradition mastered in the nineteenth century by at least one of his models, Jules Valles, who was, of all things, a left-wing pamphleteer
turned novelist. Valles's *L'Enfant* is an important inspiration for the
family portraits so tellingly employed in *Mort à crédit*.) Céline gives
his rhetoric a characteristic argotic twist, peppering the reader/vic-
tim/colleague with violent variations on a starkly limited theme, listing attributes, stereotypical clichés, elaborating profanities salted
with harsh irony and spleen, gingery with false sympathy, mass-cul-
tural catalogues that glow with rage and exuberance. To achieve the
impact, if not the precise grammar, of disruption, he breaks up his
sentences, which are often separated by his ellipses and punctuated
with exclamation points. The capacity of the words (even in my literal translation) to anger and amuse cannot be denied:

> You hype a Joseph Stalin like you do a Joan Crawford, same process,
> same gall, same con-job, same outrageous Jews pulling the strings. Be-
> tween Hollywood, Paris, New-York [sic] and Moscow nothing but a per-
> petual funny-fact factory. Even Charlie Chaplin gives his all, splendidly,
> to the cause, a great pioneer of Jewish imperialism. He's the big secret.
> Here's to good Jewish whining! Here's to the lament that works! Here's
> to immense lamentation! It softens all the good hearts, it topples with
> gold-power all walls. It makes all the goyish suckers even more weak-
> kneed, soppy, anti-prejudices, "humanitarian," that says it all, inter-na-
> tional . . . but I'm onto them! so they get propositioned! Jewish style! set
> up like bowling pins! In the sentimental muck the Jew cuts, slices, nib-
> bles, crumbles, poisons, prospers. The miseries of the exploited poor,
> the counter-jumpers at Bader's, the galley slave at Citroën, he should
> care, Chaplin, he should give a shit, with his millions. . . . Here's to the
> great jeremiad! Here's to modern times! Here's to the good Soviets, real
> yids! There's no fighting propaganda, you just have to spend enough
> gold . . . and the Jews own all the gold in the world . . . from the Urals to
> Alaska.[2]

With a few verifiable facts, rational arguments, no logical discourse, and plenty of redundancy, this text makes points by multiply-
ing myths, generating not-quite-synonyms, inventing side issues,
settling scores. (Strange that Chaplin, to whom Céline's farce owes
so much, should be a target. But then *The Great Dictator* had only
recently been released, and Céline must have felt betrayed.) The obvious effect is to immobilize the argument, turning a development
into a landscape or, at the very least, an important heap.

Bagatelles, though hardly monolithic, is an infinitely varied tan-
trum, a release of tension, a display of wild gestures implicating the

reader in language as both substance and action. Céline's "facts" are used to stun the adversary, but the attack on the reader through affective language is more immediate. Redundancy works for him precisely because he has "a way with words." He also has a way of seeming to uphold the "right," the moral. (See his condemnation of alcohol as the scourge of France, with the connivance of the Jews of course.) It will come as no surprise that Ezra Pound, who played some of the same tunes in his wartime broadcasts, loved Céline in his attack mode, singling him out for praise as a fellow truth-sayer.

Two other premonitory aspects of *Bagatelles* need emphasis. The first is its vestigial plotline. Céline, the master storyteller, motivates his harangue by pretending to hold a dialogue with a Jewish friend, whom he subjects to a barrage of insults larded with cordiality. The second is the anomalous inclusion of the curious "ballets," scenarios dedicated to an ephemeral and faeric fancy that seems to extend (and soften) the spirit of Bardamu's romance of *le roi* Krogold in *Mort à crédit*. A final noteworthy detail: it is in the pamphlets that the writer first abandons his fictional protagonist and his pseudonym, Ferdinand Bardamu, speaking directly as Dr. Destouches.

Céline's behavior after *Bagatelles* and during the war suggests that, for a time, he believed in the efficacy of the pamphlets, their capacity to destroy, if not the Jews, at least his demons. If so, he was doubly, perhaps even triply, disappointed: first, by the negative response of the Nazis; then by the postwar accusations of collaboration and prosecution; finally, by the fact that such outpourings of bile did not calm the inner turmoil that elicited them. It should be noted that he was psychologically incapable of devoting himself to any cause other than peace, that eventually he was bound to offend the authorities even while supporting them. He could not be kept in line. During the Danish exile, at a time when his future was still uncertain, his publisher (Gallimard) encouraged him to return to his fiction. By that time his anxieties had fulfilled themselves. It was natural, if only for that reason, that something significant happened to his fiction; it turned almost completely in on itself. The result was a double novel in which the need for self-exculpation is translated into an elaborate attack/defense, a novel in which the dominant discursive procedure is a parataxis that undermines and explodes syntactical hierarchies, a narrative whose plot is vestigial, and whose form is forbidding, in a context that combines theatricality and verbal spectacle.[3]

In the first volume of *Féerie*, we find Céline/Destouches shadowboxing with a hoard of absent antagonists, embodiments of a France out after his "collaborating" hide. For the first time in his fiction,

he uses his real name and recites something approximating the biographical, though still distorting historical truth; this fact underscores the curious inverse equivalence of pamphlet and novel and
prefigures the "chronicles" to come.

Féerie is a paired sequence dealing with the Destouches's precari-
ous situation in Montmartre in the days immediately preceding their
flight with the Vichy government through Germany to Sigmaringen
and then, alone, toward Denmark. Unlike the hyperactive earlier
and later fictions, it is a curiously static narrative. Most of the action
is contained in or unleashed by the rhetoric. Indeed, two-thirds of
the first volume is given over to the incarcerated Doctor's attempt
to win reader sympathy without losing self-respect or moderating his
vituperative tone. Although the death-row prisoner's associative discourse is hardly dull, its narrative is no more than a pretext: the visit
to the Destouches's apartment by Clémence Arlon, the wife of an
estranged friend. (This tactic owes something to the far shorter pre-
ludes of the earlier books, and it was even longer and certainly
richer in memories and action in the early draft in which it also
opens. Some of that material was recycled for the lengthy overture
to *D'un chateau l'autre*.) Like *Bagatelles*, but with something resem-
bling novelistic decorum, *Féerie* is characterized by a flood of images
and allegations that anesthetizes the intellect, contributing to the
text's power to badger us.

If we are initially amused by the speaker's inventiveness, by the
seemingly boundless mass of details and metaphors, we may soon
experience a mild anxiety, a dizziness, and even a need to conciliate,
to mollify his speaking text. (As in *Bagatelles*, the novel's rhetoric is
relentlessly oral and present.) Céline has managed, however, in
Féerie's diatribe/soliloquy to reverse the tactics of his pamphlets, retaining the basic metanarrative procedure and expanding the para-
tactic rhetoric. He does so while refocusing his rage and casting
himself in the triple role of malefactor/victim/assailant, a role that
combines that of the Jew with that of his attacker in *Bagatelles*. After
the war, the Holocaust had the effect of turning Céline himself into
a static embodiment of the wandering Jew and the ultimate Sebastian. All things considered, the narrative strategy is brilliant, since it
enables the writer to convict the French for hypocrisy while revealing the scabs on his own body and soul and revelling in an orgy of
unrepentent self-pity. The victimization parallels his earlier self-por-
traits, but the circumstances are no longer neutral enough to guar-
antee reader sympathy, at least at first, and the narrative occupies
the time of its telling even when it toys with the flashback. The normal
French reader of the postwar period would find the strident con-

demnation of his countrymen's behavior and the groans and whines antipathetic.

Céline's ability to combine disgust, anger, absurdity, frenzy, and rage with farce has not vanished, but it has been transformed. In the first place, no distance exists between the narrator and the events he describes, none between him and the moods he generates. The innocent, whose painful experiences are recounted with astonishing immediacy in the early novels by the jaundiced and violent voice of experience, has found his voice—that of the violent other. We should note that those earlier novels, and the novels that follow *Féerie,* all usually opened with an overture in the present tense before retreating to the past, from which the present has emerged. In each case, the present tense voice of Bardamu retreats quickly from the scene to become the source of the rhetoric that animates the experiences of a younger Bardamu. Beginning with the pamphlets, and leap-frogging the wartime novels of the *Guignol's Band* sequence, the pseudonymous author, who in true paranoid fashion (Sebastian already?) feared exposure when he wrote his first novel, while still writing under his penname, used his real name. Ferdinand Destouches was the first-person presence in *Bagatelles* and the other pamphlets, a persona both confident and versatile. In *Féerie* he still addresses us, but he speaks from his Danish prison cell; he has become a frightened, endangered, and spurned persona fighting despair and desperately attacking all and sundry in the present tense. Exceptionally, the novel begins with a flashback and moves to the present in an extraordinary and formally revolutionary diatribe. Rather than crafting an elaborate and surprisingly nuanced attack on Jews and related evils, Dr. Destouches is now attempting the impossible: clearing his name as writer while bemoaning his typically exaggerated and distorted current situation. He lashes out randomly at those who would condemn him for the behavior that got him where he is or those who force him once more to sing for his supper. The tactic is counterintuitive, but by virtue of Céline's current mode of self-abasement, it comes close to achieving its goal, especially when Jules, the legless and lubricious symbol of French resistance, is brought in as a foil.

Conversely, we may ask whether he sincerely wished to succeed, whether self-abasement had its own psychological rewards for him at that time. Was the admittedly muted, confessional mode, couched though it is in defensive language, more than strategic? Were the attacks carried out from a position of weakness on France and the French in some way provocations of opprobrium? It is impossible to say.

One thing is clear, however. Céline challenged his readers in the
first volume of his defense, that unrelenting mass of only barely narrative text. It is a whine and groan that may at first seem intermina-
ble, but one that finally intrigues and satisfies, drawing the reader,
who does not abandon it, through the wall into the web of words.[4]
It is there that, through the variety of its effects and its mastery of
style, the text succeeds at seduction even when it does not win ap-
proval. As usual, Céline's urgency is itself its own reward.

Like the pamphlet, the novel is by turns slyly ironic, bombastic,
hyperbolic, cruelly comic, and openly jaundiced, and at times per-
versely tender. Unlike it, and like the earlier fictions, it is hallucina-
tory and explosive, but above all it is a rhetorical tour de force.
Those of us who continue to read may be held not so much by a
promise of plot as by rhythmic echo, attitudinal variety, and the rhetoric, which, for all its excesses, is frequently as tensely muted and
hysterically controlled as is this snippet from the opening pages:

> Creatures act in the same way at the same time . . . the same ticks. . . .
> Like the little ducks around their mother in the parc Daumesnil, in the
> Bois de Boulogne, all together, head right . . . head left! whether they be
> ten! . . . twelve . . . fifteen! . . . same thing! all heads right! synchronized!
> Clémence Arlon sideeyes me . . . it's the times . . . Had she ten . . . twelve
> . . . fifteen sons . . . they'd sideeye in the same way! . . . I'm known as a
> notorious bribe-taker, traitor, crook, who's going to be assassinated, to-
> morrow . . . the day after . . . in eight days . . . that fascinates them from
> the bias the traitor. . . .[5]

In this exceptionally mild passage, the motif of threat is developed
in terms of ducklike, and therefore deceptively innocent, antagonism. Destouches, the poor and vulnerable clown, is put upon by a
mass of inoffensive normal citizens; the frustrated shepherd is
mowed down by a herd of sheep. Céline's rhetoric is mildly paratac-
tic, heavily accented; the attitude is an unstable blend of bemused
humor and stoic paranoia. Parataxis, humor, and paranoia, in varying degrees, are the staples in *Féerie* as in the similarly plotless pamphlets. The difference is of course in the targets and in the
particular development of Céline's rhetorical attack and the perceived nature of the attacker.

The violent pamphleteer has become the victim of an excoriated
French hypocrisy, a figure whose merits are, at first, difficult to discern. Though his rhetorical resources are astonishing, the portrait
he paints is of an unrepentent, hostile, querulous, decrepit, self-pity-
ing paranoid, a poisonous presence who blames others for all his

misfortunes. The tactic pays off later when Dr. Destouches is portrayed as a truer supporter of French values than either of his opposite-equivalents: Jules, the amputee, or Normance, the dead Halles porter whose blood washes over the second volume as symbol of a martyred France.

Two-thirds of the way through the first volume, the scene changes abruptly when Destouches's mind leaps from the claustrophobic cell back to a Paris of pantomime and ballet, a universe in which the now inoffensive doctor plays a passive voyeur, a Pierrot offended by a malevolent Harlequin/Punch. If, as I believe, *Féerie* can be read as an allegory of occupied and liberated France, the shift from claustrophobic cell-cave to sunlit Paris graphically illustrates its central destabilizing strategy. We are suddenly treated to a portrait of a consummate reprobate, in the legless, lecherous, vile-tempered, irrepressibly foul-mouthed clown: the sculptor Jules. Though seemingly a narrative, this passage is little more than an extended profile and an extension of the prisoner's meditation. Jules is a splendid monster, a happy cripple etched in harsh prose against a background of beautiful dancing legs. He appears literally out of the hallucinated context from which Destouches emerges onto the streets of Paris as if returning physically to the *fin de guerre*.

This "clown en caisse" holds the center of the stage for the rest of this volume. His gross, antisocial, comic act provides more than a lift for the reader's flagging spirits, however. Jules functions as the anti-Destouches, a vicious, vengeful, and hyperactive plastic artist vs. a silently suffering, if inwardly vituperative, collabo novelist. Art is, after all, at the center of this allegory in which writing cedes center stage to painting, dance, and, ultimately, spectacle. Here we find a last echo of the pamphlet mode with its broad and crude categories. We may read Destouches's wife, Lili, as an embodiment of the cleansing spirit disclosed by the ballet scenarios of *Bagatelles*. Indeed, this is the role she shares with the Destouches's much-traveled cat in the postwar trilogy: *D'un chateau l'autre*, *Nord*, and *Rigodon*.

Of course, paranoia is not susceptible to easy cures. Even palliation has its costs. Doubtless, Céline wrote in part because he needed money. He may even have gotten some profound pleasure or relief from self-expression. Driven as he was by the nagging power of his anger, anguish, and unrepentent guilt, it seems that ultimately he had no choice but to write; nothing he had written or would write could assuage present torment, and he was, even at his most catastrophically comic, subject to forces similar to the constant buzzing sound (*"bourdonnements"*) he claimed echoed in his head as a result of the wound he received in World War I.[6] Finally, despite evidence that he was aware of himself, intractable, and even paranoid, it made no difference whether he reacted as a Harlequin (Mars) or a Pierrot (Sebastian). He craved an adequate focus for his anxieties, a way to say them over and over again forcefully, artfully, aiming at an unachievable catharsis. Céline, like all the artists in the Janus-faced class I have been describing, must draw his satisfaction not only from the power and efficiency of his verbal action, but also from the *pains* he takes and receive's with/from expression, the barriers he himself has erected to completion, to the end-stopping period of his prose/ poetry. In this sense, the act of writing itself becomes the obstacle-in-progress. It is of this complex dynamic that Céline is a sublime and troubling illustration.

Notes

1. Very early on, he feared the consequences of the attacks he made on French society in *Voyage au bout de la nuit*. Witness his use of a pseudonym and the preface he added to the postwar edition.

2. *Bagatelles pour un massacre*, (Paris: Denoël, Paris, 1937), 38–39.

3. In the second draft of *Féerie pour une autre fois* (see *Maudits soupirs pour une autre fois: Une version primitive de* Féerie pour une autre fois, ed. Henry Godard [Paris: Gallimard, 1985]), the anguish and violence, the verbal rhythms, the Paris setting, and the major actors have been mobilized, but the focus is radically different. Before he finished revising, Céline reversed his procedures, altering in the process the structure, tone, and hence the impact while deleting a huge amount of background material, including the details of the Paris setting. His most brilliant and telling decision was to turn a rational narrative development on its head, filling fully two-thirds of the first volume with the hectic monologue of Destouches as the underground man. Hence Destouches is bounded on one side by the visit of a predatory friend and on the other by the semi-allegorical antics of an unconscionable clown.

4. To appreciate the revolutionary nature of this procedure, one has only to compare the *Féerie* monologue with the next necessary step: the voice of Samuel Beckett's Unnamable in *Texts for Nothing*, another great breakthrough novel in the Sebastian mode.

5. Louis-Ferdinand Céline, *Féerie pour une autre fois* (Paris: Gallimard, 1952), 11–12. My translation. Note the care Céline takes with timing, gesture (both physical and verbal), and punctuation. Typical also is that this comic but ominous passage should be followed by an equally comic description of Clémence's son.

6. On this topic, see Philippe Alméras's fine biographical study, which cuts through much of the confusion created by Céline's fabri-fictions. (*Céline: entre haines et passions* [Paris: Robert Laffont, 1994], 42.)

Writing to Overcome (Escribir superar): Luisa Valenzuela

DEBRA A. CASTILLO

THE FINAL STORY IN LUISA VALENZUELA'S 1975 COLLECTION, *AQUÍ pasan cosas raras (Strange Things Happen Here)*, is a chilling autobiographical fantasy about the role of writing, and of the writer, in a police state. The story, "El lugar de su puietud" ("The Place of Its Quietude"), is one of a series of stories written by Valenzuela upon her relatively brief return to Argentina just before the crackdown that led to the "dirty war" (1976–1983) begun under Jorge Rafael Videla's regime and waged against Argentina's citizens by its military. Presciently, the weight of the coming period of oppression already saturates these stories. The collection as a whole points to the terror perpetuated by the government and at the same time to the complacency of Argentine citizenry that allowed all the worst human rights violations to continue unabated for years. Such an environment compels the writer to speak out. Says Valenzuela in an interview, "Politics has forced itself on us . . . the time comes when you can't detach yourself from it, the horror was so great that it is worse to keep quiet" (García Pinto 232).

"Horror," "detachment," and "quietude" are all key words in this literary-political enterprise, for if Valenzuela cannot separate herself from the ongoing state terror, in her narrative practice her protagonists are often strangely detached from the horrors around them. Thus, for example, "The Place of Its Quietude" offers an ironic and apparently contemplative commentary both on the thin veneer of organized calm overlying massive violence as well as on the inevitable outcome of that violence: the quietude of death. At the very end of her book *Powers of Horror*, Julia Kristeva asks herself a question highly pertinent to Valenzuela's work: "Is it the quiet shore of contemplation that I set aside for myself, as I lay bare, under the cunning, orderly surface of civilizations, the nurturing horror that they attend to pushing aside by purifying, systematizing, thinking; the horror that they seize on in order to build themselves

175

up and function?" She answers her question: "I rather conceive it as a work of disappointment, of frustration, and hollowing—probably the only counterweight to abjection. While everything else—its archeology and its exhaustion—is only literature . . ." (210). Valenzuela too knows of the work of disappointment, the fury and frustration of hollowing out an as-yet-undefined space for difference. But "only" literature? For a woman living in a context of daily horrors that operate on a far more literal level than those suggested in *Powers of Horror,* Valenzuela likely would find Kristeva's echo of Verlaine's famous line almost unbearably precious and conventionally intertextual. I suspect that Valenzuela would say, rather, that everything—the horrifying surface of civilization and its counterpart, abjection—is itself countered by the force of literature. Despite her stories' highly ironic surface tranquility, Valenzuela reminds us that her work derives not from a quiet shore, but rather from the experience of trying to process and understand horror when it is itself laid bare, rather than masked under an orderly, civilized veneer: "I went back . . . in 1975, upon returning to my city after a long absence to find it wasn't mine any longer. Buenos Aires belonged then to violence and to state terrorism" *(Open Door* viii). Her project in this book is apparently contemplative, ultimately contestatory.

Yet, as is typical of all Valenzuela's work, such calls to arms are issued diffidently and ambiguously. "The Place of Its Quietude" operates as if it were written from an impossible "quiet shore of contemplation" and concludes with a writer's meditation on the role of writing in a police state: "If they [the people in the interior] go on writing they may someday reach the present and overcome it, in all meanings of the verb *to overcome:* leave it behind them, modify it, and with a little luck even improve it." ("Escribiendo sin descanso puede que [los del interior] algún día alcancen el presente y lo superen, en todos los sentidos del verbo superar: que lo degen atrás, lo modifiquen y hasta con un poco de suerte lo mejoren" 139, 134).[1] The charge of this story hinges upon the minuscule gap between writing "to overcome" (a literary project) and writing to overcome oppression (a political effort). At the same time, the story encodes two different types of such writing; one, by the unnamed Luisa Valenzuela–like narrator, is a private project, a phosphorescent, forbidden writing in the dark intended for no audience but the author herself with the intention of narrativizing her experience and so to comprehend her personal fear. The other writing to overcome, that theorized in the hypothetical existence of a writing authored by "them" from the interior, is imagined as a public rehistoricization that will redirect the nation's understanding of itself.

At the same time, the effect of this story's performance of its own literariness operates in the exchange between these two writers and two audiences, as well as two meaning structures captured in the conjunction of "to write" and "to overcome" and, with the Spanish text at least, in the ubiquity of subjunctive verb constructions that implicitly cast both the act of writing and that of overcoming into a hypothetical and contingent mode. The subjective mood tradition-ally recalls a history of such relational states—linguistic and social—ordered and arranged according to a well-defined institutional hierarchy: of the sentence, of the society. ("Subjunctive: Mood of the verb that indicates an action is conceived as subordinate to an-other, as doubtful, possible, or desired" [*Larousse*]. "Subjunctive: That which is subjoined or dependent; designating a mood the forms of which are employed to denote an action or state as con-ceived [and not as fact] and therefore used to express a wish, a com-mand, exhortation, or a contingent, hypothetical, or prospective event" *(The Oxford English Dictionary)*. The subjunctive, then, has no independent existence in standard grammar; it is other-directed in the modes of request, subordinated in complex structures as a reac-tion or as a secondary action existing only in relation to some other act.

Such a tight coupling reminds us that the narrative exchange never opens itself to simplistic politics nor to recuperation in the service of any national allegorical construction, however defined. This is particularly true in countries like Argentina, where tight cen-sorship along implicit knowledge of state abuses have put extreme pressure on such formulations. Marta Morello-Frosch has pointed out that the ritual exercise of rhetorical appeals to national solidar-ity not only furthers the political agenda of the repressive state appa-ratus in maintaining the status quo, but also paradoxically helps cover over the gaps and resistances "where practical control is lack-ing but deemed necessary" (691). While "The Place of Its Qui-etude" points ineluctably to the operation of the militaristic state apparatus, it also reminds us of the subtle perversities of national allegorical constructions that legitimize extraordinary violence against its own citizens as an inalienable right: what Valenzuela de-scribes in the story as the "Gobierno" (government with a capitol "g"), the shadowy presence authorizing "the usual shootings, police raids, customary patrols" ("los consabidos tiroteos, alguna que otra razzia policial, los patrullajes de siempre" 130, 123). Valenzuela's marking of the "usual" and the "ordinary" in this quote rubs against a formulation that is anything but, and reminds us how the Government manipulates certain kinds of ritual discourse in an attempt to tranquilize the general population and forward its own political purposes.

In this story, the shadowy response to a shadowed violence comes in the form of another ritual response: the city fills gradually with the sounds of indigenous flutes and the smell of burning incense issuing from unidentifiable sources. As the ubiquity of both the police sirens and of the counterritual flutes impinges ever more forcefully on people's daily lives, the effort to maintain neutrality also wears thin, and the veneer of detachment reveals itself as an inadequate mask: "Nothing to fear. The escalation of violence only touches those who are looking for it, not us humble citizens who don't allow ourselves so much as a wry face or the least sign of discontent." ("Nada hay que temer. La escalada de violencia sólo alcanza a los que la buscan, no a nosotros humildes ciudadanos que no nos permitimos ni una mueca de discontento ni la menor señal de descontento" 133, 127.) Here the closed system of official discourse ("nothing to fear") serves as a shield or mask for the citizens, who cower under its inadequate protection in the hope that the (officially nonexistent) violence will pass them by.

Inelectuably then, both state discourse and rebellious response are tightly imbricated in analogous ritual actions. Insofar as they appeal to ritual, both discourses stand only outside the historical implications of the inscription by those from the interior who are writing in this threshold moment but also against it, to overturn the state's official discourse. All the while, they are taking care that this overcoming is not just another renegotiation of tired concepts but also a strategic operation to usher in a reconceptualization as well as a reinscription of the national project. The narrator's appeal to these others, and to another writing, suggests as well that at some point in this process the individual narrative becomes a collective understanding and that her tardily admitted fear has an objective form. Writing, then, points toward another kind of action rather than a ritual by which fear can be comprehended.

Inevitably, the individual's inability to admit to a fear that might isolate her from the rest of the citizenry and so place her life in danger gives way to a collective recognition of a shared societal nightmare: We might speak of sensorial or ideological infiltration, if in some remote corner of our national being we didn't feel that it's for our own good—a form of redemption. And this vague sensation restores to us the luxury of being afraid." ("Podríamos hablar de penetración sensorial e ideológica si en algún remoto rincón de nuestro ser nacional no sintiéramos que es para nuestro bien, que alguna forma de redención nos ha de llegar de ellos. Y esta vaguísima esperanza nos devuele el lujo de tener miedo" 134, 128.) In this recognition, the citizenry at large rejects the official discourse of a peaceful state where well-meaning citizens have nothing to fear. Instead, Valenzuela projects a fragile, newly consolidated sense of a national being excluding the official Government and defined by a fear of its actions. Paradoxically, people are experiencing that fear as a form of redemption, even though their fear is never expressed openly but remains "behind closed doors, silent, barren, with a low vibration that emerges in fits of temper on the streets or conjugal violence at home" ("un miedo a puertas cerradas, silencioso, estéril, de vibración muy baja que se traduce en iras callejeras o en arranques de violencia conyugal" (134, 128).

Ironically, fear itself serves as the occasion for salvation, for recuperation of a sense of self. The narrator speaks of the ubiquity of disappearances and torture, of the individual bad dream becoming a collective nightmare, of the familiar yet alien rituals of flute and copal incense, only to conclude: "None of that can save us. Perhaps only fear, a little fear that makes us see our urban selves clearly." ("Nada de todo esto podrá salvarnos. Quizá tan sólo el miedo, un poco de miedo que nos haga ver claro a nosotros los hombres de la ciudad" 135, 129.) Interestingly enough, fear and hope are reborn together out of the disjunction between Government rhetoric evoking the sacred truths of national culture and the sensed reality of Government actions, out of the reappearance of indigenous ritual as an oppositional force, even if its pertinence for national life, and especially urban life in the capital city, remains unresolved. The return of fear motivates the hope that some redemption can derive from the new sense of national self constituted in and by the impact of state terror. This is precisely the import of Fernanco Ainsa's observation that "the power, the courage to rise up against fear emerges from the knowledge and the recovery of memory. . . . What can one do, however, so that memory does not disappear with life itself? How can one make it 'stick' and last, so that it becomes a testimony that is transmitted and remembered years later? There is only one answer, and it seems clear: in order to last, memories must be fixed in the written word" (689). Out of the anguish produced by ambiguity about the signs of fear come the resurgence of hope and a fragile new sense of a national project that can speak and write, if only in a tentative manner, of overcoming and modifying the present by rewriting it from the inside out; if not now, then soon; if not here, then someplace nearby. Ainsa concludes: "Thus, if literature requires fear, this is because it is not possible to write without fear, or because all memory is forever made up of those fragments that will not succumb to definitive silence" (690).

It is, of course, as the last sentence of the story reminds us, a "question of language" ("Es cuestión de lenguaje" 139, 134). This too suggests a reconstitution, a recuperation or reinvention of what Valenzuela has described under the general term of myth. "I write myths," says Valenzuela in an interview, "in order to reinvent myths" (Ordóñez 518). In this story, too, a problematized and remotivated myth serves as the crucial figure for change. In meditating on the monumental task before the hypothetical writers from the interior, the narrator of this story reminds herself that she must have patience, for "they have to go a long way back in time to arrive at the origin of the myth, dust the cobwebs off it, and demythicize it (in order to restore to the truth its essence . . .)" ("van a tener que remontarse tan profundamente en el tiempo para llegar hasta la base del mito y quitarles las telarañas y demitificarlo [para devolverle a esa verdad su esencis . . .]" 138, 132). Writing to overcome is a tedious and painstaking process, one both outside the workings of state power and located deeply within it—inhabiting its interior, its collective heart, and the byways of its blood. From the place of horror derives the space of quietude; "they" are "us," and "we" becomes "I." Once the sirens and the flutes have fallen silent, the tear gas and the copal incense blown away, then and only then will the writers from the interior come into their own; their writing can only overcome the future once it has already overcome the past.

The narrator of "The Place of Its Quietude" has a secretive compulsion to leave her own record of these events on the phosphorescent board she has created so as to scribble down her fragmentary tales late at night, in the dark. Her stories, "The Best Shod," "The Gift of Words," and so on, are all titles of stories included in this volume by Luisa Valenzuela, *Strange Things Happen Here*, the same collection in which "The Place of Its Quietude" is the final story. Ostensibly, this Luisa Valenzuela–like narrator leaves the task of writing for the future to those other writers, the posited people in the interior, who are compiling more complete histories of current events, and through whose efforts present horrors may be modified or overcome. The character in this story can only hypothesize the existence of these other writers; her project, like that of Valenzuela's book as a whole, is located *in medias res*. The narrator, writing secretly in the dark, calls her work a "modest contribution and I hope it never gets into the hands of readers" ("un aporte muy modesto y además espero que nunca llegue a manos de lector alguno" 139, 133). She writes in silence and against silence, in the dark and in phosphorescent colors, writing through and of her own fear, and in fear of the potential audience of readers comprising agents of the police state who could well make her disappear for the transgressive nature of her writings. Yet, of course, the words written against the fear of the enemy reader are those very tales we have nearly finished perusing; the narrator's personal writing to understand and to overcome her own fear collapses with the more general political intent of those verbs.

Thus, the narrator's reasons for undertaking this solitary and silent task echo Luisa Valenzuela's commentary in a 1994 interview with Gwendolyn Díaz: "I had to confront the horror because it was the only way I had of not continuing to be terrified. Now I believe I do the same in writing. It is a recognition of fear and a confrontation with it so as to see what it is about and of what it is made." ("Iba a enfrentar el horror porque era la única manera que tenía yo de no seguir aterrada. Ahora creo que hago lo mismo escribiendo. Es un reconociemiento del miedo y un enfrentamiento con él para ver de qué se trata y de que está hecho" 45.) In "The Place of Its Quietude," the narrator notes: "Though I'm quiet these days, I go on jotting it all down in bold strokes (and at great risk) because it's the only form of freedom left us." ("Yo, cada vez más calladita, sigo anotando todo esto aún a grandes rasgos [¡grandes riesgos!] porque es la única forma de libertad que nos queda" 138, 133.) We have writing about writing here, and about writing this story in particular, but we also have the displacement back and forth from plural "we" to the singular "I." Notable narrative stumblings can be seen in this respect, from the "we" who fear, to the "I" who serves as fear's particular expression: "It's true that we are—I am—afraid." ("Cierto que tenemos—tengo—miedo" 137, 132.) This narrative "I" materializes the memory of that fear in the individual's secret storywriting, and does so as an expression of a more generalized sense of "our" possibilities for a mediated sense of freedom.

Strangely enough, writing in the dark allows the narrator to throw off other narrative disguises, including—eventually—that of gender as well as point of view: "I have no fear of playing their game or giving them ideas. I can even do away with the subterfuge of referring to myself in the plural or the masculine. I can be myself" ("no temo estar haciéndoles el juego ni dándoles ideas. Hasta puedo dejar el subterfugio de hablar de mí en plural o en masculino. Puedo ser yo" 137, 132). The shift from "we" to "I" implies a specifically feminine take on these questions, positing that in these narrative exchanges between "we" and "they," between the capital and the interior, between the police state and the countervaling indigenous rituals the first-person female narrator appropriates—to borrow a term from Ruth Salvaggio—her pivot point. Salvaggio writes: "There is not a subject continually reaching for an object, not the one eternally in quest of the other. Instead, women write the unhinging of this dangerous pivot. Subject meets subject not at a closed door, but at the frame where the door opens" (160). In an analogous use of the same metaphor of the door, Anne McLeod describes the effects of feminism for women as a process of unhinging, of imagining "antithetical relations between the arts in such a way that the ontological framework within which they have been thought comes unhinged" (59). To the degree that the feminine "I" serves as the story's pivot, and is, by the semi-autobiographical quality of the tale also revealed as the secret narrative pivot of the other stories as well, the project of writing to overcome is already encoded in these apparently preliminary hinge texts of an incipient dirty war.

At the same time, Valenzuela is less certain, or perhaps less optimistic, than Salvaggio and McLeod; for her, to dislocate narrative frames may offer new vistas; it also risks unhinging in the second, colloquial sense of madness. It is no coincidence that she has chosen *Open Door* as the title for the U.S. reissue of these stories in English; as she reminds us in the prologue to the volume, "Open Door" is literally "the name of the most traditional, least threatening lunatic asylum in Argentina" (viii).[2] At the same time, if "Open Door" evokes a nonthreatening lunacy, it also reminds us of the ritual of asylum in the other sense, as a place of refuge from unlawful terror. The actual Argentine asylum is located outside Luján, near the capital city of Buenos Aires but already at the threshold of the interior; it too is a hinge site framing the social body and projecting a ritual of retirement and return.

It is wholly to be expected in such a context that the hinging, or unhinging, of narrative in "The Place of Its Quietude" rests on the act of writing itself. At the same time, in contrast with another of Valenzuela's hermetic tales from this volume, "Camino al ministerio" ("On the Way to the Ministry"), in which "the protagonist's itinerary figures the motion of the text and the only story that such a writing can tell, is the story of its own materialization and displacements" (Guitiérrez Mouat 715); in this story the literalization of the act of writing offers two models: in one the peculiar intertextuality consumes itself in its foregrounding of the writing process; in another Valenzuela points to the heuristic potential of the nonallegorical writing about writing as a personal and political effort to overcome the limitations encoded in the rituals of government and the formal rigors of grammatical narrative structure. Gutiérrez Mouat writes perceptively: "much of Valenzuela's writing is generated by the literal interpretation of tropes, a strategy that exploits the gap between the proper and the figurative meaning of words and that implies the subversion of representation" (709). I would add that Valenzuela's practice not only exploits gaps/thresholds of various sorts, including that of literalizing tropes, but also valorizes the strategic displacement/unhinging of a propensity to organize discourse around seemingly incontestable structures.

It is above all to assert the *différance* in her words, differing from and deferring to the language of patriarchy as she defers her definition of it. Margo Glantz asks whether such subtle games of appropriation, literalization, and censorship might not at some level mask textually the idea of failure (25). I prefer to figure her practice in Valenzuela's own self-effacing circuitous terms: "I believe in the existence of a feminine language, even though it may not yet have been completely defined, and even though the boundary between it and the other language . . . may be too subtle and ambiguous to be delineated" ("Word" 96). This feminine language is ambiguously marked in the collection of short stories, *Strange Things Happen Here;* only in "The Place of Its Quietude," and only as a by-product of a writerly fantasy, does the final text in the volume force a reevaluation of the narrative stance in the rest of the stories. Valenzuela's narrator in this story—gendered female and author of numerous well-known Valenzuela fictions—becomes the only source of information about the shadowy "los del interior" who write in splendid isolation from the horrors (of the horrors) in the capital city, and whose texts are eternally unavailable to the reader of this book.

Fellow Argentine novelist Julio Cortázar once said of Valenzuela: "To read her is to enter our reality fully" (quoted Magnarelli 157)—perhaps (given Cortázar's well-known gender bias) more fully than he imagined, and with a more expansive understanding of the word "our." Valenzuela's literary practice challenges readers to rethink the category of the woman as discursive subject/object outside the essentialist frame into which she has so traditionally been cast, as she also forces us to return to a question relative to the field of literary study at large—that of the struggle with and against the power of words. In putting pressure on the doubled verbs—"escribir superar," writing to overcome—Valenzuela suggests not only a model for revitalizing national myth, but also a method for dislocating the hinge between linguistic and extralinguistic binaries such as the one that has exercised us over the last few pages. These insights are not the least of her contributions to international literary studies.

Notes

1. Page numbers within the text cite first the English translation, then the Spanish edition.
2. Mariano Plotkin reminds us that in the Argentine context the use of this metaphor is particularly resonant because of the deep penetration of psychoanalysis into the national culture. Argentina is a well-known international center of psychoanalysis, so much so that political speeches are frequently laden with psychoanalytically derived terms. For example, in his speech of April 25, 1995, apologizing for the military's role in the dirty war, General Martín Balza spoke of "the collective unconscious" and the need to "work through mourning" (271).

Works Cited

Ainsa, Fernando. "Journey to Luisa Valenzuela's Land of Fear." *World Literature Today*. 69.4 (1995): 683–90.

Díaz, Gwendolyn. "Entrevista con Luisa Valenzuela, Emory University, Atlanta, 1994," in Gwendolyn Díaz y María Inés Lagos, ed. *La palabra en vilo: Narrativa de Luisa Valenzuela*. Santiago de Chile: Cuarto Propio, 1996: 27–52.

García Pinto, Magdalena. *Historias íntimas: Conversaciones con diez escritoras latinoamericanas*. Hanover, N.H.: Ediciones del norte, 1988.

Glantz, Margo. "Reflexiones sobre *Simetrías*," in Gwendolyn Díaz and María Inés Lagod, ed., *La palabra en vilo: Narrativo de Luisa Valenzuela*. Santiago de Chile: Cuarto Propio, 1996: 247–52.

Gutiérrez Mouat, Ricardo. "Luisa Valenzuela's Literal Writing." *World Literature Today*. 69.4 (1995): 709–16.

Kristeva, Julia. *Powers of Horror: An Essay on Abjection*. Trans. Leon S. Roudiez. New York: Columbia University Press, 1982.

Magnarelli, Sharon. "Women, Discourse, and Politics in the Works of Luisa Valenzuela." *Antipodas*. 6–7 (1994–95): 157–71.

McLeod, Anne. "Gender Difference Relativity in GDR-Writing or: How to Oppose Without Really Trying." *Oxford Literary Review* 7 (1985): 41–61.

Morello-Frosch, Marta. "The Subversion of Ritual in Luisa Valenzuela's *Other Weapons*." *World Literature Today*. 69.4 (1995): 691–96.

Ordóñez, Monserrat. "Máscara de espejos, un juego especular: Entrevista-asociaciones con la escritora argentina Luisa Valenzuela." *Revista iberoamericana*. 51 (1985): 511–17.

Plotkin, Mariano. "The Diffusion of Psychoanalysis in Argentina." *Latin American Research Review*. 32.2 (1998): 271–77.

Salvaggio, Ruth. "Psychoanalysis and Deconstruction and Woman," in Richard Feldstein and Henry Sussman, ed., *Psychoanalysis and—*. New York: Routledge, Chapman and Hall, 1990: 151–60.

Valenzuela, Luisa. *Aquí pasan cosas raras*. Buenos Aires: Ed. de la Flor, 1975. Trans. Helen Lane as *Strange Things Happen Here*. New York: Harcourt, Brace, Jovanovich, 1979, and reprinted in *Open Door*. San Francisco: North Point Press, 1988.

———. "The Word, that Milk Cow," in Doris Meyer and Margarite Fernández Olmos, ed., *Contemporary Women Authors of Latin America*. 2 vols. New York: Brooklyn College Press, 1983: 96–97.

Ethnicity and Authenticity: Wilson Harris and Other "Black" Writing

MARK WILLIAMS

WILSON HARRIS'S FICTION IS GENERALLY ENCOUNTERED IN COURSES IN post-colonial literature; sometimes he is taught as a Caribbean writer. In the United States, where the term "African American" is sometimes considered to include black Caribbean writing, he is honored by a special issue of the journal *Callaloo*. As a long-time British resident, he might be regarded as a black British or an expatriate Guyanese writer. These problems with the definition of the author are compounded by those associated with the writing, which is even more resistant to categorization. Is his fiction modernist or post-modernist? None of these competing terms seems entirely satisfactory, although each explains some aspect of his work. My purpose here is not to resolve this problem by arguing for any single category, but to point to the limitations of consigning a writer as curious and as distinctive as Harris to *any* category and to relate the elusiveness of his writing to the situation of the novel in the post-colonial world.

I do not mean that we should pretend that Harris is *sui generis* as a writer, and that questions of influence, tradition, and antecedents are merely irrelevant. Nor do I mean to imply that nothing is to be achieved by acknowledging that Harris's thought and writing arise from and have been shaped by the historical and social conditions he shares with other writers from the Caribbean region. To deny that something useful in literary and literary-historical terms is achieved by locating writers within racial, national, or religious categories would be foolish. Great caution, however, must be exercised in the process. Our categories should be open, flexible, nuanced, and subject to continual revision. This is particularly the case with Harris, whose thought, "like the linguistic fabric of his prose," as Hena Maes-Jelinek has argued, "defies categorization."[1]

The difficulties involved in associating Harris as a writer with terms such as modern, post-colonial, or, most problematically,

"black," go to the heart of the multiple problems involved in reading and attempting to make sense of his work. It is Harris's ability to
slip away from his readers whenever they feel they have at last seized
the essence of his work, and encountered and understood the vision
that lies behind it, that interests me. This elusiveness runs counter
to the view of him as a Blakean seer, whose vision of reality transformed by the imagination is plain, however impenetrable the prose
in which it is conveyed.

Harris is one of those rare writers in whose work difficulty is
wholly justified because it is never mannerism or affectation. He can
express his sense of reality in no other way, and part of that sense of
reality involves a final refusal to endorse any or all of the constructions, what Blake would call "systems," in terms of which we approach it. His style in an absolute and uncompromising sense *is* his
subject, because his subject is the impenetrability of the world regarded as a text (or the text regarded as a world), which continually
intimates the presence of a lucid center behind or within the opaci-
ties of nature or syntax.

> When I travelled in the rain forests of Guyana for the first time—when
> I faced the immensity of the rain forests, all the connections, the subtle-
> ties, all those remarkable connections, I realised that I could *not* describe
> what I saw within a story-line frame that reduced nature to a passive abso-
> lute. I attempted to describe it by saying: "The river is black. The trees
> are green." But that was hopeless. "Black" meant passivity of colour,
> "green" passivity of fertility. I discovered then, for the first time, that
> there were two kinds of immediacy. One immediacy I will call realistic
> immediacy. For example, I would have my camp table before me, I
> would rub the passive surface of the table, I would place my maps on the
> table, I would place drawing paper on the table, and the table therefore
> served an immediate purpose. It had a realistic purpose, a realistic im-
> mediacy. In so doing I was naturally tempted to reduce the world to con-
> venient passivities and to enshrine a deprivation of the senses into tools
> of communication.
>
> On the other hand, the table comes from a tree in the forest, the for-
> est is the lungs of the globe, and the lungs of the globe breathe on the
> stars. There are all sorts of connections and those are quantum connec-
> tions. Quantum mechanics and physics would embrace those connec-
> tions. At that stage I had read nothing of quantum mechanics and I
> simply addressed my repudiation of absolute chains upon nature (my
> repudiation of a nature there to serve me, to prop up my structures) as
> an intuitive, disturbing necessity. I needed to immerse myself in the liv-
> ing, disturbing but immensely rich text of landscapes/riverscapes/sky-
> scapes. Language began to break its contract with mere tools framed to
> enshrine a progressive deprivation. There was a more complex and intu-

itive approach to language in which one suffers and through which one perceives the peculiar ecstasies of dimensionality.[2]

This is a moment that figures as recurring motif, an epiphanic insight that organizes the design of the novels. Significantly it serves the purpose of what has come to be seen as Harris's essential "vision" of reality and his sense of the proper function of the novel as a form in terms of that vision. We can isolate features of this vision. It involves a repudiation of nineteenth-century realism, of a materialistic construction of the universe. In place of that Harris's novels offer intimations of a concealed order of connections and correspondences one grasps only by way of intuition. But the embodying of that "vision" in the verbal texture of Harris's novels involves a kind of shrugging of the shoulders by the author, an acknowledgment that our common usages of language can take us only so far. Harris refuses to smooth the reader's path toward those "peculiar ecstasies" of mystical insight that lie within or behind ordinary language.

This refusal bears not only on the metaphysical dimension of Harris's writing—the concern with essence, center, God—but also on the social dimension—the concern with race, culture, nationality, history. Ultimately, metaphysics and politics are not separable concerns in Harris's writing. Both are functions of the imagination. We need, then, to attend to the *provisional* nature of imaginative constructs in Harris's novels; we encounter metaphors and myths, not literal truths. We must also attend to the productive contradictions and ambivalences in his stance as a novelist. Harris is a visionary whose work embodies a profoundly practical sense of human social realities. He is a modernist and a cosmopolitan whose writing is deeply rooted in a particular geographical experience.

A special sense exists in which Harris escapes his categorizers: the mysterious or elusive quality characteristic of his thought, the deviations and circularities of his writing. The problem of categorizing is not, however, peculiar to Harris as an individual writer. It is a function of the kind of modernism he represents that the works of its major figures tend to straddle competing kinds and styles. This "straddling" is a particularly marked feature of writers like Janet Frame, Patrick White, and Harris, who fall uneasily between the descriptions modernism, post-modernism, and, most problematically, post-colonialism. Perhaps to write modernism in a post-colonial society or from a post-colonial perspective is not to write modernism at all, but to enter some stubbornly resisting ground where the features seem familiar but the relations among them have changed in some profound way. The problem, in other words, is one fundamental to post-colonial writing.

In the post-colonial literatures generally, an obvious and pressing need exists to map and organize a relatively new field of knowledge without distorting the features within it. The problem is that, the more encompassing the classifications employed to make sense of such a field, the less satisfactory they tend to be. Ambitious and vague terms, especially those that denote ethnic or cultural identity, are necessarily tricky. "Black" is an especially troublesome term because it is so slippery. It seeks to include too many heterogeneous elements. Ultimately, it is precisely as limiting as its opposite term. We do not usually talk about "white" writing because too many differences of culture, taste, class, and outlook are embraced by the description. When J. M. Coetzee entitled a book *White Writing*, he did so from within a South African context in which the Manichaean dualism regarding race that has governed modern South African history makes possible, indeed makes inescapable, such self-limiting descriptions.[3]

Inside South Africa the savage binaries of race have been kept intact not only by the force of historical memory but also by the continuing prestige of the idea of purity, the desire for authentic belonging to the group. Not only right-wing Boers but also traditionally minded Zulus have sought to preserve by violence what they see as the "essence" of their cultural being. Even in South Africa, however, skin color is no longer the only determinent of racial identity, as it was under apartheid when children from within a single family could be sent to separate schools on the basis of degree of color.

In the rest of the world, even overtly racist cultures have long been obliged to acknowledge the difficulties involved in ascribing racial qualities on the basis of color. Color, like physiognomy, is at best a haphazard indicator of racial identity. Hence the Nazis' need for genealogical tables to check for concealed Jewishness and calipers to justify racist ideology with a grotesque parody of the scientific method. A story, possibly spurious, is told about Haitian dictator Papa Doc Duvalier that illustrates the problem. As Barbara Fields tells it, an American journalist once asked Papa Doc what percentage of the Haitian population was white and received the extraordinary reply: "Ninety-eight percent." The astonished journalist put his question again. Duvalier assured him that he had heard and understood the question perfectly well and had given the correct answer. The American finally asked Duvalier how he defined white. Duvalier answered with a question: "How do you define black in your country?" Receiving the explanation that in the United States anyone with black blood was considered black, Duvalier nodded and said, "Well, that's the way we define white in my country."[4]

This unreliability at the basis of racism—the failure of race to manifest itself unambiguously in external characteristics once the process of mixing has begun—has long allowed for shifting self-definitions. Traditionally, it has meant that people of mixed ancestry whose physical appearance is deceptive have sought to identify with the "white" part of themselves. The effect of thus identifying against a part of the self is to produce a form of schizophrenia, as when the Guyanese novelist Edgar Mittleholzer, embarrassed by the dark complexion he inherited from his mother, chose to idealize the paternal, German side of his background. In a curious contemporary reversal of this cultural schizophrenia that deepens the sense of self-division by identifying with the dominant culture, we sometimes see individuals in white settler countries—Australia, New Zealand, Canada—choosing to redefine themselves around the indigenous portion of their ancestry.

"Blackness" is never the exact outward sign of any definite quality or fixed essence of being; to conceive it as such is to reaffirm the conditions of slavery. Under slavery a seemingly exact method of measuring color was devised that involved what Edward Brathwaite has called "an elaborate ladder of skin coloring." A sambo was the child of a mulatto and a negro; a mulatto was the child of a white man and a negress; a quadroon was the child of mulatto woman and a white man, and so forth.[5] Such divisions rested on the notion of what Herman Melville called a "blackness of darkness,"[6] an original and essential quality of race, and this concept is impossible to sustain indefinitely once the process of racial intermixing has begun. The problem, of course, is that race is not a biologically determined condition, and percentage of "blood" is not precisely manifested in skin color. Hence the need for increasingly minute gradations of color—mustiphinis, quintoons, and octoroons. Not surprisingly, from the earliest period, racial identity for those with mixed backgrounds took on extremely complex *psychological* qualities. In the late twentieth century, this sense of internal duality or multiplicity, for so long a condition of shame and distress, is in the process of becoming something positive (allowing for some notable recidivisms).

Wilson Harris is one of those writers, Salman Rushdie and Derek Walcott are others, for whom the antagonisms within those who live in post-colonial countries—the multiplicities of possible identities—are a source of value and the cause of optimism rather than the occasion of shame. The various traces of ethnic, religious, and cultural belonging enable cross-fertilization and the formation of new fluid identities within the individual subject and within the general culture. Harris's attitude toward indigenousness rests on his "Caribbean" sense that no way back exists to the worlds before the voyage to the New World, termed by Caribbeans "the middle passage." More than other colonized peoples, Caribbeans have been condemned by their history to the knowledge that no essential and immutable characteristics of race might serve to fix the identity of groups or individuals with absolute security and connect modern West Indians in a direct line to their ancestors in Africa, India, Europe, or the Americas. This is not to suggest that Caribbeans generally, or Harris in particular, accept that the precontact worlds have been erased by history. In his continual drawing upon indigenous mythologies, Harris signals a time of what Edward Said sceptically describes as "geographical spaces with indigenous, radically 'different' inhabitants who [could] be defined on the basis of some religion, culture, or racial essence proper to that geographical space."[7] Nevertheless, all of Harris's writing rests on the recognition that in the Caribbean—and in this sense the region is *exemplary* of contemporary culture everywhere—the myths and tales that carry the memory of vanished or vanishing cultures are never more than traces of the realities they once represented and participated in; now, moreover, they participate in new social orders.[8]

In this sense Harris is a very different writer from all the Third World writers for whom the experience of an intact oral culture was part of childhood. Here Tongan novelist Epeli Hau'ofa describes the place of storytelling in the island society of his boyhood:

> The spoken word, especially in the form of stories, was central to social and cultural life. Indeed a people could not be known and understood sufficiently without their stories. Pacific Island societies were held together by a series of stories; and divisions in a society were delineated by stories. One's links to a social group were by virtue of one's connections to the stories of one's ancestors; where they originated, how they came to be where their descendants lived, by what means they acquired what they bequeathed through generations, and who, and how and where they married, procreated, died and were buried. The physical universe of Island peoples was related and explained through stories; their moral universe was anchored in stories. . . . In short, people lived in a world made sense of and quickened by stories.[9]

Similar descriptions are readily found in the writing of Ngugu wa Thiongo, Festus Iyayi, and many widely dispersed writers who experienced firsthand an oral culture that had persisted into an antagonis-

tic world. The same pattern is to be found in the stories of Witi
Ihimaera recounting a childhood in a remote Maori community in
the 1950s, one still based in oral and tribal values before the drift to
the cities in the postwar period.

For "black" American or Caribbean writers, however, no such direct memory of a non-European oral community is available, although many speak of the power of oral tradition in their
childhood. African-American novelist Charles Johnson seems to be
confirming the same kind of experience when he observes that
"[m]any black authors confess in interviews that the origin of their
artistic journey began when, as children, they heard folktales or
ghost stories in the South from elders."[10] Yet when he comes to the
oral influences on American writers of his own generation, black
and white, he lists comics, the Bible, science fiction, and Nancy Drew
novels. In other words, modern African Americans as children are
subject to the same mix of popular cultural sources as Italian or Jewish or Irish Americans. This is not to suggest that American blacks
can claim no legacy from Africa, that they have become completely
"Americanized . . . of the African culture not a trace" remaining.[11]
It is merely to observe that the African heritage, scattered and sub-
merged by the process of transportation, has been mediated
through layers of alien influence. It exists within modern African
Americans as part of a complex and continually evolving identity,
one no less *African* for being also American.[12] Like contemporary
Maori, Samoans, or Tongans, modern black Americans find it difficult to disentangle the layers of Christianity and the influences from
the general culture from their sense of their past. Yet they remain
free to identify with the part of their past they choose to learn about
and value. Ironically, in a world where "authentic" belonging to
some ethnicity is under ever-increasing threat from a homogenizing
global culture, the freedom to choose one's identity means that
many define their own authenticity, their difference, in terms of a
past from which their ancestors had struggled to free themselves.

Perhaps the vanishing worlds in which people were tribally rooted
in particular places through generations, what F. R. Leavis used to
call "organic communities," were never "whole" in reality, although a romantic aura still clings to tribal and oral cultures even
today. Certainly, once such worlds have been disturbed, no way back
remains except that of romantic nostalgia. The only *practical* way
back is by violence and exclusion, by the fantasies of racial purity
that have been acted out not only by the Nazis against Jews but also
by indigenous Fijians and some decolonized African countries
against Asians, and, most recently, by the Serbians in the former Yu-

goslavia against Croats and Muslims. "Ethnic cleansing" is the logical outcome of the desire to recapture that post world deemed in retrospect to be whole and satisfying.

Opposed to the closure of the ideology of racial purity is Harris's "Caribbean" sense of radical openness to cross-fertilization, hybridity, to the continual bleeding of one culture into others that enriches rather than erases. Yet even this is to present a Manichaean duality that simplifies what it describes. Seeing this antagonism between the forces of openness and closure in global or static terms is distorting: the Ayatollah's Islamic fundamentalism in Iran versus novelist Salman Rushdie's secular India, ethnic nationalism versus multiculturalism. Such antagonisms are constantly being played out at local and particular levels within every country, and the opposing terms are continually modifying each other out of the contact, assuming fresh forms. This is precisely the point of Harris's journey into the interior of Guyana in *Palace of the Peacock,* wherein the monolithic imperialist, Donne, confronts and ultimately merges with his dreaming other, the narrator.) The militant form of Islam that was (and still is) directed at Rushdie, for example, is not a permanent feature of the religion as such; it corresponds to no essence of the religion, although many of its champions as well as its detractors believe that it does. Certainly, Islam itself is not a monolithic religion. As Akeel Bilgrami puts it, "there is no reason to doubt that Muslims, even devout Muslims, will and do take their commitment to Islam not only as one among other values, but also as something that is itself differentiated internally into a number of, in principle, negotiable detailed commitments."[13]

At the same time, it must be acknowledged that the tendency toward essentialism is an ineradicable bias that turns up in various guises and in different levels of intensity at particular stages within the evolutions of separate religions and nationalisms. But this bias is never unchallenged; it is always engaged in disputation with counterimpulses within the larger culture. In contemporary New Zealand, for example, the disputes about race, culture, and language prominent since the 1970s focus on a difference between traditionalist efforts to preserve the ancient and "pure" forms of Maori culture and language and the approach that accepts that Maori cultural forms are undergoing continual modification in their interaction with European forms, and that this process of change is irreversible and not wholly regrettable. In the case of Maori language, the Maori Language Commission funded by the government acts to find Maori words for things or concepts that have none by discovering authentic and traditional forms rather than accepting hybrids. Conversely, enthusiastic younger Maori teachers work in the schools with alienated teenagers struggling to keep the language alive as a *used* language—infected by English diction and syntax, yet distinct and evolving.[14]

Such disputes are inescapably part of being post-colonial: struggling to assert identity in the face of a sense of fracture and dislocation, continually reinventing the past to assuage the doubts of the present, loudly asserting the truth of myths that conceal anxieties about meaning and belonging. Yet they exist in a larger context we call unsatisfactorily "postmodernity," where the past is seen as irrecoverable in the pure forms of its original presence, where myths are a source of playful consolation for the loss of transcendent meanings, and where identity is a matter of imaginative self-invention rather than a matter of searching for some authentic center.

In parts of the cosmopolitan First World, race, like gender, is increasingly becoming a matter of choice (which is not to deny that it remains a matter of imposed fate for most of those in south central Los Angeles or Soweto). To some extent this is a function of modernity generally, where from Katherine Mansfield to Sam Shepard the self has been defined not as an integrated, predictable, and consistent set of qualities or features imposed on individuals, but as a free-floating set of possibilities. For post-colonial subjects this sense of the self as multiple and unstable is made more anxious and acute by the failure of the social context in which they exist to affirm their identity. The individual in post-colonial societies shifts between codes in ways that might be likened to a practice called by linguists "code-switching," which describes the way in which bi- or multilingual individuals switch from one language to another, often within a single sentence. Identity-switching is the cultural equivalent of this, where the subject, experiencing ambivalence about cultural belonging, crosses the divisions of ethnicity or religion.[15] Harris describes this practice in *Black Marsden:*

> (A newspaper column I had read some time back floated into consciousness; a "white" woman made herself invisible by playing "black" in an American economic theatre: real life rather than fiction. And then the right-handed real world to which she belonged (or with which she secretly identified) saw her as a left-handed unreal chair to sit upon—or left-handed door to knock upon—mental cross-lateral furniture. In crossing and re-crossing an economic racial or religious or political divide (right to left, left to right) one could draw down upon oneself the implacable biases of cross-lateral reification or malfunction. . . .)[16]

The problem of the unstable and shifting nature of defining terms related to race also exists in contemporary culture generally.

"Black" means very different things in different places. In America the word black usually means descended from Africa; East Indians are not generally defined as black there. In Britain, however, Asians often designate themselves as black. In New Zealand, Maori radicals sometimes use the word because it points to their difference from the dominant white culture in terms conveniently binary. Even vaguer uses of the word can be seen, such as the expression "Black Irish," which refers to Irish people supposedly descended from Spanish sailors, or "Black Maoris," who are believed by other Maoris to be descended from black sailors who jumped ship in the northern parts of New Zealand in the early contact period. The flexibility of the signifier in different cultures indicates the vagueness of what it signifies and the falseness of race as a signifier. Blackness no longer designates simply racial origins, skin color, or what previously was called "blood," but is the sign of identity that individuals or groups within a given society *choose* to adopt to signal their difference from other groups. No authentic and universal experience of blackness as racial identity is behind the word. As Akeel Bilgrami puts it, in recent years "the concept of identity has had its corset removed and hangs loosely and precariously in the domain of culture and politics."[17]

James Clifford in *The Predicament of Culture* makes the sense of "lost authenticity," or lack of essence, loss of source, the defining feature of modernity. Harris is one of the key figures he cites, along with other Caribbean writers, as those who suggest a positive response to this condition. Clifford does not mean that modern individuals no longer have any access to cultural experience other than that of an amorphous global culture. On the contrary, they experience within particular societies local and special cultures that are themselves in a constant process of change. By the 1920s, according to Clifford, "a truly global space of cultural connections and dissolutions had become imaginable." At the same time "local authenticities" were already meeting and merging "in transient urban and suburban settings" from America to Africa.[18]

For Clifford, the desire for purity, essence and authentic connection to origins is inescapably nostalgic. This means that the past is recoverable only by way of the myths and evasions that have interposed themselves between the present and the imagined past. Nevertheless, modern humans are linked by a sense of the past or by locality, and thus they continually redefine themselves against the homogenization of culture. Global culture is resisted in multiple instances of assertion and discovery of those problematic and shifting concepts: tribe, culture, identity. These are always contested terms, and the stakes involved in conflicts over their precise interpretation are always high. Clifford cites an Indian tribe in New England fighting a legal battle over land as an example of the kind of interpretive problems posed by the notions of culture, tribe, and authenticity. Clifford asks: "Were the plaintiffs of 1977 the 'same' Indians" as those who had inhabited the land in dispute before the arrival of Europeans?[19]

Blacks in the United States exist in a context entirely different from that of native Americans. Their way back to authentic roots is inevitably more doubtful, although Clifford points out that it is perilous even for indigenous people: "Questionable acts of purification are involved in any attainment of a promised land, return to 'original' sources, or gathering up of a true tradition. Such claims to purity are in any event always subverted by the need to stage authenticity in opposition to external, often dominating, alternatives." When New Zealand novelist Keri Hulme identified herself as a Maori writer and laid claim to an authentic Maori presence in *the bone people* (1983), she was attacked by C. K. Stead on the grounds that one Maori grandparent was insufficient grounds to justify such claims.[20] Hulme has responded to such attacks by asserting her Maoriness all the more strenuously.[21] However, her fierce determination to privilege a part of her ethnic background over the predominant one, felt to be contaminated by colonial and masculine forms of power, raises the question put by Margerie Fee: "who can speak for the other"?[22] Hulme sidesteps the question by insisting that she *is* the other, but this is a suspect claim, given that the versions of pre-European Maori reality offered in the novel have necessarily been affected by the utter permeation of New Zealand society, Maori and Pakeha, by the typologies of Christianity and romanticism.[23] How then can contemporary writers, whatever their degree of ethnicity (and arguing about the fractions of "blood" is surely vulgar and irrelevant), represent that pristine order *authentically* in a work of fiction? How do we get back to what we were, or to what we imagine we were, before our "true" origins were caught up in the commerce of cultures?

In a recent essay in *The New York Times Book Review*, Henry Louis Gates, Jr. reflects on the problem of racial authenticity by focusing on *The Education of Little Tree*, a book written by Forrest Carter, which was widely praised as a "true" autobiographical account of a boy raised by Cherokee Indians and an authentic work of Native American literature. The problem was that Carter was a white racist, the man who wrote George Wallace's notorious "Segregation today. . . . Segregation tomorrow. . . . Segregation forever" speech. Gates's conclusion is that Carter's "crossing" of a racial divide, to use Harris's terms, demonstrates that segregation "is as difficult to maintain in the literary realm as it is in the civic one."[24] The ideology of authenticity is dangerous because, by defining identity in terms of specific traits, it inhibits that fruitful exchange between cultures that makes our various identities as blacks, whites, natives, or whoever continually open to new kinds of knowledge.

Gates begins his essay with an anecdote about a wager between a black jazz musician, Roy Eldridge, and music critic Leonard Feather that Eldridge could distinguish black musicians from white ones—blindfolded. When Feather dropped the needle onto a selection of records, however, "more than half the time Eldridge guessed wrong."[25] The lesson Gates draws from this is not that "our social identities don't matter" or that our histories as individuals or groups do not "affect what we wish to write and what we are able to write," but that "that relation is never one of fixed determinism."[26] The raggedness of culture, its failure to fit neatly and exclusively to individuals, allows us to enter other cultures, learn about them, albeit in a provisional sense, inhabit them, and this capacity is always enriching.

Salman Rushdie has said that authenticity is "the respectable child of old-fashioned exoticism. It demands that sources, forms, style and language and symbol all derive from a supposedly homogeneous and unbroken tradition."[27] It assumes an unchanging and ahistorical tradition similar to sacred time. It is opposed to what Clifford sees as the "pervasive condition of off-centredness in a world of distinct meaning systems," which condition he identifies with the twentieth century's "unprecedented overlay of traditions." This brings us back to Harris, for whom identity also is never an unchanging essence. (Hena Maes-Jelinek points out that, while Harris's concern with concepts like "inimitable truth" seem to mark him out as an essentialist," what Harris has in mind in terms of 'essence' or 'centre' remains . . . forever 'unnameable' or 'unfathomable.'")[28] For Harris, difference and cultural distinctness are inescapable values that have not been eradicated, but they can no longer be 'located solely in the continuity of a culture or tradition," as Clifford puts it.[29]

One response to the loss of authenticity that characterizes modernity is what Clifford calls "the great narrative of entropy": the modernists' lament for the falling away of the modern world from their visions of wholeness. Clifford suggest that the Caribbean, with its ambiguous experience of cultural identity, offers a useful counterpoint to this lament. By "Caribbean" he means roughly what Rushdie understands by India—the open and inclusive India rather than the pure one of the religious fundamentalists. In this model the modern world is grasped as the relentless movement of informations from a huge variety of cultures and sources across national and ethnic barriers, yet allowing for a flourishing of cultures as they intersect. Postmodernity means this in its most positive and affirmative sense: the opening out to reality as an optimistic act of faith in the human capacity to be enriched by experience, painful as well as consoling, to make new, provisional wholes out of the fractures of history, to draw on, imitate, and celebrate the past without seeking to close the world around some nostalgic conception of its meaning for the present.

Clifford offers Aimé Césaire as example of this. Césaire is "a practitioner of 'neologistic' cultural politics." That is to say, he reconceives organic culture "as inventive process or creolized 'interculture.' "[30] The same sort of thing might be said of Harris, whom Clifford also sees as an exemplar of that universal Caribbean we all now inhabit in our "urban archipelagos."[31] None of us can return to a "native land," as Ulysses did in the *Odyssey*. Too many different worlds and traditions now inhabit all of us. Thus, according to Clifford, we must accept Harris's " 'principle of juxtaposition' as a way to account for 'the making of tradition . . . the heterogeneous groundwork of authentic community.' "[32]

This "principle of juxtaposition" involves texts as well as individuals, the locus of contending traditions. Soyinka points out that African writers occupy and draw on both European and African heritage. Their writing is thus "two-toned.'[33] For Gates, this doubleness means that in Soyinka, Césaire, and Ellison, the text is both "like its French or Spanish, American or English antecedents, yet differently 'black.' "[34] Gates's ambivalence here points to the possibility of a more open and accommodating species of négritude than that which seeks to affirm the African element at the expense of the European: he admires the effort to "will into being . . . an essence called 'blackness,' " yet acknowledges the idealism, the notion of essence, fatally present in the project.[35] He accepts the force of the concept of Africa for black people, but does not simplify its meaning for the present.

Perhaps we must construct a more capacious and complex definition of négritude. In its most limited sense it means an essentialist idea of African origins and personality. Conceivably, a more open sense exists where the collective memory of the African past, modified over time, has accommodated itself to various pressures and influences. There is no need to hierarchize those influences, either in favor of white canonical texts, as colonialism did, or in favor of indigenous and oral traditions, as Ngugi wa Thiongo does.[36] Rather, we might learn to see the *variety* of cultural traditions that modern black people, quite as much as white people, inherit as a source of cross-cultural possibility. As Harris puts it:

> Homer, Dante, Shakespeare, Goethe are as much the heritage of black men and women as of white men and women because the triggers of conflicting tradition . . . lie in, and need to be re-activated through, the cross-cultural psyche of humanity, a cross-cultural psyche that bristles with the tone and fabric of encounters between so–called savage cultures and so-called civilised cultures.[37]

Even in the 1950s alternatives to négritude could be found among black writers, and competing versions of négritude were within the movement itself. Aimé Césaire turned to surrealism as a means of cultural decolonization. The problem here, as Michael Dash puts it, was that surrealism was useful as a means of attacking the concepts, confidences, and myths of the Western worldview; it signified a violent rejection of Europe as the inherited structure of meanings, values, and narratives that had presumed to define all alterity as inferiority. It could not, however, recover the African past; it could not release the Africa in Césaire's unconscious.[38] Clifford, however, talks about Césaire's "inventive and tactical 'négritude,' " which conceives of Caribbean history not only as characterized by degradation, mimicry, violence, and blocked possibilities, but also by rebellion, syncreticism, and a creative response to the ambivalent legacy of colonialism.[39] This is very close to Harris's sense of the past, especially if we stress the syncreticism and creativity and add the concept of the intuitive imagination.

Dash has described Harris's version of magical realism, which he terms "marvellous realism," as "the way out of négritude." The defining characteristic of négritude, for Dash, was the view that the violence and loss of the black past meant that nothing had survived, the past was an emptiness, and that this emptiness called for a violent and total kind of protest against the past. History involved "a spiritual loss as complete as their [the black peoples'] protest was violent." From this arose "the necessity of forgetting and replacing such a past by the process of decolonisation, and the consequent urgency to substantiate the originality and authenticity of the African Presence—based on the racial 'essence' inherited from ancestral Africa."[40]

Négritude, in Dash's definition, reached its definitive expression in the post–World War II years with a vision of the African presence as a pan-national and pan-linguistic essence of black identity. Senghor's concept of négritude, for instance, is not merely a political protest; it involves an African ontology, an essentially African way of perceiving reality and the spiritual forces in the universe."[41] Events as diverse as protest poetry in the United States and the decolonization of Africa were shaped by this ontology. Behind the various expressions—musical, literary, plastic, political—of négritude lay the effort to substitute a positive version of the African past for the actual one by linking the subjects of that history around an idealized essence, what Abiola Irele calls the "African personality."[42]

Irele, in fact, offers the most positive case for négritude in recent years. He discovers the origins of a distinctive black consciousness in the contact between Africa and Europe and describes it as representing "the profound subjective response to the peculiar pressures of the colonial situation." More importantly, he sees négritude as an evolving ideology, which he characterizes thus:

Today, this awareness has been prolonged into an intellectual and ideological exploration of those avenues of endeavour which might give a meaning to the collective experience, into a quest for a positive orientation of African ideas and action in the contemporary world. One might say then that there is abroad among us, governing our feelings and consequently our expression, a certain idea of Africa, a certain ideal vision of ourselves founded upon our awareness of our specific constitution as a race and as a people, of our fundamental attachment to a distinctive culture and spiritual background. The consciousness of our singularity as Africans thus forms the live core of the intellectual idea we hold of Africa and by implication of our destiny.[43]

The attraction for black people of the idea of négritude, and ultimately the source of its redundancy, was that it offered a myth of universal black identity to oppose the myth of white supremacy. This notion of the homogeneity of black identity, the idea of blackness itself, was necessarily derived from the condition it opposed. Without the experience of racism directed at blacks by whites confident of their superiority, the African peoples who suffered slavery and colonization would not have come to see themselves as more unified than diverse. This idea of a homogeneous black culture denies the variety of kinds within the category. Barbara Fields comments on this as follows:

[Black people] do not look alike; they came originally from different countries, spoke different languages, and had different cultures. In the heyday of the Atlantic slave trade, both traders and their customers understood that the cargoes of the slave ships included Africans of different national, cultural and linguistic backgrounds. Slave-buying planters talked in voluble, if no doubt misguided, detail about the varied characteristics of Coromantees, Mandingoes, Foulahs, Congoes, Angolas, Eboes, Whydahs, Nagoes, Pawpaws, and Gaboons. Experienced buyers and sellers could distinguish them by sight and speech, and prices would vary accordingly. Black people, in other words, were initially no more a racial group than Hispanics. In the era of the slave trade a social fact—that these people all came from the same exotic continent and that they were all destined for slavery—made the similarities among them more important, in principle, than the differences. Their subsequent experience in slavery, particularly in its mainland North American form, eventually caused the similarities to overwhelm the differences in reality as well.[44]

A general effect of colonization is that it dissolves the internal differences among the colonized. Paradoxically, this deprivation of cultural resonance and specificity becomes at the close of the period of explicit oppression a means of reasserting identity. It is, however, a necessarily circumscribed one. As James Baldwin puts it, "The anatomizing of the great injustice which is the irreducible fact of colonialism was yet not enough to give the victims of that injustice a new sense of themselves."[45] This is very close to what Harris means by "self-righteous deprivation." Baldwin's stance ushers us toward Harris's attitude to the past, to colonialism, to tradition, to culture, and to the composite nature of individual identity in post-colonial societies. Above all, Harris's sense of the local specificities of culture, the layerings of traditions within individuals, ethnic groups, and nationalities, agrees with those who object to the ahistoricism of négritude.

For Harris, the history of colonization is not a wholly unproductive one. Rather he sees in the formation of post-colonial national cultures the synthesizing of various influences into distinctive new wholes. This creative approach to colonial history denies the notion of a specific black identity or essence of being. It also denies a universal black experience, except in most general terms, and hence has no need for a universal black aesthetic. Above all, Harris articulates a philosophy of Third World history, which négritude never managed to address satisfactorily.

Harris's sense of history is "visionary" in that he envisages, or imagines, syntheses in the place of brokenness, finds value and meaning in the experiences of those victimized by historical processes, makes present in fictive terms what history had made absent. Harris turns to myths and legends of the "folk" to find traces of a complex process of survival, adaption, and assertion. The experience of transplanted and indigenous peoples in the Caribbean is part of this process. History is recovered as a valuable source of memories and resistances. Locked within the unconscious collective memory of the people are signs of the imaginative forms that constitute a necessary and healthy response to oppression and loss. These forms are extraordinarily varied in their expression, ranging from Limbo and rap poetry to Augustan couplets in Latin written by an eighteenth-century former slave. We find this range not only in Carribbean anthologies like Paula Burnett's *Penguin Book of Caribbean Verse* (1986) but also within the individual texts of Harris, who shows an astonishing ability to switch from high to low registers, from the hieratic to the demotic, from literary allusions to folk traditions. In other words, the problems of cultural belonging, of historical memory and the layering of traditions, are to be found *within* the texts of individual authors as well as within the societies from which they come. Reading Harris takes us into the same knotty complexities of social being that Clifford, the anthropologist, encounters entering and reading modern cultures.

Notes

1. Hena Maes-Jelinek, " 'Numinous Proportions': Wilson Harris's Alternative to All the 'posts'," in Ian Adam and Helen Tiffin, ed., *Past the Last Post: Theorizing Post-Colonialism and Post-Modernism* (Calgary: University of Calgary Press, 1990), 51.

2. Wilson Harris, *The Radical Imagination: Lectures and Talks*, ed. Alan Riach and Mark Williams (Liège: University of Liège, 1992), 72.

3. J. M. Coetzee, *White Writing: On the Culture of Letters in South Africa* (New Haven: Yale University Press, 1988).

4. Barbara Fields, "Ideology and Race in American History," in J. Morgan Kousser and James M. McPherson, ed., in *Region, Race and Reconstruction: Essays in Honour of C. Vann Woodward* (New York: Oxford University Press, 1982), 146.

5. Edward Brathwaite, *The Development of Creole Society in Jamaica, 1770–1820* (Oxford: Clarendon Press, 1978), 167.

6. Herman Melville, *Moby-Dick* (1851; New York: Norton, 1967), 18.

7. Edward Said, *Orientalism* (New York: Vintage, 1979), 322.

8. Hena Maes-Jelinek comments on this: "Through their experiences and encounters with a vanished past, lost cultures or deprived individuals and groups (apparently non-existent yet agents of the sacred in his fiction), his protagonists confront 'areas of tradition that have sunken away and apparently disappeared and vanished and yet are still active at some level,' " "Numinous Proportions," 52.

9. Epeli Hau'ofa, "Oral Traditions and Writing," paper read at Conference of Pacific Writers, Commonwealth Institute, London, October 1988, published in *Landfall*, vol. 44, no. 4 (December 1990), 402–3.

10. Charles Johnson, *Being and Race: Black Writing Since 1970* (Bloomington: Indiana University Press, 1988), 4.

11. Melville J. Herskovits, "The Negro's Americanism," quoted in Walter Mi-

chael Benns, "Race into Culture: A Critical Genealogy of Cultural identity," *Critical Inquiry*, 4 (Summer 1992), 675. According to Arthur M. Schlesinger, Jr., in *The Disuniting of America* (New York: Norton, 1992), until 1965 few African Americans saw much "African" in the black person in America.

12. The Maori novelist Witi Ihimaera, who was for a time New Zealand Consul in New York, has claimed that, looking out from his upper West Side apartment, he recognized a Maori, not an alien, world. In other words, Maori culture is sufficiently strong to encompass the various realities to which it had been exposed since contact with Europeans. Witi Ihimaera interviewed by Mark Williams in Elizabeth Alley and Mark Williams, ed., *In the Same Room: Conversations with New Zealand Writers* (Auckland: Auckland University Press, 1992), 223.

13. "What Is a Muslim?," 824.

14. See *Dirty Silence: Aspects of Language and Literature in New Zealand,* ed., Graham McGregor and Mark Williams (Auckland: Oxford University Press, 1991), especially the essays by Harlow and Hollings.

15. The film *Europa Europa,* which traces the apparently true adventures of a young Jewish boy in World War II Europe who managed to pass himself off as a Nazi and a communist, brilliantly illustrates what I mean by "identity-switching."

16. Wilson Harris, *Black Marsden* (London: Faber & Faber, 1972), 18–19.

17. Bilgrami, "What Is a Muslim?," 821.

18. Clifford, *The Predicament of Culture,* 4.

19. Ibid., 8. Compare Clifford's citing of a difficult instance of cross-cultural litigation with Harris's discussion in *Carnival* of a conflict between Amerindian tribal law and the law of the colonizing power in a case involving matricide according to ancestral custom; see also *The Radical Imagination,* 121–23.

20. C. K. Stead, *Answering to the Language: Essays on Modern Writers* (Auckland: Auckland University Press, 1989), 179–80.

21. Keri Hulme interviewed by Elizabeth Alley, *In the Same Room: Conversations with New Zealand Writers,* ed. Elizabeth Alley and Mark Williams (Auckland: Auckland University Press, 1992), 151–53.

22. See Margerie Fee, "Why C. K. Stead Didn't Like *the bone people*," *Australian and New Zealand Studies in Canada,* no. 1 (spring 1989), 151–53.

23. See my *Leaving the Highway: Six Contemporary New Zealand Novelists* (Auckland: Auckland University Press, 1992), 98.

24. Henry Louis Gates, Jr., " 'Authenticity' or the Lesson of Little Tree," *The New York Times Book Review,* 24 November 1991, 30.

25. Gates, "The Lesson of Little Tree," 1.

26. Gates, "The Lesson of Little Tree," 30.

27. Rushdie, *Imaginary Homelands,* 67.

28. Maes-Jelinek, "Numinous Proportions," 58.

29. Clifford, *The Predicament of Culture,* 11.

30. Ibid., 15.

31. Ibid., 173.

32. Ibid., 173–74.

33. Henry Louis Gates, Jr., ed., *Black Literature and Literary Theory* (London: Methuen, 1984), 4.

34. Gates, *Black Literature and Literary Theory,* 6.

35. Ngugi wa Thiongo, "The Abolition of the English Department," in *Homecoming: Essays on African and Caribbean Literature, Culture and Politics* (1972); quoted in Gates, *Black Literature and Literary Theory,* 7.

36. See Gates, *Black Literature and Literary Theory,* 11.

37. Wilson Harris, "Comedy and Modern Allegory," quoted in Maes-Jelinek, "Numinous Proportions," 59.

38. J. Michael Dash, "Marvellous Realism: The Way out of Négritude," *Caribbean Studies*, vol. 13, no. 4 (1973), 59.

39. Clifford, *The Predicament of Culture*, 15.

40. Dash, "Marvellous Realism, 57.

41. Lewis Nkosi, *Tasks and Masks: Themes and Styles of African Literature* (Harlow: Longman, 1981), 12. For a sophisticated and up-to-date defense of négritude, see Rex Nettleford, "The Aesthetics of Négritude: A Metaphor for Liberation," in Alistair Hennessy, ed., *Intellectuals in the Twentieth-Century Caribbean*, Vol. I, *Spectre of the New Class: The Commonwealth Caribbean* (London: Macmillan, 1992), 80–97.

42. Irele, *The African Experience*, 12.

43. Ibid., 89.

44. Fields, "Ideology and Race in American History," 144–45.

45. James Baldwin, "Princes and Powers," in *Nobody Knows My Name*, quoted in Dash, 61.

Part VI
Bibliography

Melvin J. Friedman: A Bibliography

This listing of Melvin J. Friedman's publications is drawn primarily from his own curriculum vitae. It was edited by Jackson R. Bryer, with the assistance of Judith Friedman, Judith Couillard, and Marc Singer.

Books

Stream of Consciousness: A Study in Literary Method. New Haven, CT: Yale University Press, 1955.

Configuration Critique de Samuel Beckett. Paris: Lettres Modernes, 1964. Edited and with an introduction by Melvin J. Friedman.

The Added Dimension: The Art and Mind of Flannery O'Connor. New York: Fordham University Press, 1966. Coedited and with an introduction by Melvin J. Friedman; second revised edition (paperback), 1977.

Configuration Critique de William Styron. Paris: Lettres Modernes, 1967. Coedited and with an introduction by Melvin J. Friedman.

The Shaken Realist: Essays in Modern Literature in Honor of Frederick J. Hoffman. Baton Rouge: Louisiana State University Press, 1970. Coedited and with an introduction by Melvin J. Friedman.

Samuel Beckett Now: Critical Approaches to His Novels, Poetry, and Plays. Chicago: University of Chicago Press, 1970. Edited and with an introduction by Melvin J. Friedman; second revised edition (paperback), 1975.

William Styron's "The Confessions of Nat Turner": A Critical Handbook. Belmont, CA: Wadsworth Publishing Company, 1970. Coedited and with a preface by Melvin J. Friedman.

Calépins de Bibliographie Samuel Beckett. with J. R. Bryer, Peter Hoy, and R. J. Davis. Paris: Lettres Modernes, 1971 and 1972.

William Styron. Popular Writers Series, No. 3. Bowling Green, OH: Bowling Green University Popular Press, 1974.

The Two Faces of Ionesco. Troy, NY: Whitston Publishing Company, 1978. Coedited and with an introduction by Melvin J. Friedman.

Academics View Sports. Special issue of *Journal of American Culture,* 4 (Fall 1981). Edited and with an introduction by Melvin J. Friedman.

Critical Essays on Flannery O'Connor. Boston: G. K. Hall, 1985. Coedited and with an introduction by Melvin J. Friedman.

Special William Styron Issue of *Papers on Language and Literature,* 23 ·(Fall 1987). Coedited and with an introduction by Melvin J. Friedman.

Pound/The "Little Review": The Letters of Ezra Pound to Margaret Anderson. New York:

New Directions, 1988; London: Faber and Faber, 1989. Coedited and with an introduction by Melvin J. Friedman.

Aesthetics and the Literature of Ideas: Essays in Honor of A. Owen Aldridge. Newark: University of Delaware Press, 1990. Edited by François Jost with the assistance of Melvin J. Friedman.

Joycean Occasions. Newark: University of Delaware Press, 1991. Coedited and with an introduction by Melvin J. Friedman.

Traditions, Voices, and Dreams: The American Novel Since the 1960s. Newark: University of Delaware Press, 1995. Coedited and with an introduction by Melvin J. Friedman.

Critical Essays on Carson McCullers. New York: G. K. Hall, 1996. Coedited by Melvin J. Friedman.

Contributions to Books

"Le Monologue intérieur dans *As I Lay Dying.*" In *Configuration Critique de William Faulkner.* Ed. Michel J. Minard. Paris: Lettres Modernes, 1958–59. 331-44.

Lexikon der Weltliteratur im 20. Jahrhundert. Freiburg: Verlag Herder. Vol. I, 1960: "Fitzgerald," pp. 651–53; "Irische Literatur," pp. 979–85; "Henry James," 1022–31; Vol. II, 1961: "James Starkey," 1003–4.

"*Amphitryon 38:* Some Notes on Jean Giraudoux and Myth." In *Hereditas: Seven Essays on the Modern Experience of the Classical.* Ed. Frederic Will (Austin: University of Texas Press, 1964. 133–49.

"Les Romans de Samuel Beckett et la tradition du Grotesque." In *Un Nouveau Roman?* Ed. J. H. Matthews. Paris: Lettres Modernes, 1964. 31–50.

"F. Scott Fitzgerald." In *Encyclopedia of World Literature in the 20th Century.* Ed. W. B. Fleischmann. New York: Frederick Ungar, 1967. I, 387–88.

"Towards an Aesthetic: Truman Capote's Other Voices." In *Truman Capote's "In Cold Blood": A Critical Handbook.* Ed. Irving Malin. Belmont, CA: Wadsworth Publishing Company, 1968. 163–76.

"Three Experiences of the War: A Triptych." In *Promise of Greatness: The War of 1914–1918.* Ed. George A. Panichas. New York: John Day; London: Cassells; Toronto: Longmans, 1968. 542–55.

"Isaac Bashevis Singer: The Appeal of Numbers." In *Critical Views of Isaac Bashevis Singer.* Ed. Irving Malin. New York: New York University Press, 1969. 178–93.

"Flannery O'Connor (1925–1964)." In *A Bibliographical Guide to the Study of Southern Literature.* Ed. Louis D. Rubin, Jr. Baton Rouge: Louisiana State University Press, 1969. 250–53.

"Irish Literature." In *Encyclopedia of World Literature in the 20th Century.* Ed. W. B. Fleischmann. New York: Frederick Ungar, 1969. 146–50.

"Henry James." In *Encyclopedia of World Literature in the 20th Century.* Ed. W. B. Fleischmann. New York: Frederick Ungar, 1969. II, 166–71.

"Flannery O'Connor." In *Encyclopedia of World Literature in the 20th Century.* Ed. W. B. Fleischmann. New York: Frederick Ungar, 1969. III, 7–8.

"Seumus O'Sullivan." In *Encyclopedia of World Literature in the 20th Century.* Ed. W. B. Fleischmann. New York: Frederick Ungar, 1969. III, 27.

"Some Notes on the Technique of *Man's Fate.*" In *The Shaken Realist: Essays in Mod-*

ern Literature in Honor of Frederick J. Hoffman. Ed. Melvin J. Friedman and John B. Vickery. Baton Rouge: Louisiana State University Press, 1970. 128–43.

"Flannery O'Connor's Sacred Objects." In *The Vision Obscured: Perceptions of Some Twentieth-Century Catholic Novelists.* Ed. Melvin J. Friedman. New York: Fordham University Press, 1970. 67–77.

"William Styron." In *The Politics of Twentieth-Century Novelists.* Ed. George A. Panichas. New York: Hawthorn, 1971. 335–50.

"William Styron and the *Nouveau Roman.*" In *Proceedings of the Comparative Literature Symposium.* Ed. W. T. Zyla and W. M. Aycock. Lubbock: Texas Tech University, 1972. 121–37.

Contemporary Novelists. Ed. James Vinson. London: St. James Press; New York: St. Martin's Press, 1972. "Robie Macauley," 796–98; "Wallace Markfield," 843–44; "Philip Roth," 1077–80; "Sloan Wilson," 1388–91.

"Jewish Mothers and Sons: The Expense of *Chutzpah.*" In *Contemporary American-Jewish Literature.* Ed. Irving Malin. Bloomington and London: Indiana University Press, 1973. 156–74.

"Bruce Jay Friedman." In *Contemporary Dramatists.* Ed. James Vinson. London: St. James Press; New York: St. Martin's Press, 1973. 264–67.

"Ernest Hemingway." In *Sixteen Modern American Authors: A Survey of Research and Criticism.* Ed. Jackson R. Bryer. New York: Norton, 1973; Durham: Duke University Press, 1974. 392–416.

"Lestrygonians." In *James Joyce's "Ulysses": Critical Essays.* Ed. David Hayman and Clive Hart. Berkeley and Los Angeles: University of California Press, 1974. 131–46.

"Samuel Beckett und seine Kritiker zu Anfang der siebziger Jahre." In *Das Werk von Samuel Beckett Berliner Colloquium.* Ed. Hans Mayer and Uwe Johnson. Frankfurt, Germany: Suhrkamp, 1975. 135–38, 234.

"The Symbolist Novel: Huysmans to Malraux." In *Modernism.* Ed. Malcolm Bradbury and James McFarlane. Harmondsworth, Middlesex, England: Penguin Books, 1976. 453–66.

"Introductory Notes to Beckett's Poetry." In *Samuel Beckett: The Art of Rhetoric.* Ed. Edouard Morot-Sir, Howard Harper, and Dougald McMillan III. Chapel Hill: North Carolina Studies in the Romance Languages and Literature, 1976. 143–49.

" 'The Perplex Business': Flannery O'Connor and Her Critics Enter the 1970s." In *The Added Dimension: The Art and Mind of Flannery O'Connor.* Second edition. Ed. Melvin J. Friedman and Lewis A. Lawson. New York: Fordham University Press, 1977. 207–34.

"Dislocations of Setting and Word: Notes on American Fiction Since 1950." In *American Fiction: Historical and Critical Essays.* Ed. James Nagel. Boston: Twayne Publishers and Northeastern University Press, 1977. 79–98. Reprinted from "Dislocations of Setting and Word: Notes on American Fiction Since 1970," *Studies in American Fiction,* 5 (Spring 1977): 79–98.

"Some Notes on John Hawkes and Flannery O'Connor: The French Backgrounds." In *The Savage Comedy of John Hawkes.* Ed. James Green. Deland, FL: Everett/Edwards, 1978. 47–66. Reprinted from "John Hawkes and Flannery O'Connor: The French Background," *Boston University Journal,* 21 (Fall 1973): 34–44.

"*The Mortgaged Heart:* The Workshop of Carson McCullers." In *Carson McCullers: Essays in Criticism.* Ed. Irving Malin. Deland, FL: Everett/Edwards, 1978. 187–204.

Reprinted from "*The Mortgaged Heart: The Workshop of Carson McCullers,*" *Revue des Langues Vivantes,* U.S. Bicentennial Issue (1976): 143–55.

"Anthony Burgess." In *Collier's Encyclopedia.* New York and London: Macmillan, 1978. IV, 739–40.

"R. K. Narayan." In *Collier's Encyclopedia.* New York and London: Macmillan, 1978. XVII, 141.

"The Enigma of Unpopularity and Critical Neglect: The Case for Wallace Markfield." In *Seasoned Authors for a New Season: The Search for Standards in Popular Writing.* Ed. Louis Filler. Bowling Green, OH: Bowling Green University Popular Press, 1980. 33–42.

"Samuel Beckett." In *A Critical Bibliography of French Literature.* Ed. Douglas W. Alden and Richard A. Brooks. Syracuse, NY: Syracuse University Press, 1980. 3: 1865–86.

"Foreword." In P. G. Rama Rao, *Ernest Hemingway: A Study in Narrative Technique.* New Delhi: S. Chand & Company, 1980. v–vi.

"Samuel Beckett." In *Columbia Dictionary of Modern European Literature.* second edition. New York: Columbia University Press, 1980. 59–60.

"Valery Larbaud." In *Columbia Dictionary of Modern European Literature.* second edition. New York: Columbia University Press, 1980. 460–61.

"Recent New England Fiction: Outsiders and Insiders." In *American Literature: The New England Heritage.* Ed. James Nagel and Richard Astro. New York and London: Garland Publishing, 1981. 167–82.

" 'The Swimmers': Paris and Virginia Reconciled." In *The Short Stories of F. Scott Fitzgerald: New Approaches in Criticism.* Ed. Jackson R. Bryer. Madison: University of Wisconsin Press, 1982. 251–60.

"Prefatory Note on Joyce and Beckett." In *The Seventh of Joyce.* Ed. Bernard Benstock. Bloomington: Indiana University Press; Sussex: The Harvester Press, 1982. 27–28.

"William Styron and the *Nouveau Roman.*" In *Critical Essays on William Styron.* Ed. Arthur D. Casciato and James L. W. West III. Boston: G. K. Hall, 1982. 289–305. Reprinted from *William Styron.* Bowling Green, OH: Bowling Green University Popular Press, 1974. 19–36.

"Raymond Federman." In *Contemporary Novelists.* third edition. Ed. James Vinson. New York: St. Martin's Press, 1982. 209–10.

"Malcolm Bradbury." In *British Novelists Since 1960.* Ed. Jay L. Halio. Detroit: Gale, 1983. I, 108-16.

"George Moore and Samuel Beckett: Cross Currents and Correspondences." In *George Moore in Perspective.* Ed. Janet Dunleavy. Ireland, England, and New York: The Malton Press, Colin Smythe, Barnes and Noble, 1983. 116–31.

"Flannery O'Connor's *Via Extrema et Negativa.*" In *Review.* Ed. James O. Hoge and James L. W. West, III. Charlottesville: University Press of Virginia, 1983. 149–54.

"Something Jewish Happened: Some Thoughts About Joseph Heller's *Good as Gold.*" In *Critical Essays on Joseph Heller.* Ed. James Nagel. Boston: G. K. Hall, 1984. 196–204.

"Malcolm Bradbury's 'Plot of History.' " In *Essays on the Contemporary British Novel.* Ed. Hedwig Bock and Albert Wertheim. Munich: Max Hueber Verlag, 1986. 213–26.

"The Novels of Samuel Beckett: An Amalgam of Joyce and Proust." In *Critical Essays on Samuel Beckett.* Ed. Patrick A. McCarthy. Boston: G. K. Hall, 1986. 11–21. Reprinted from *Comparative Literature,* 12 (Winter 1960): 47–58.

"William Styron." In *Fifty Southern Writers After 1900: A Bio-Bibliographical Sourcebook.* Ed. Joseph M. Flora and Robert Bain. Westport, CT: Greenwood Press, 1987. 444–56.

"Foreword." *Beckett's Later Fiction and Drama: Texts for Company.* Ed. James Acheson and Kateryna Arthur. London: Macmillan, 1987. vii–xi.

"William Styron's Fiction and Essays: A Franco-American Perspective." In *The Comparative Perspective on Literature: Approaches to Theory and Practice.* Ed. Clayton Koelb and Susan Noakes. Ithaca and London: Cornell University Press, 1988. 117–29.

"Making the Best of Two Worlds: Raymond Federman, Beckett, and the University." In *The American Writer and the University.* Ed. Ben Siegel. Newark: University of Delaware Press, 1989. 136–45.

"Flannery O'Connor." In *Biographical Dictionary of Contemporary Catholic American Writing.* Ed. Daniel J. Tynan. Westport, CT: Greenwood Press, 1989. 221–24.

"Ellmann on Joyce." In *Re-Viewing Classics of Joyce Criticism.* Ed. Janet Egleson Dunleavy. Urbana and Chicago: University of Illinois Press, 1991. 131–41.

Articles in Journals

"Valery Larbaud: The Two Traditions of Eros." *Yale French Studies,* No. 11 (1953): 91–100. Reprinted in part in *Twentieth-Century Literary Criticism.* Ed. Dennis Poupard. Detroit: Gale, 1983. 9, 199–200.

"A Revaluation of *Axël,*" *Modern Drama,* February 1959, 236–43.

"Recent French Fiction," *Palinarus,* April 1959, 55–59.

"The Achievement of Samuel Beckett," *Books Abroad,* Summer 1959, 278–81. Reprinted in part in *A Library of Literary Criticism: Modern Romance Literature.* New York: Frederick Ungar, 1967. 49–50.

"The Creative Writer as Polyglot: Valery Larbaud and Samuel Beckett," *Transactions of the Wisconsin Academy of Sciences, Arts, and Letters,* 49 (1960): 229–36.

"The Novels of Samuel Beckett: An Amalgam of Joyce and Proust," *Comparative Literature,* Winter 1960, 47–58.

"Samuel Beckett and the *Nouveau Roman,*" *Wisconsin Studies in Contemporary Literature,* Spring–Summer 1960, 22–36.

"William Styron: An Interim Appraisal," *English Journal,* March 1961, 149–58, 192; reprinted in *William Styron's "The Confessions of Nat Turner": A Critical Handbook,* 176–86.

"The Neglect of Time: France's Novel of the Fifties," *Books Abroad,* Spring 1962, 125–30.

"Flannery O'Connor: Another Legend in Southern Fiction," *English Journal,* April 1962, 233–43. Reprinted in *Recent American Fiction: Some Critical Views.* Ed. Joseph J. Waldmeir. Boston: Houghton Mifflin, 1963. 231–45. Reprinted in *Flannery O'Connor.* Ed. Robert Reiter. St. Louis: B. Herder Book Co., 1968. 5–24.

"A Note on Leibniz and Samuel Beckett," *Romance Notes,* Spring 1963, 93–96.

"American and European Fiction: The Contemporary Interaction," *Comparative Literature,* Fall 1965, 342–45.

"The Cracked Vase," *Romance Notes,* Spring 1966, 127–29.

"Crritic!," *Modern Drama,* December 1966, 300–308.

"Anthony Burgess Fa I Conti Con Joyce," *Umanesimo: Quarterly of Italian and American Culture,* 1: 5 (1967): 21–30.

"Beckett Criticism: Its Early Prime," *Symposium,* Spring 1967, 82–89.

"*The Confessions of Nat Turner:* The Convergence of 'Nonfiction Novel' and 'Meditation on History,' " *Journal of Popular Culture,* Fall 1967, 166–75. Reprinted in *William Styron's "The Confessions of Nat Turner": A Critical Handbook,* 63–72.

"Molloy's 'Sacred' Stones," *Romance Notes,* Fall 1967, 8–11.

"Anthony Burgess and James Joyce: A Literary Confrontation," *Literary Criterion,* Summer 1971, 71–83.

"John Hawkes and Flannery O'Connor: The French Background," *Boston University Journal,* Fall 1973, 34–44.

"Samuel Beckett and His Critics Enter the 1970s," *Studies in the Novel,* Fall 1973, 383–99.

"William Styron Now," *The Blue Guitar,* December 1975, 337–46.

"*The Mortgaged Heart:* The Workshop of Carson McCullers," *Revue des Langues Vivantes,* U.S. Bicentennial Issue (1976), 143–55.

"The Schlemiel: Jew and Non-Jew," *Studies in the Literary Imagination,* Spring 1976, 139–53.

"William Styron," *Fer de Lance,* January–June 1977, 53–60; July–September 1977, 52–59; January–June 1978, 47–52; July–September 1978, 40–48; October–December 1978, 33–44.

"Dislocations of Setting and Word: Notes on American Fiction Since 1950," *Studies in American Fiction,* Spring 1977, 79–98.

"Flannery O'Connor in France: An Interim Report," *Revue des Langues Vivantes,* October 1977, 432–42.

"To 'Make It New': The American Novel Since 1945," *Wilson Quarterly,* Winter 1978, 133–42.

"Michel Benamou (1929–1978)," *French Review,* October 1978, 11–12.

"Beckett's Life Story," *Contemporary Literature,* Summer 1979, 377–85.

" 'The Human Comes Before Art': Flannery O'Connor Viewed Through Her Letters and Her Critics," *Southern Literary Journal,* Spring 1980, 114–24.

"The American Jewish Literary Scene, 1979: A Review Essay," *Studies in American Fiction,* Autumn 1980, 239–46.

"Some Notes on John O'Hara," *John O'Hara Journal,* Fall/Winter 1980, 135–37.

"The Enigma of Unpopularity and Critical Neglect: The Case for Wallace Markfield," *Review of Contemporary Fiction,* Spring 1982, 36–44. Reprinted from *Seasoned Authors for a New Season.* Ed. Louis Filler. Bowling Green, OH: Bowling Green University Popular Press, 1980. 33–42.

"Robert Coles's South and Other Approaches to Flannery O'Connor," *Southern Literary Journal,* Fall 1982, 120–29.

"The 'French Face' of William Styron," *International Fiction Review,* Winter 1983, 33–37.

"William Styron's Criticism: More French than American," *Delta* (Montpellier), October 1986, 61–75.

"Texts and Countertexts: Philip Roth Unbound," *Studies in American Jewish Literature,* Fall 1989, 224–30.

"Lives of the Poets," *The World and I,* December 1990, 423–29.

"Art and Madness," *The World and I,* January 1991, 428–35.

"Our Difficult Bellow," *The World and I,* July 1991, 392–98.

"Samuel Beckett: Tradition and Innovation," *Contemporary Literature,* Spring 1995, 350–61.

Partial List of Reviews in Journals

"Out of His Brother's Shadow," *New Republic,* February 10, 1958, 18–20.

Review of *The Picaresque Saint, Comparative Literature,* Fall 1959, 371–75.

"Joyce's Life," *The Progressive,* December 1959, 49–50.

"Literary Panorama," *The Progressive,* June 1960, 44–46.

"Book Reviews," *Wisconsin Studies in Contemporary Literature,* Fall 1962, 100–106.

Review of *Samuel Beckett: The Comic Gamut* and *Four Playwrights and a Postscript, Comparative Literature,* Summer 1964, 264–69.

Review of *Les Romans de Robbe-Grillet, Symposium,* Fall 1964, 279–85.

Review of *Mallarmé and the Symbolist Drama, French Review,* December 1964, 269–71.

"The Achievement of Frederick Hoffmann," *Massachusetts Review,* Fall 1965, 862–67.

Review of *Journey to Chaos: Beckett's Early Fiction, French Review,* April 1966, 817–18.

Review of *Configuration Critique de James Joyce II, Comparative Literature Studies,* 4 (1967): 216–18.

Review of *Tolstoy and the Novel, Commonweal,* 28 July 1967, 477–78.

"A Critical Garland," *Modern Age,* Fall 1967, 417–19.

Review of *La Vision du Monde d'Alain Robbe-Grillet, L'Esprit Créateur,* Fall 1967, 216–17.

Review of *The Imagination's New Beginning, Commonweal,* November 17, 1967, 217–19.

"The Joys of Joyceana," *Modern Age,* Winter 1967–68, 93–96.

Review of *Samuel Beckett's Art, Style,* Winter 1968, 79–82.

"Joyce the Jansenist," *Modern Age,* Fall 1967, 406–408.

Review of *The Literature of Silence: Henry Miller and Samuel Beckett, French Review,* October 1968, 167–68.

Review of *Samuel Beckett: A Critical Study, French Review,* March 1969, 610–11.

Review of *William Styron's Nat Turner: Ten Black Writers Respond, Journal of Popular Culture,* Summer 1969, 153–59.

Review of *Black Thunder, Journal of Popular Culture,* Fall 1969, 370–72.

"Singer and the Tradition," *Journal of Religion,* October 1969, 388–91.

Review of *Joseph and Potiphar's Wife in World Literature, Classical Journal,* December 1969, 126–28.

Review of *Critics of Consciousness, Comparative Literature Studies,* December 1969, 126–28.

"André Malraux and Anaïs Nin," *Contemporary Literature,* Winter 1970, 104–13.

Review of *Comparative Literature: Matter and Method, Comparative Literature Studies,* March 1970, 136–39.

"More Joycean Exegesis," *Modern Age*, Summer–Fall 1970, 345–47.

"By and About Flannery O'Connor," *Journal of Modern Literature*, 2: 1970, 288–92.

Review of Existential Thought and Fictional Technique, Modern Language Quarterly, March 1971, 119–22.

Review of *The World of Marcel Proust*, Symposium, Spring 1971, 87–90.

"The Faces of Professional Football," *Journal of Popular Culture*, Summer 1971, 241–43.

"The Anatomy of Silence," *Modern Age*, Spring 1972, 215–18.

Review of *Marguerite Duras*, Journal of European Studies, June 1972, 208–209.

Review of *Ulysses on the Liffey*, Journal of European Studies, September 1972, 296.

Review of *Negative Capability: Studies in the New Literature and the Religious Situation*, Boundary 2, Fall 1972, 225–27.

Review of *Henry Becque*, French Review, February 1973, 617–18.

"Flannery O'Connor: The Canon Completed, The Commentary Continuing," *Southern Literary Journal*, Spring 1973, 116–23.

Review of *Invisible Parade: The Fiction of Flannery O'Connor*, American Literature, May 1973, 313–14.

Review of *Hawkes: A Guide to His Fictions*, Studies in American Fiction, Autumn 1973, 228–29.

Review of *The Schlemiel as Metaphor* and *The Schlemiel as Modern Hero*, Journal of Modern Literature, February 1974, 436–38.

Review of *Golden Codgers: Biographical Speculations*, Journal of European Studies, March 1974, 73.

"Flannery O'Connor: The Tonal Dilemma," *Southern Literary Journal*, Spring 1974, 124–29.

Review of *About Harry Towns*, New Republic, 27 July 1974, 28, and August 3, 1974, 28.

Review of *The Hermit*, New Republic, 7 December 1974, 26–27.

" 'Unexampled Versatility': The Critical Performance of Nathan Scott," *Journal of Religion*, January 1975, 110–15.

Review of *Here at the "New Yorker*,*"* Journal of Popular Culture, Spring 1975, 913.

Review of *Space, Time and Structure in the Modern Novel*, Symposium, Spring–Summer 1975, 180-82.

"The New Criticism in France," *Clio*, June 1975, 409–11.

Review of *Whence the Power?: The Artistry and Humanity of Saul Bellow, Saul Bellow's Enigmatic Laughter*, and *The Fiction of Philip Roth*, Modern Fiction Studies, Summer 1975, 294–97.

Review of *The Implied Reader: Patterns of Communication in Prose Fiction from Bunyan to Beckett*, Studies in the Novel, Summer 1975, 309–10.

"The Author of the Malgudi Novels," *The Nation*, 28 June 1975, 790–92.

Review of *The Literary Impact of "The Golden Bough*,*"* Comparative Literature, Fall 1975, 363–65.

Review of *Flannery O'Connor*, Studies in American Fiction, Autumn 1975, 226–28.

"Alain Robbe-Grillet," *Contemporary Literature*, Winter 1976, 132–37.

Review of *John Hawkes and the Craft of Conflict*, American Literature, January 1976, 648–49.

"Nihilism," *Contemporary Literature*, Spring 1977, 255–58.

Review of *The Controversial Sholem Asch, American Literature,* May 1977, 291–92.

Review of three books on James Joyce, *Modern Fiction Studies,* Winter 1977–78, 610–14.

Review of *Yeats, Joyce, and Beckett: New Light on Three Modern Irish Writers, American Committee for Irish Studies Newsletter,* February 1978, 2–3.

Review of *The Art of Djuna Barnes: Duality and Damnation, American Literature,* March 1978, 133–34.

Review of *The Literature of Memory* and *The Achievement of William Styron, Studies in American Fiction,* Autumn 1978, 241–43.

Review of *Samuel Beckett and the Pessimistic Tradition, Comparative Literature Studies,* December 1978, 439–41.

Review of *The Twentieth-Century English Novel: An Annotated Bibliography of General Criticism, Literary Research Newsletter,* Spring 1979, 95–98.

Review of *Four Postwar American Novelists: Bellow, Mailer, Barth, and Pynchon, Journal of American Culture,* Summer 1979, 347–48.

Review of *Sophie's Choice, American Book Review,* October 1979, 17.

Review of *The Resisting Reader: A Feminist Approach to American Fiction, American Literature,* November 1979, 426–27.

Review of *Beckett and Joyce: Friendship and Fiction, Journal of Beckett Studies,* Autumn 1980, 138–41.

Review of *Isaac Bashevis Singer: The Magician of West 86th Street* and *Old Love, Hollins Critic,* October 1980, 14–15.

"Back to Beckett's Theater," *Contemporary Literature,* Summer 1981, 370–73.

"Chinese Boxes," *Novel,* Winter 1982, 175–78.

Review of *Studies on Samuel Beckett, American Committee for Irish Studies Newsletter,* April 1982, 4.

Review of *The Tie that Binds, Religious Studies Review,* April 1982, 176–77.

Review of *Beyond Egotism: The Fiction of James Joyce, Virginia Woolf, and D. H. Lawrence, English Language Notes,* September 1982, 95–98.

Review of *The Presence of Grace and Other Book Reviews, Resources for American Literary Study,* Spring and Autumn 1984, 239–42.

"Systematic Realism," *Novel,* Fall 1984, 92–94.

"Beckett's Early Fiction," *Contemporary Literature,* Winter 1985, 516–19.

Review of *The Self-Apparent Word: Fiction as Language/Language as Fiction, American Literature,* March 1985, 184–85.

Review of *The New Covenant: Jewish Writers and the American Idea, Studies in American Fiction,* Spring 1985, 114–15.

Review of *The Root of All Evil: The Thematic Unity of William Styron's Fiction, Centennial Review,* Fall 1985, 475–77.

Review of *Flannery O'Connor's Library: Resources of Being, International Fiction Review,* Winter 1986, 32–33.

Review of *Three Catholic Writers of the Modern South, Studies in American Fiction,* Autumn 1986, 234–36.

Review-essay on Louis D. Rubin's *The History of Southern Literature, American Literature,* October 1986, 427–30.

Review of *The Novel as Performance: The Fiction of Ronald Sukenick and Raymond Federman, International Fiction Review*, Winter 1987, 55–57.

"Flannery O'Connor and the Language of Apocalypse," *Clio*, Spring 1987, 294–96.

"William Styron in Eden," *Papers on Language and Literature*, Fall 1987, 544–48.

Review-essay on David Herbert Donald's *Look Homeward: A Life of Thomas Wolfe, English Language Notes*, March 1988, 93–96.

Review of *Risen Sons: Flannery O'Connor's Vision of History, International Fiction Review*, Summer 1988, 179–81.

Review-essay on Daniel R. Schwartz's *Reading Joyce's "Ulysses," James Joyce Quarterly*, Fall 1988, 152–56.

"A Day, a Life," *The Progressive*, December 1988, 44–45.

"Joyce's Heirs," *Novel*, Spring 1989, 341–43.

Review of *Flannery O'Connor: A Study of the Short Fiction* and *Flannery O'Connor: Collected Works, International Fiction Review*, Summer 1989, 139–42.

"British Inside and Out," *The Progressive*, July 1989, 40–42.

"Boy in Gangland," *The Progressive*, August 1989, 38–39.

"British Woes," *The Progressive*, December 1989, 40–42.

Review of *The Lyre of Orpheus* and *Flannery O'Connor and the Mystery of Love, International Fiction Review*, Winter 1990, 55–57 and 70–72.

"Love and Art," *Congress Monthly*, February 1990, 18–20.

"More on G.B.S.," *The Progressive*, February 1990, 41–42.

Review-essay on Henry Serrano Villard and James Nagel's *Hemingway in Love and War, Studies in American Fiction*, Autumn 1990, 252–53.

Review of *William Styron's "Sophie's Choice": Crime and Self-Punishment, Studies in American Jewish Literature*, Fall 1990, 279–280.

Review of *Cambridge, Review of Contemporary Fiction*, Fall 1992, 195–96.

Review of *Accidents of Influence: Writing as a Woman and a Jew in America, International Fiction Review*, Winter 1993, 71-73.

"Nat Turner Once More," *Review*, 1993, 247–57.

Bibliography

Yearly contribution to the annual bibliography published in *The Yearbook of Comparative and General Literature*, vols. 7–9 (1958–1960).

Translations

"Passages on Aesthetics from Flaubert's Correspondence," *Quarterly Review of Literature*, 4 (No. 4, 1949): 390–400.

"D. H. Lawrence and Eroticism: Concerning *Lady Chatterly's Lover*," *Yale French Studies*, No. 11 (1953): 55–58.

"The Hour with the Human Face," *Palinurus*, April 1959, 8–10.

Contributors

JAMES ACHESON is senior lecturer in English at the University of Canterbury in Christchurch, New Zealand. He is the author of *Samuel Beckett's Artistic Theory and Practice* and coeditor of *Beckett's Later Fiction and Drama: Texts for Company.* A member of the editorial board of the *Journal of Beckett Studies,* he has published essays on Beckett as well as other writers in books and journals.

OWEN ALDRIDGE is Emeritus Professor of Comparative Literature at the University of Illinois. He is cofounder with Melvin Friedman of the journal *Comparative Literature Studies.* (The latter coedited a *festschrift* in Professor Aldridge's honor, *Aesthetics and the Literature of Ideas.*) Aldridge has published books on American, European, and comparative literature. The most recent of these is *The Dragon and the Eagle: The Presence of China in the American Enlightenment.*

HASKELL M. BLOCK is Professor Emeritus of Comparative Literature at State University of New York–Binghamton. A past president of the American Comparative Literature Association, he is a *Chevalier dans l'Ordre des Palmes Academiques* (France). He has published essays on European dramatic naturalism, symbolist drama, expressionism in the modern American theater, as well as individual studies of Hofmannsthal, Yeats, and Camus. His many publications include *Masters of Modern Drama* (with Robert G. Shedd), *The Teaching of World Literature, Mallarmé and the Symbolist Drama, The Poetry of Paul Celan,* and (with Herman Salinger) *The Creative Vision: Modern European Writers on Their Art.*

ZACK BOWEN is professor of English at the University of Miami. He has published nine books and written approximately 150 articles, notes, and reviews, mostly on Irish and modern literature topics. He is the editor of Hall/Twayne/Macmillan's Essays in British Literature series. In addition, he edits the Florida Press Joyce Series and the *James Joyce Literary Supplement.* He is also president of the International James Joyce Foundation.

JACKSON R. BRYER is Professor of English at the University of Maryland. He is the author, editor, or co-editor of a number of books by or about F. Scott Fitzgerald. These include *The Critical Reputation of F. Scott Fitzgerald, Dear Scott/Dear Max: The Fitzgerald-Perkins Correspondence, F. Scott Fitzgerald in His Own Time: A Miscellany, The Basil and Josephine Stories, F. Scott Fitzgerald: The Critical Reception, The Short Stories of F. Scott Fitzgerald: New Approaches in Criticism, New Essays on F. Scott Fitzgerald's Neglected Stories,* and *French Connections: Hemingway and Fitzgerald Abroad.*

DEBRA A. CASTILLO is Stephen H. Weiss Presidential Fellow and professor of romance studies and comparative literature at Cornell University. She also serves as director of the Latin American Studies Program and director of Graduate Studies for the Women's Studies Program. She finished her Ph.D. thesis at University of Wisconsin–Milwaukee under the direction of Mel Friedman in 1982. Her most recent book is *Easy Women: Sex and Gender in Modern Mexican Fiction.*

LIVIO DOBREZ is reader in English at the Australian National University, Canberra, and he formerly held the chair of Australian Studies at Bond University (1989–91). He has published numerous articles in comparative literature and edited *Review of National Literature* (volume XI) and *Identifying Australia in Postmodern Times.* His books include *The Existential and Its Exits: Literary and Philosophical Perspectives on the Work of Beckett, Ionesco, Genet, and Pinter* and *Parnassus Mad Ward: Michael Dransfield and the New Australian Poetry.*

RAYMOND FEDERMAN is the Melodia E. Jones Distinguished Professor of English at the State University of New York–Buffalo. He has written criticism, essays, and poetry, but he is recognized especially as an experimental surfictionist with such novels as *Double or Nothing; Amer Eldorado, Take It or Leave It; The Voice in the Closet; The Twofold Vibration; Smiles on Washington Square; To Whom It May Concern;* and *La Fourrure de ma Tante Rachel.* His novels have been translated into thirteen languages.

MICHAEL PATRICK GILLESPIE is professor of English at Marquette University. He has published three studies on the works of James Joyce, coedited a volume of essays on Joyce, and written a monograph on Oscar Wilde. He has written more than two dozen essays on modernist writers and their precursors. He is an advisory editor of the *James Joyce Quarterly* and is on the board of consultants of the Zurich James Joyce Foundation. He has received fellowships from the National Endowment for the Humanities, the American Philosophical Society, the American Council of Learned Societies, the Harry Ransom Humanities Research Center, and the William Andrews Clark Memorial Library.

JAY L. HALIO is professor of English at the University of Delaware. He has edited the *Dictionary of Literary Biography: British Novelists Since 1960* and (with Ben Siegel) *Daughters of Valor: Contemporary Jewish American Women Writers.* Among his books is a study of Philip Roth. A Shakespearean scholar, he has edited *Shakespeare's "Romeo and Juliet": Texts, Contexts, and Interpretations* and new editions of *King Lear* and *The Merchant of Venice.*

DAVID HAYMAN is Professor Emeritus of Comparative Literature at the University of Wisconsin–Madison. He has written or edited more than fifteen books in modern literature. His books include *Joyce et Mallarmé; Louis-Ferdinand Céline; Reforming the Narrative; Toward a Mechanics of Modernist Fiction;* and *The Wake in Transit.*

CLAYTON KOELB is Guy B. Johnson Professor of German and Comparative Literature and chair of the Department of Germanic Languages at the University of North Carolina–Chapel Hill. He focuses primarily on reading and rhetoric in Western European literature. His books include *The Incredulous Reader; Reading and the Function of Disbelief; Inventions of Reading; Rhetoric and the Literary Imagination; Kafka's Rhetoric; the Passion of Reading;* and most recently *Legendary Figures: Ancient History in Modern Novels.*

JAMES LIDDY is professor of English at the University of Wisconsin–Milwaukee, where he was Mel Friedman's long-time colleague. His many volumes of poetry include *At the Grave of Fr. Sweatmen; Baudelaire's Bar Flowers; Collected Poems;* and *Art Is Not for Grownups.*

RICHARD PEARCE is professor of English at Wheaton College and long-time book-review editor of *Novel.* His published works include *The Politics of Narration: Joyce, Faulkner, Woolf; The Novel in Motion: An Approach to Modern Fiction; Molly Blooms: A Polylogue on "Penelope" and Cultural Studies;* and *Critical Essays on Thomas Pynchon.*

MARGARET ROGERS is an American musician, singer, and composer who was for twenty years in the Chicago Symphony Chorus and currently directs a chorus, composes, and teaches individual voice students. She has written a series of choral pieces based on James

Joyce's works. These include "A Babble of Earwigs, or Sinnegan with Finnegan," which premiered at the Joyce conference in Milwaukee (June 1987), and draws its inspiration from the general structure of *Finnegans Wake*. Her "The Washerwomen Duet" derives from the ALP section of the same work. Her "Sirens Fugue" and "Sirens Duet" were inspired by the Sirens episode of *Ulysses*.

BEN SIEGEL is professor of English at California State Polytechnic University–Pomona. He is the author, editor, or coeditor of twelve books on a variety of literary subjects. These include *The Puritan Heritage: America's Roots in the Bible; Biography Past and Present; Isaac Bashevis Singer; The Controversial Sholem Asch; The American Writer and the University; Traditions, Voices, and Dreams: The American Novel Since the 1960s* (with Melvin Friedman); *Critical Essays on Nathanael West; Conversations with Saul Bellow;* and *Daughters of Valor: Contemporary Jewish American Women Writers* (with Jay Halio). He is also president of the International Saul Bellow Society.

MARK WILLIAMS is senior lecturer in the English Department at Canterbury University, Christchurch, New Zealand. His publications include *Leaving the Highway: Six Contemporary New Zealand Novelists; Patrick White;* and *Post-Colonial Literature in English: Southeast Asia, New Zealand, and the Pacific.* He has edited a number of books, including (with Jenny Bornholdt and Gregory O'Brien) *The Oxford Anthology of New Zealand Poetry* in English.

Index

221